Billy Ball

BILLY MARTIN
AND THE
RESURRECTION
OF THE
OAKLAND A's

DALE TAFOYA

Foreword by Ken Korach

LYONS
PRESS

Essex, Connecticut

An imprint of Globe Pequot, the trade division of
The Rowman & Littlefield Publishing Group, Inc.
4501 Forbes Blvd., Ste. 200
Lanham, MD 20706
www.rowman.com

Distributed by NATIONAL BOOK NETWORK

British Library Cataloguing in Publication Information available

Library of Congress Control Number: 2019957605

ISBN 978-1-4930-4362-0 (hardcover)
ISBN 978-1-4930-7119-7 (pbk. : alk. Paper)
ISBN 978-1-4930-4363-7 (e-book)

♾™ The paper used in this publication meets the minimum requirements of American National
Standard for Information Sciences—Permanence of Paper for Printed Library Materials, ANSI/NISO
Z39.48-1992.

TO CUTIE

My late loving dachshund—my best friend—who brought me so much joy.
I miss you.

If Billy goes, only he himself will go. The things he has left here—they will remain.
—MIKE NORRIS, 1980

CONTENTS

FOREWORD
by Ken Korach   1

PROLOGUE
Finley's Last Manager   5

CHAPTER ONE
The Triple A's   11

CHAPTER TWO
Baseball's Boat People   25

CHAPTER THREE
Forever Young   28

CHAPTER FOUR
Casey's Boy   47

CHAPTER FIVE
The Odd Couple   69

CHAPTER SIX
Billy Ball   81

CHAPTER SEVEN
The Renaissance   91

CHAPTER EIGHT
Haas-Minded   109

CHAPTER NINE
The Miracle Worker   121

CHAPTER TEN
Aces and the Outfield   129

CHAPTER ELEVEN
The Resurrection   143

CHAPTER TWELVE
Urban Cowboy   157

CHAPTER THIRTEEN
The Revival   165

CHAPTER FOURTEEN
Postseason Dreams   183

CHAPTER FIFTEEN
Rainy Days   193

CHAPTER SIXTEEN
The Steinbrenner Siren   211

EPILOGUE
Organization of the Year   217

ACKNOWLEDGMENTS   219

NOTES ON RESEARCH AND SOURCES   221

BIBLIOGRAPHY   225

INDEX   231

FOREWORD
BY KEN KORACH

I MIGHT HAVE BEEN THE ONLY PERSON WHO ENJOYED THE OAKLAND A's slip down into the abyss in the late 1970s. They drew only 306,000 fans in 1979 and lost close to 110 games, but that was great with me.

I was searching for a job in broadcasting but didn't have a tape to send out. The Oakland Coliseum was the perfect place since I could have whole sections to myself. I'd sit down the left field line in total solitude and that's how I made the play-by-play tape that helped me get my first job.

None of this would have been possible just a year later because Billy Martin was on the scene and a rebirth was taking place.

Billy Ball brought more than just credibility and hope to a once moribund franchise. Yes, Martin was cantankerous and flammable, but even as a manager he was must-see entertainment. He was also brilliant and dynamic, and there was the anticipation that with Billy at the helm anything could happen, and with the A's—beginning in 1980—that meant that the Coliseum was now home to a exciting brand of baseball played by a team that mirrored Billy's personality.

It didn't hurt that Billy Martin was a local kid who had prepped in nearby Berkeley before debuting with the Yankees in 1950. It also didn't hurt that the team's young core featured another local—the dashing Rickey

Henderson, who, at twenty-one, was setting out on a career that would take him to Cooperstown.

Nineteen eighty was a building block year as the A's won 83 games and stunned the baseball establishment with a starting rotation that combined for 94 complete games.

As Dale Tafoya beautifully chronicles in this book, the 1981 season was one of the most seminal in baseball history. New ownership took over the club, two legends were now in the broadcast booth, but Billy was still in the dugout and the Coliseum—once dubbed "The Mausoleum"—was the place to be.

After returning home from an undefeated trip that began the season, the A's christened the new era before 50,000 fans at the home opener and walloped the Seattle Mariners 16–1. Long after the final out had been recorded, Bill King sat alone in the broadcast booth enjoying the quiet and reflecting on what he had just chronicled.

Soon, A's president Roy Eisenhardt joined him and as they sat together they talked about how everything in their world seemed perfect.

As Bill later told broadcaster Marty Lurie, "Roy's eyes were just glistening as he looked out onto the field and reflected on a ninth consecutive victory. The sprinklers had been turned on, the grass was green, and it seemed the sky was the limit for that A's ballclub."

And, indeed, with a talented team often driven to success by the mere force of Billy Martin's will, the A's would make the playoffs in 1981. And, even in a strike-interrupted season, they drew 1.3 million fans—a million more than they drew just two years earlier and the most since moving to Oakland in 1968.

I broadcast my first minor-league season in 1981, and had plenty of time once the season ended to visit the Coliseum in September. I was blown away. It was like magic. The sound system, the new look of the scoreboards, the energy in the park, the quality of the team on the field—just walking into the ballpark it all felt divine.

This short foreword is a mere snippet of what happened in Oakland once Billy Martin took over the club.

Dale's writing, his attention to detail, and the insight that comes from a lifetime of following the A's, gives readers a fascinating account of one of the greatest eras in the history of one of baseball's storied franchises.

Anyone watching the A's play in three straight World Series beginning in 1988 wouldn't have likely remembered how close the A's were to moving a decade earlier. As Dale tells the story, a transformation had taken place, with Billy Martin at the center of everything.

PROLOGUE

FINLEY'S LAST MANAGER

*It was the merger of an owner who has been trying to get out of base-
ball and a manager who repeatedly has been thrown out of baseball,
and it is an effort to pick up the pieces of a sick franchise.*
—Dave Nightingale, *Chicago Tribune*, February 22, 1980

February 21, 1980: It was a union of convenience for two of
the most controversial figures in Major League Baseball. Billy Martin, baseball's fiery gunslinger of a manager, flew to Chicago—not Oakland—for
that Thursday's 3:00 p.m. presser. Inside an eighth-floor suite at the Drake
Hotel in Chicago, sixty-one-year-old Charles Oscar Finley, the Oakland
Athletics' colorful owner, introduced the firebrand Martin, the franchise
shaker with drawing power, as his new manager. Billy was Finley's fifteenth
different manager in twenty years.

On the eve of spring training, the A's were scrambling to mount a
competitive season in Oakland. For years, uncertainty had clouded the
once-celebrated franchise, and the future of Oakland A's baseball was bleak.
Major League Baseball's new financial structure, free agency, allowed veteran
players to shop their services at the expiration of their contracts to the highest bidder. Introduced as the result of an independent arbitrator's decision
in 1975, free agency was, in effect, forcing Finley to sell his club, the one

he moved to Oakland from Kansas City in 1968. Finley had brought three straight World Series titles to Oakland from 1972 to '74, but he'd lost his stars to wealthier owners and slashed payroll in half, keeping the franchise alive on a shoestring. Some wondered why Martin took the job. At any rate, if any franchise needed saving, the A's fit the bill.

Attendance at A's games was so bad that many baseball owners, along with American League president, Lee MacPhail, wanted to take the team off life support in Oakland and move it elsewhere. Many were convinced that the San Francisco Bay Area could only support one major-league club, the San Francisco Giants, who arrived there first in 1958. The A's nadir was reached at a chilly home game on April 17, 1979, when a tiny crowd of 653 was announced. Some witnesses have insisted that figure was generous, estimating that only about 250 people were there. "I probably knew everybody sitting in the stands," chuckled Jeff Newman, the A's starting catcher that night. And only 1,215 fans showed up the next day. Alienated fans, resigned to the fact that the team would likely be moving, lost interest and stopped showing up.

Drawing only 306,763 fans in 1979, the A's were hemorrhaging money, averaging only 3,787 fans for each home game. American League clubs traveling to Oakland rarely met budget. Earning the nickname the "Triple A's" and "Oakland Pathetics," the last-place A's lost 108 games in 1979. Trying to hit on a winning formula, the A's shuffled managers and broadcasters every year. The falloff reached the point where a local college radio station broadcasted their games in 1978.

Behind the scenes, Finley had, since 1977, been trying to reach a deal for the sale of the team to wealthy, Colorado-based oil magnate Marvin Davis. Davis planned to take the A's to Denver. Finley had been embroiled in a costly divorce, and finally reached a settlement in January 1980. Among other benefits for the A's owner, the settlement ended an order that any sale of the A's needed court approval. The family was ready to sell. Finley dropped his $200 California business license and the A's cleaned out their offices four days later, leaving everyone in the dark about the A's future in Oakland. In fact, MacPhail had delayed printing the 1980 schedule because of the A's limbo.

Oakland officials, just eleven days before the press conference, had rejected a $4 million buyout proposal from Finley, Davis, the American League, and San Francisco Giants' owner Bob Lurie that would have released the A's to Denver, and announced there would be another A's season in Oakland in 1980. Davis's efforts to bring the A's to Denver had tanked one last time. The A's instability forced such updates for anyone who cared.

In 1979, the city of Oakland and Alameda County had sued Finley for not promoting the club in the community. Oakland A's baseball in 1980 was up in the air—in the hands of a conglomerate of local political forces, including the Oakland Raiders, and engulfed in litigation. Shackling the A's to Oakland was a twenty-year ironclad lease agreement that Finley signed with Oakland officials in 1967. Under its terms, Finley's A's were essentially stuck in Oakland until 1987 unless local officials freed them from their lease. Also part of this backdrop was Oakland Raiders owner Al Davis, who was eyeing a larger market down south, and threatening a possible move to Los Angeles.

Fifty-one-year-old Billy, who signed a two-year contract worth $250,000, showed up in the thick of this uncertainty. He'd been fired by New York Yankees owner George Steinbrenner the previous October, following a fight with a marshmallow salesman in Minnesota. It was the fifth time in eleven years that Martin had either been fired or forced to resign.

The A's were a moribund franchise in need of a boost the aggressive Martin could provide. But Martin, who was born in nearby Berkeley, needed some hometown cooking. Returning home to manage the A's meant Billy could reunite with his seventy-eight-year-old mother, Joan Downey, and focus on his health after a few turbulent years in New York. His main goal was to bring excitement back to Oakland A's baseball. "I think I can get the fans to come back in Oakland," Martin assured the press. "They like exciting baseball, and that's my style of managing. I'm happy to be here. Charlie made me a wonderful offer and I'm pleased with the opportunity to keep baseball in Oakland, which is my hometown."

Billy had been a part of Oakland baseball championship lore in the past. In 1948, starring for Casey Stengel's Oakland Oaks, he helped lead them to their first Pacific Coast League title since 1927, sparking civic pride in the community. After an 11-year career as a major-league player, Billy managed his first big-league club, the Minnesota Twins, in 1969. He went on to manage the Detroit Tigers, Texas Rangers, and, in 1975, the Yankees. Martin brought wins and excitement wherever he managed, but he also had a tendency to cause trouble, which eventually led to his dismissal. Although he warred with front offices, fans—particularly working-class fans—adored him. "He was the most fascinating manager and—in a baseball sense—the best manager I've ever covered," said Bruce Jenkins, longtime columnist for the *San Francisco Chronicle*.

Finley had flirted with bringing Billy on board as manager intermittently since the A's were in Kansas City in the 1960s and Martin was coaching in Minnesota, but they never joined forces. Finley admired Martin's baseball acumen and knew he could fill the stands despite his pugnacious reputation. Martin's hiring was announced a day before A's pitchers and catchers were scheduled to report to spring training in Scottsdale, Arizona. Finley had decided only a week before not to bring back Jim Marshall, his former manager, opening the door for Billy.

Desperate to generate excitement in order to attract a buyer for his club, Finley turned to the unemployed Martin because Billy had a reputation for conquering fan apathy and hypnotizing players into believing they could win. He'd done it in Minnesota, Detroit, and Texas, and he'd taken the 1977 Yankees to a World Series championship. He seemed to have a formula for bringing baseball fever to a city from scratch. The declining A's were the perfect landing spot after Martin's unceremonious exit from New York. "Billy was the epitome of what the A's had been in the past," said Steve McCatty, one of Billy's former A's pitchers. "That was Billy growing up. He wasn't the best player, but he fought his way through it. He was the perfect fit for our organization."

The A's in 1980 were like a desperately ill patient in need of a bold physician, a miracle cure, and a good deal of hope. Billy Martin was the doctor, and what came to be known as "Billy Ball" was the remedy.

1

THE TRIPLE A'S

It was a catastrophe. We were basically a Triple-A ballclub until Billy [Martin] got there. We didn't really feel like a big-league team at that point.
— MIKE NORRIS, FORMER A'S STARTING PITCHER, AUGUST 2018

IN 1977, OAKLAND WAS BASEBALL'S VERSION OF ALCATRAZ, THE island prison located not far away in San Francisco Bay. Players were sentenced there. The A's home field, the desolate Oakland-Alameda County Coliseum—an empty, drab concrete mausoleum constructed for football—reminded some players of a prison yard. Only the contrasting A's uniform colors of Kelly green and California gold slightly brightened up the concrete dungeon in front of crowds that averaged just 6,100. Alienated fans had lost interest.

When twenty-three-year-old Bob Lacey trotted onto the field, what few fans there were could still see the ghost image of "Fingers" on the back of his uniform. The A's tall rookie lefty reliever had just arrived in Oakland after the club promoted him from the San Jose Missions of the Pacific Coast League on May 12. Frank Ciensczyk, the A's equipment manager, handed Lacey the old uniform jersey of the club's former All-Star closer Rollie Fingers—No. 34. Lacey, standing at 6-foot-5 and weighing about 190 pounds, had a similar body size to Fingers. Fingers's old jersey was available because he had left the A's to sign with the San Diego Padres during the inaugural free agency carnival in 1976. Lacey's teammates chuckled when they saw him hop out of the dugout with Fingers's old uniform. That was a sign of the times for Oakland A's baseball in the late 1970s. Uniforms were recycled. New managers were the only fresh commodities on the A's unpredictable conveyor belt of skippers.

Charlie Finley, the fifty-nine-year-old maverick owner of the A's who brought three world championships to Oakland from 1972 to '74, didn't purchase new uniforms often in 1977. The A's owner—once heralded as the Barnum and Bailey of the baseball world for the revolutionary ideas he introduced to the game—was notoriously cheap. He scrutinized laundry bill after laundry bill and grilled Ciensczyk on why ten uniforms were washed when only nine players played in the game. "He was so cheap that he wouldn't even buy new uniforms," said Bob Lacey, who pitched for the A's from 1977 to '80. "We had to use the same stuff."

Finley's parsimony had other drawbacks. For example, A's batting practice was unconventional for a major-league team. Finley never bought new bats for spring training; therefore, players were forced to use leftover bats from the previous season. There were only about two dozen balls to hit; so players rounded up balls after they hit them. And while many teams analyzed game tape as part of their training and preparation, the A's lacked video equipment. So players who wanted to watch a recording of a game had to visit a local restaurant. Finley, a Chicago insurance tycoon, operated with a conviction that if he felt it wasn't necessary, he wouldn't buy it.

Finley and his A's were in transition and declining fast. The window had closed for the A's glorious run of three consecutive world championships and five consecutive division titles from 1971 to '75. The honeymoon in Oakland was over. Free agency, which allowed players to test the market for their services, was forcing Finley out of the business. He was spending the bare minimum to keep his operation alive in Oakland until he found a buyer.

The limbo made playing in Oakland unattractive. "Ballplayers don't perform in Oakland. They do time. Most of them spend their idle hours plotting an escape. Most of the talented A's—the Reggie Jacksons, and the Joe Rudis—managed to go over the wall. Left behind were the lame, the halt and the blind," wrote Paul Oberjuerge of the Gannett News Service in 1980. Finley was plotting an escape himself.

The unraveling began on December 16, 1974, when arbitrator Peter Seitz ruled that Finley violated the contract of his prized ace Jim "Catfish" Hunter. The twenty-eight-year-old Hunter, baseball's premier pitcher, was coming off another celebrated championship season. He won the American League Cy Young Award in 1974 by virtue of a 25–12 record and stingy 2.49 ERA. But Finley had failed to pay Hunter half of his annual $100,000 salary in the form of deferred payments to a North Carolina–based insurance firm as agreed to in their contract. Hunter's dismay over what he considered Finley's breach of contract was leaked to the media. At the time, Finley claimed the payment language confused him. Under pressure from Commissioner Bowie Kuhn, Finley offered to pay Hunter the $50,000 in a lump sum. But it was too late. Since the contract stipulated that Finley must make annuity payments, and since Finley failed to do so, Seitz voided Hunter's two-year contract and declared him the first free agent in baseball's modern era. The ruling sent shockwaves around the league. Hunter, who'd tossed a perfect game for the A's in 1968, was a free man and could render his services to the highest-bidding club.

Hunter was the first star of the celebrated A's dynasty to bolt. But initially upon learning of the arbitrator's ruling, the pitcher was nervous. "I hung up the phone, turned to my wife and said, 'We don't belong to anybody.' I was scared. I didn't have a job. I didn't realize the implications."

He needn't have worried. After a major bidding war for Hunter's services ensued, he signed a five-year, $3.7 million contract with the New York Yankees on New Year's Eve, making him baseball's highest paid player. Hunter also received a $1 million signing bonus. "He really liked his teammates and playing in Oakland, but he didn't like the lying and scheming that came from Finley," recalled George "Doc" Medich, who was Hunter's roommate in New York in 1975. "He was very happy to get out of there."

Hunter's historic deal set a precedent for future free agent salaries and foreshadowed what was to come when star players came up for bid. His departure was a harsh sign of things to come for Finley and his soon-to-be folding dynasty. The Major League Baseball Players Association was getting stronger under the negotiating muscle of Marvin Miller, the executive director, and players were finally gaining independence. The business of baseball was changing fast. It threatened Finley's ownership model.

Finley's worst nightmare came true in 1976. Thanks to continued adept negotiating by Miller, and prompted by the case of Dodgers pitcher Andy Messersmith, baseball's reserve clause was effectively wiped out. Free agency was introduced and allowed players with at least six years in the major leagues to shop their services to the highest-bidding team. For the first time, players now had options and leverage. Baseball's richest owners could attract the best players, placing modest-spending owners like Finley at a disadvantage. Finley was a master talent evaluator, but free agency loosened his control of players. It shifted the power to the players and wealthiest owners, and would inevitably cost Finley his best talent and weaken his club.

It didn't take long for the ruling to have an effect on Oakland baseball. Eight of the twenty-five players on Finley's A's roster would test the market after the 1976 season. One of Finley's strategies was to receive compensation in return for them before they walked. His biggest fear was receiving nothing for them. Free agency forced Finley to adjust to the idea of locking up players to long-term deals. In 1977, Stan Bahnsen, a thirty-two-year-old A's pitcher, inked a four-year deal with Finley worth $500,000, the longest contract Finley ever awarded a player. Bahnsen remembered how free agency changed how Finley offered him a contract. "If it weren't for free agency, he wouldn't have offered me more than a one-year contract. That's why he was so against free agency. He knew he couldn't afford it and we weren't drawing a lot of fans. I don't think Finley could really afford free agency."

Finley, seeing the writing on the wall, had already shipped a pair of All-Stars, slugger Reggie Jackson and starting pitcher Ken Holtzman, to the Baltimore Orioles for Don Baylor, Paul Mitchell, and Mike Torrez on April 2, a week before the 1976 season. Then on June 15, 1976, in what was called a "Tuesday night massacre," Finley stunned baseball by selling three of his superstars for $3.5 million. He sold three-time 20-game winner Vida Blue to the Yankees for $1.5 million and Fingers and Rudi to the Red Sox for $1 million each. The sales would have dramatically impacted the balance of power in the American League. Two days later, however, Major League Baseball commissioner Bowie Kuhn voided both sales in order to maintain competitive balance, which he deemed in the "best interest of baseball." Blue, Fingers, and Rudi returned to the A's and a furious Finley began suing and battling Kuhn, with litigation continuing into the following season.

The race for the exits in Oakland became official during baseball's first free agent draft in November 1976 when a bunch of A's talent jumped ship. Fingers and catcher Gene Tenace signed with the San Diego Padres; third baseman and team captain Sal Bando signed with the Milwaukee Brewers; Rudi and another outfielder, Don Baylor, joined the California Angels; and shortstop Bert Campaneris inked a deal with the Texas Rangers. In a short period of time, Finley lost premier talent and received nothing in return.

What a difference a decade had made. In 1967, he'd moved the A's from Kansas City to Oakland with its population of 400,000 and close proximity to four million others with easy freeway access. Many had encouraged Finley to consider moving the A's to Seattle, but he insisted on Oakland, even though the Giants of the National League had already occupied the San Francisco Bay Area since 1958. "He wanted the bigger market in the Bay Area," said John Hickey, former A's beat writer for the *Oakland Tribune*. "He figured it was better to be the second team in a huge market than the first team in a smaller market."

Finley was also intrigued by Oakland's newly constructed spectacular $25-million-dollar Oakland-Alameda County Coliseum, which opened in 1966 on 140 acres of land and featured a three-tiered 50,000-seat stadium and 16,000-seat indoor arena joined by an exhibit hall in the center. The Oakland Raiders of the American Football League were already tenants. The Coliseum also featured four removal wedges of seats to convert the stadium from football to baseball. At the time, it was considered a groundbreaking multipurpose entertainment complex, and marketed as a "launching pad for East Bay greatness." The Nimitz Freeway, which ran alongside the Coliseum, provided quick and easy access from the neighboring cities. Studies conducted in Oakland had forecast a population of six million within an hour's drive by 1970 and 8.8 million by 1990. The A's drew 50,164 fans on Opening Night in 1968 for their inaugural season in Oakland. But only 5,304 showed up the next night.

After Finley's stars left, he watched his franchise decline in Oakland from his South Michigan Avenue insurance office in Chicago. Rumors of Finley selling the A's were common. "There was a lot of negative publicity coming out about the A's organization with Finley wanting to sell and move them," said Dave Heaverlo, a former A's reliever who was acquired by the A's in a trade that sent Blue to the Giants on March 15, 1978. "I had heard he was getting rid of everyone. I began to realize quickly how dysfunctional the organization was. It was disheartening."

The once star-studded swingin' A's had become a stripped-down product of Finley's contempt for free agency and his railing against the establishment. By 1977, only Vida Blue and Billy North from the A's championship clubs remained on the team. Blue's teammates nicknamed him "the captive" because Finley held him prisoner. Writers started calling them the Oakland Apathetics, Awful A's, and Triple A's. "We were a bad team," remembered Steve Dunning, who pitched for the A's in 1977. "It wasn't the best of situations from a player's perspective. Finley was pretty much controlling everything. Our manager Bobby Winkles didn't have any control or authority to do anything. I don't know if Finley made out the lineup and pitching rotation, but everything was mostly preapproved by him."

Former A's pitcher Steve McCatty, who signed as an undrafted amateur free agent in 1973, remembered the circus of player turnover in the late 1970s. "We were like the island of misfit toys," said McCatty. "There was a rotation of different players coming in and out. We were in the minors and he was bringing in these guys who had done nothing in the big leagues. We weren't getting a chance and it became a little frustrating. You were always getting pushed back by these older guys."

There were numerous signs of a franchise in decline. World Series trophies earned in the early '70s were used in the A's office to file mail and stationery in between the trophy flagpoles. Former A's catcher Jim Essian described calling the A's offices one winter only to get a message that the phone was disconnected. Finley was demanding that A's players turn in any half-fare airline coupons they collected on team flights. "Finley had given Oakland three straight World Series championships, but he stripped that team," said Dave Newhouse, longtime sports columnist for the *Oakland Tribune*. "There was nobody in the front office except for his cousin, Carl, and MC Hammer, Stanley Burrell Jr." The fare served up by the A's in the Coliseum press box was Kentucky Fried Chicken.

The University of California's 10-watt student radio station, KALX-FM, broadcasted A's games in 1978. Twenty-year-old student Larry Baer, the chief executive officer of the Giants today, was the A's play-by-play voice. None of the Bay Area radio stations were interested in carrying the A's. The A's instability scared them away. Judge Eddie Sapir, Billy Martin's longtime friend and legal advisor, said the A's cupboards were bare when they arrived in 1980. "They didn't even have a copy machine. When we got there, Lee MacPhail, the American League president, told me, 'We have major-league standards for these owners and you might find the A's a little short when you arrive to spring training. If you need the cooperation of our office, we will get you everything you need to meet our standards.'"

Because fans weren't showing up at the gate, the A's became a financial drain for the American League as a whole. Clubs were losing money traveling to Oakland. "It's a good idea to get out of the Bay Area because it's been costing us money every time we go to Oakland," Calvin Griffith, former owner of the Minnesota Twins, said in 1977. "We don't meet our expenses when we go to play the A's."

As the A's tumbled badly in the standings, Finley ran a conveyor belt for managers. After Dick Williams resigned following the 1973 season, Finley ran through managers Alvin Dark, Chuck Tanner, Jack McKeon, and Bobby Winkles from 1974 to '78. In June 1977, Finley fired Jack McKeon and replaced him with Winkles, a coach for the Giants who had previously coached in Oakland under Dark and had captured championships on the collegiate level at Arizona State. But the following season, in 1978, Winkles, fed up with Finley's meddling, quit on May 23 after leading the A's into first place with a 24–15 record. Winkles once explained to Beachwoodreporter. com why he resigned: "I just couldn't take his crap anymore. [I'd be up] every morning at 6 o'clock. When you're the manager, you get home at 12 or 12:30 every night. At 2 o'clock he's calling, 'Why didn't you do this, why didn't you run that guy?' We're leading the league by two games. So I said, 'Well, I'm going to quit on top. Now's the time. I'm going to do it.'"

Jeff Newman, a former catcher who played for the A's from 1976 to '82, remembered when Winkles called it quits. "We saw papers announcing his resignation on our chairs when we walked in," recalled Newman. "Winkles was exceptionally nice, but he couldn't deal with Charlie anymore, and I could understand that. Winkles was on the phone a lot in the dugout and everyone knew he was talking to Charlie."

Finley replaced Winkles with McKeon, his third-base coach whom he'd fired as manager the previous season. "Standing here, I feel as secure as the manager of the Oakland A's," Willie Mays joked during a Dean Martin TV roast in 1977. "When I arrived in Oakland in 1977, I noticed that the place was being run on a shoestring," remembered Medich. "It just didn't have the touches the more mature and better funded franchises had. We flew only one charter flight during the season I was there. I remember the chaos the most. We had players coming and going all season. I don't know how many people were on the big-league roster that season, but there were a whole bunch. We never knew who would be in the clubhouse the next day."

The 1977 A's finished in last place in the American League West with a 63–98 record, and while the 1978 club got off to a sizzling 19–5 start, they ended up 69–93, only finishing ahead of the last-place second-year Seattle Mariners. "The struggle was always to avoid losing 100 games," said Hickey. "They were so overmatched."

Mike Norris refused to carry the team luggage sporting the A's logo during road trips. He was embarrassed. "It was a catastrophe," said Norris, who pitched parts of 10 seasons for the A's. "We were basically a Triple-A ballclub until Billy got there. We really didn't feel like a big-league team at that point. Other than McKeon, we didn't have any major-league managers. Winkles had just came out of Arizona State and didn't know how to treat us like men because he was transitioning from working with college kids, so that didn't go over too well with us, and Marshall wasn't a major-league manager, period. We didn't have a proven major-league manager."

Finley offered Rene Lachemann the A's managerial job in 1979. Lachemann, who had deep roots in the franchise, had been a manager in the A's organization from 1973 to '77 and helped schedule spring training workouts for farm director Norm Koselke. He signed as an eighteen-year-old catcher with the Kansas City A's in 1963.

Lachemann flew to Chicago in severe snowy conditions to meet with Finley about the managerial vacancy. "He told me that if I turned it down, I need a psychiatrist," Lachemann said. "Two days later, I called him and asked if he knew any numbers to any psychiatrists." Lachemann declined the offer. He was concerned about Finley meddling with his lineups. Finley ended up choosing Jim Marshall to manage the 1979 A's. Lachemann went back to managing the Mariners' Triple-A affiliate in Spokane.

Attendance was so bad that A's reliever Dave Heaverlo volunteered to shave his head if the A's drew 40,000 fans. By 1979, the A's hit rock bottom in the stands and on the field. On April 17, the A's announced a crowd of 653 on a freezing, gloomy, windy, and locally televised night game against the Mariners. Insiders claimed that was a generous estimate, however. "An unofficial census of players, coaches, security, press, ushers and others who earn a living at the game totaled 223," wrote Tom Weir, an A's beat writer who covered the game for the *Oakland Tribune*. "Considering there are nine more A's home games to be televised, the fans may get outnumbered by the workers before this season is over." The late Herb Caen, former columnist for the *San Francisco Chronicle*, got into the act: "The A's drew 653 fans Tuesday night," he wrote. "Can you name them?"

Newman remembered the nasty weather and historically tiny crowd on that chilly night at the Oakland Coliseum. "I probably knew everybody sitting in the stands," chuckled Newman. "Charlie just didn't make it a very enjoyable experience for the fans to come out at that point. We weren't the best team, but it was still the big leagues. He had alienated the people in Oakland by always telling them he was going to move the club."

The A's finished the 1979 season in last place with a record of 54–108, the worst in franchise history since Connie Mack's Philadelphia A's were 36–117 in 1916. A's attendance stayed embarrassingly low, drawing 495,599 in 1977, 526,999 in '78, and 306,763 in '79. The season attendance in 1979 was the lowest since they arrived in Oakland and lowest in franchise history since the Philadelphia A's drew 304,666 in 1954, their final season there before relocating to Kansas City. From 1977 to '79, the A's combined attendance was 1,329,361. Across the bay, the Giants alone drew 1,456,402 in 1979, while the Dodgers led the pack that year with a season attendance of 2,860,954. Even the expansion Mariners outdrew the A's in 1979 with a season total of 844,447. "The attendance was unbelievably bad," remembered Bruce Jenkins, a longtime Bay Area columnist. "The teams were terrible and they were on a treadmill to nowhere. As long as Finley was in charge of the club, having dismantled what was one of the greatest teams of all time, it seemed like he had given up at that point."

Finley was fielding expansion-like teams in the late 1970s, and drafted and acquired some talent that began showing up in Oakland. He drafted prep standout Rickey Henderson, who played locally at Oakland Technical High School, in the fourth round in 1976. Henderson sparked the A's during his debut in 1979 and was on his way to superstardom. Finley had also drafted center fielder and soon-to-be-captain Dwayne Murphy, third baseman Wayne Gross, and outfielder Mike Davis. Pitcher Rick Langford— along with talented hitting prospects Mitchell Page and Tony Armas—came from Pittsburgh in a blockbuster trade that Finley authored before the 1977 season. Toiling in the minors were a group of young A's hurlers, Mike Norris, Brian Kingman, Steve McCatty, and Matt Keough, a former shortstop who converted to a pitcher in 1976. Norris, the A's first-round draft selection in 1973 and heralded as Catfish Hunter's heir apparent, was struggling and battling nagging arm issues through the minors.

On June 15, 1979, the A's acquired twenty-four-year-old catcher Mike Heath, infielder Dave Chalk, and cash from the Texas Rangers in exchange for lefty starting pitcher John Henry Johnson. The A's already had Jeff Newman and Jim Essian, two established catchers, so Heath played outfield most of the time for the remainder of the season. "We were a bunch of young guys ready to pop and needed a no-nonsense manager to make us believe in ourselves," said Heath, who played for the A's until 1985.

These were the Oakland A's of boom boxes, gold jewelry, and swagger. The endless shuffling of the A's roster and player turnover kept players on their toes. No one was safe. Infielder Rodney Scott got the message quickly when he came to the A's in a trade from the Rangers for Claudell Washington in the spring of 1977. "We never knew what was going to happen on a daily basis," said Scott.

Scott remembered flying out to right field to lead off a game against the Brewers at Milwaukee's County Stadium on June 22, 1977. He trotted back inside the dugout to grab his glove to play shortstop, but before he could get on the field, Rob Picciolo had taken over at short. A's manager Bobby Winkles had taken Scott out of the game in the first inning without telling him.

Since Winkles removed him from the game so early, Scott figured he would shower early and wait for the game to end in the clubhouse. But after Winkles saw Scott walking toward the clubhouse, he directed Scott to the A's bullpen to warm up pitchers. Scott told Winkles that he wasn't a catcher, so he wasn't going to warm up pitchers. Winkles warned Scott that there would be consequences if he refused to report to the bullpen. Scott reported to the bullpen. Teammate Billy North stuck up for Scott, but Finley later confirmed that as long as he's paying a player, the organization could assign him wherever they wanted. "I had never seen that before and was not accustomed to that treatment," said Scott. "That made me realize anything goes here. It was pretty wild."

It was wild in the air, too. The A's rarely flew charter planes. They flew commercial flights that stopped in several towns before landing in the next city they were playing in. Finley didn't usually pay for charter flights. Medich remembered the club being caught in a vicious thunderstorm one night as they flew on a Boeing 737 to Kansas City to play the Royals for a four-game series in September 1977. Medich was just celebrating Finley placing him on waivers so he could escape Oakland. The thunderstorm was so ferocious that everyone thought they were going down. "This happened right after he finally put me on waivers," said Medich. "I was finally getting away from Finley, but I was going to die in Kansas first. I saw Dorothy and Toto fly by six times."

The pilot finally made an emergency landing at a tiny airport in Salina, Kansas, which was a five-hour drive from Kansas City. After being stuck for five hours at the tiny airport, the team bused to Kansas City from there. "We looked like clowns stuck at that airport," said Medich. "The farmers arrived to catch a plane and they looked at us like we were the circus in town."

Stan Bahnsen remembered the traveling nightmares that came with playing for the thrifty A's. He said that while most teams flew to the next city directly after getaway games, the A's flew commercial the next morning on game day to avoid paying lodging the night before. "It was inconvenient and giving other teams an edge over us because of how we traveled," said Bahnsen. "After we played a night game in Oakland, if we had to play in Chicago or New York the next day, we'd have to get up early in the morning and fly all day. When we finally got to the hotel, we had to report to the ballpark for the game. That's the way he did things. I remember arriving in Milwaukee at 5:00 p.m. once for a 7:30 p.m. game."

Bahnsen was shocked one day when they arrived at Burbank Airport after playing the Angels and a rare charter flight back to Oakland was waiting for them on the runway. "When we started boarding the plane, I was wondering why the flight attendants were seating us on the back of the plane," said Bahnsen. "We found out cargo was stored in the front half of the plane. We were on a cargo plane. Are you kidding me? I'm sure it was discounted."

Most major-league clubs employed at least thirty front office staff at that time, but Finley only had six. "He was great with players in the early part," said Lachemann. "If you'd get called up, he'd give you money for clothes. He'd send you beautiful Christmas presents. But free agency killed him."

The A's depended on the Major League Scouting Bureau to select players from the amateur draft. The A's didn't have any scouts, so they scouted and drafted by phone. Finley once had a stable of twenty to twenty-five scouts, but when the scouting bureau began centralizing and computerizing intelligence on prospects in 1974, he dismantled his scouting department and relied on their information, although most teams used the bureau service as an option. "He was trying to get out of baseball and he wasn't going to put anything into it," said Lachemann. "Believe it or not, the farm system wasn't that bad."

Late legendary scout Dick Wiencek, whom Billy Martin brought over to revitalize the A's scouting department in 1980 when he took over as manager, recalled the disaster he inherited when he arrived. "When we first took over there, we didn't have any scouts and our minor league teams were bankrupt," Wiencek said in 2004. "The place was left a mess. We didn't even have any forms. So we had to start from scratch."

Everyone wondered how the A's drab situation would end. "I kind of felt bad for Charlie because only a few years before he knew he was going to lose a bunch of stars to free agency, and he was trying to get money for them, but Kuhn negated all the deals. I didn't think that was right," said Medich, who finally escaped and joined the Mariners in September.

Many baseball insiders concluded that moving the A's from Oakland was the only solution to save the franchise. But moving the A's out of Oakland wasn't so simple.

2

BASEBALL'S BOAT PEOPLE

The A's lease is a strong, valid contract which we fully intend to enforce. We shall make every effort to assist the A's in making baseball a success in Oakland.

—LIONEL WILSON, FORMER MAYOR, OAKLAND, 1978

ON DECEMBER 14, 1977, COLORADO-BASED OIL MILLIONAIRE MARVIN Davis announced that he had purchased the Oakland A's from Finley and the team would be playing at Mile High Stadium in Denver for the 1978 season. The bombshell generated national headlines. The insatiable Davis was a wealthy Colorado real estate developer who'd made his fortune as CEO of the Davis Oil Company, the world's largest independent oil company. He was believed to be one of the wealthiest men in America and was touted as being as rich as Greek shipping mogul Aristotle Onassis, the second husband of Jackie Kennedy.

Davis was the real deal and walked in powerful circles. He moved millions of dollars for a living and rubbed shoulders with the likes of then President Gerald Ford and former secretary of state Henry Kissinger. He flew on his private Gulfstream G2 plane and lived in a 33,000-square-foot mansion in the luxurious Cherry Hills Village, south of Denver. He was also very private and preferred not to discuss his wealth. Finley knew Davis had deep pockets and was serious about bringing the A's to Denver. Finley, during his failed courtship of Rene Lachemann to manage his 1979 club, apprised him about Davis. "He told me he was going to sell the club to Marvin Davis, a millionaire oilman in Colorado," said Lachemann, who was serving as a minor-league manager in the A's organization. "He said Davis had enough money to buy all the clubs in the American League. He said he would sign me for $45,000 and if Davis decided to get rid of me, he'd put a stipulation in my contract that he would have to pay me $100,000 to get rid of me."

The fifty-two-year-old Davis agreed to purchase the franchise from Finley for $12.5 million, including a $5 million deposit. Finley had purchased the team in Kansas City for $4 million in 1960. Denver would be the A's fourth home since 1954.

Nancy Finley, the daughter of Carl Finley, the club's director of public relations in 1977 and Charlie's cousin, said that Finley's agreement on the A's move to Denver was fueled by his frustration with the Coliseum board for failing to follow through on promised front offices since they arrived in 1968: "We were angry at Oakland for not finishing our front offices. Davis offered dad a great package and he was going to keep working under him. We were ready to go because it felt like Oakland didn't want us. They kept promising our front offices would be done, and after three championships, they still weren't done. That was a slap in the face."

Davis alone could solve baseball's Oakland A's crisis with his bank account. But the sale was contingent on whether Finley could actually transfer the team to Denver, a city baseball executives were eyeing. Denver was receiving a lot of notoriety for being the hub of the Rocky Mountains and a promising location for major league baseball. The perception and landscape of Denver was changing. It was no longer being considered a cow town. It was a fast-growing metropolis.

Developers were building and expanding the downtown area to enhance the mile-high skyline. The city was a perfect fit for an American League team, far away from other major-league cities, and the A's schedule could be maintained easier with the transfer. Former commissioner Ford Frick had always promoted Denver as a prime candidate for a major-league baseball club. "In the end, it was the dollar that made the difference," Davis said during the Denver press conference. "Our main course is to produce a winning team. Someday we will have a winning team in Denver."

Denver was baseball ready. Mile High Stadium was refurbished for baseball in 1974 at a cost of $24 million and the climate was perfect during the early months of baseball season. The Denver Bears, baseball champions of the American Association, drew 195,000 at Mile High the previous season. While the Denver Broncos were the toast of the town, many city insiders insisted that a major-league baseball team would easily dominate the region's professional sports market. Big-league baseball in Denver would lure fans from neighboring states such as Nebraska, Utah, Kansas, Wyoming, New Mexico, and Arizona. The radio and television contract would be astronomical because of the vast territory to cover. To Denver fans, it was the beginning of a baseball revival. "They assumed it was a done deal," remembered Alan Fallick, who covered the A's aborted move to Denver for the *Colorado Springs Gazette Telegraph* in 1977–78. "Davis was a man of his word."

The media reported the A's pending move to Denver and ownership change. It was inevitable and expected. Columnists were writing Finley's baseball ownership obituary. By that time, some Oakland fans were so disgusted with Finley they didn't care anymore. Fan interest in the A's had hit an all-time low. The move would close the chapter on the wandering team's decade-long legacy in Oakland, which began in celebration but ended in apathy. The A's were being called "baseball's boat people" because of their lack of stability and direction.

Not so fast. The following day, the Coliseum board, the city of Oakland, and Alameda County filed a $35 million lawsuit against Finley and Davis because the team was trying to break their stadium lease. They also obtained a temporary restraining order from a federal judge to suspend the sale immediately and keep American League owners from voting on the move. Finally, they demanded a payment of $200,000 from Finley for unpaid Coliseum services rendered during the 1977 season.

What made A's move talks moot was the twenty-year lease with the Coliseum board that shackled them to Oakland until 1987. Finley signed the lease in 1967 with four five-year options. Every time Finley engaged in public discussions about selling the club to a group threatening to move them to another city, Oakland officials pulled out their trump card, the ironclad lease he signed in 1967.

According to the lease, the A's could not play anywhere else while the agreement was in effect. Any potential A's move would breach the contract Part of Paragraph 7 of Finley's ironclad Coliseum lease:

Licensee [Finley] agrees that because of the particular nature of [the] business of professional baseball, a breach of any of the covenants contained in this paragraph cannot be reasonably or adequately compensated for in damages at law and that a breach of said covenants will cause Coliseum great and irreparable injury and damages. Licensee agrees that in addition to all other remedies under this agreement whatsoever, Coliseum shall be entitled to injunctive and other equitable relief to prevent a breach of any of the covenants contained in this paragraph.

The Coliseum board protected itself from tenants breaking their lease agreement and costing them revenue from lost rent and concessions. They charged Finley a minimum of $125,000 annually for rent. Even if Finley struck a deal with a potential buyer, he knew it was his responsibility to settle the lease. Lee MacPhail also publicly offered to help any potential buyer with a plan to free the A's from Oakland. The only hope of Finley escaping the lease was either to come up with some sort of buyout that would satisfy Oakland officials or sell the franchise to a local buyer who would keep them in Oakland.

Davis was obviously aware of the lease agreement, but he quickly discovered that Finley's confidence that he could somehow extricate himself from the contract was misplaced. It was clearly going to take more than Davis's $12.5 million to get the A's to Denver. The sale needed approval from American League owners first, but all of them knew their votes were meaningless unless Finley's lease problem was solved. Owners had their own agenda of forcing Finley out of the game. "Even perhaps more than getting the A's out of Oakland, the owners were looking forward to Finley handing over the reigns to someone else who would fall more in line with fellow owners," said Alan Fallick. "He was ahead of his time in many ways, but fellow owners were not thrilled with him owning a team at the time."

A concerned Finley soon flew to Oakland to meet with Giants owner Bob Lurie, Coliseum president Robert T. Nahas, George Moscone, the mayor of San Francisco, and Oakland Mayor Lionel Wilson to come up with a peaceful resolution to release the A's to Davis and Denver. Oakland leaders, however, couldn't meet with him because of the restraining order. "There never has been a lease that couldn't be broken," Finley insisted in 1977. "I could move the team. They might take me to court, and it might cost me a lot, but I could move the team."

Finley and Nahas were no strangers. Nahas, president of Coliseum Inc. and a prominent international land developer, began wooing Finley to move his Kansas City A's to Oakland in 1962. In 1959, Nahas, at age thirty-six, became the youngest ever president-elect of the Oakland Chamber of Commerce. Nahas was an ambassador for the East Bay. The Chamber later tasked Nahas to design and operate the Coliseum, a multipurpose complex on Hegenberger Road and the Nimitz Freeway, for major sports entertainment. He was well connected in Alameda County political circles. He was also the head of Alameda County Land Development Committee and helped revive Oakland's downtown business district. Nahas saw greatness in Oakland and loved to build. He injected confidence in a city that many felt had an inferiority complex to San Francisco.

"Don't paint me as a saint or give me any credit, "Nahas told the *Oakland Tribune* in 1961. "I'm selfish. I believe in this community, I want to be able to brag about it to my friends in other parts of the country and I love to build. I'm having a ball. Take the Coliseum. I just love to take some rejected land with water running through and tin cans all over it and transform it into a beautiful, functional facility."

Nahas was present when Finley signed the twenty-year lease in 1967. Now, a decade later, Nahas and Finley haggled over the A's leaving Oakland. One of the negotiating points for a settlement to free the A's was the Giants playing some games at the Coliseum to generate parking and concession revenue in the absence of the A's. Lurie was willing to approve the Giants playing 20 to 25 games at the Coliseum. But he would first need approval from the city of San Francisco and Recreation and Park Commission to make that happen. The Giants had their own lease agreement for Candlestick Park to worry about. Lurie, who purchased the Giants in 1976 to keep them from moving to Toronto, wanted the A's to leave town so his Giants could have the Bay Area to themselves. The A's fate was partly in the hands of the team from across the Bay.

The prevailing sentiment was that the A's presence in the Bay Area was affecting attendance at Giants' games. Both franchises drew only 1.2 million combined in 1977. They both were last in attendance in their leagues. Major League Baseball had witnessed a significant spike in attendance in 1977, but the A's drew just 495,599 fans. Baseball's surge in popularity was not manifesting in Oakland. "Should the Denver deal go through, Finley will be rewarded for his incompetence and maliciousness on one hand, and his acute business sense on the other. Not many people can sell a failing operation at a huge profit," wrote *Oakland Tribune* columnist Ron Bergman in 1977.

The temporary restraining order to halt the A's sale was dissolved by Judge William Orrick Jr. on December 23, after Finley promised he would not sell unless the Coliseum board relieved him from the ironclad lease. Growing impatient, Davis insisted that he needed the deal completed in thirty days so he could hire enough staff to run the team in time for spring training. The clock was ticking. Finley needed to solve the problem fast.

On December 30, 1977, Finley, Kuhn, Nahas, William Cunningham, general manager of the Coliseum, Neil Papiano, Finley's attorney, and James P. Garner, an attorney for the American League, met in Palm Springs, California, for almost four hours to discuss a possible resolution. It soon became apparent that four hours was not enough time. Kuhn tabled the recommendations for another meeting with the Coliseum board in Oakland the following week. "This could be one of a series of meetings," Kuhn told reporters. "The lease situation is not unsolvable."

Oakland and Alameda County officials met and settled on their demands to free the A's. Most of them involved the Giants and Bay Area parity. Nahas, insisting on parity with the Giants, wanted them to play half of their home games at the Coliseum. "My primary concern is to put together a good package for the people in the East Bay," Nahas said at the time. "Money isn't the principal objective."

Some of Nahas's demands required civic approval:

1. A name change of the Giants to reflect both sides of the Bay Area.

2. The home schedule divided equally between the Coliseum and Candlestick Park.

3. The Coliseum guaranteed against losses in rent should the A's move.

4. The Coliseum and the Giants will be indemnified for any losses in concession sales.

5. In the event of playoffs, the games will be divided equally between both stadiums.

"The A's lease is a strong, valid contract which we fully intend to enforce," Oakland mayor Lionel Wilson said in 1978. "We shall make every effort to assist the A's in making baseball a success in Oakland."

Davis set a deadline of January 23, 1978, more than a month after the sale was announced, for Finley to settle his tangled legal mess with Oakland officials. When Davis didn't hear anything that day, he announced through a spokesman that he would withdraw his offer to purchase the A's. But Kuhn and MacPhail convinced him to give them more time to work out a deal. Davis extended his offer again on February 2. By this time, Davis felt that if he couldn't land the A's in time for the 1978 season, he would keep his options open for the following season. The roadblocks began frustrating Davis. The future of Denver baseball rested on the shoulders of Bay Area politicians. "It was an incredible rollercoaster," said Fallick. "One day it looked like they were coming and the principles agreed. A few days later, we're told, 'don't go so fast.' It was a rollercoaster throughout the negotiations. The longer it went on, the more challenging Finley, and to some degree, the Coliseum board became. Davis eventually threw up his hands. He was tired of the games Finley was playing. He started being more frustrated as the days, weeks and months dragged on."

On February 9, 1978, Nahas, Lurie, Moscone, Deputy Mayor Mel Wax, and Chub Feeney, president of the National League, met in the morning for seventy-five-minutes and reached a complete impasse. A disappointed MacPhail phoned Davis to tell him the deal was off. Moscone refused to approve the name change or approve of the Giants playing half of their games in Oakland. "All negotiations regarding the possibility of the Giants games in the Oakland Coliseum have ended," the Giants said in a statement later that day. The principles also recognized they wouldn't be able to strike a deal, draw up documents and garner the necessary approvals in time for the season.

The political posturing and flexing continued into March, though. They decided to resume negotiations. The discussions gained momentum and Moscone eventually gave in to Nahas and approved the Giants playing 40 games at the Coliseum. They also agreed on a $4 million buyout to free the

A's. Oakland officials planned on using the $4 million to help finance the sixty-four luxury boxes Al Davis was asking for in negotiations.

Los Angeles was charming the Raiders away from Oakland, and Oakland officials knew Raiders owner Al Davis was flirting back. Davis was lusting for the larger market in Southern California. A few weeks later, on April 4, the Coliseum board announced they would not let the A's out of their lease and stopped negotiations with the Giants to play games at the Coliseum during the 1978 season. The A's were staying. Again.

They were close, but it became more apparent the Raiders would be moving to Los Angeles. Lurie remembered Nahas verbally agreeing to accept the buyout with a handshake, but Nahas later told him they had changed their minds. "We were trying to gather a lot of money between Finley, Davis, the American League and myself, to send the A's to Denver," recalled Lurie. "We all had dinner at the Bank of America building in San Francisco and Nahas pretty much agreed to the buyout to let the A's go. He agreed verbally, and as far as I knew, they started drawing up the papers. A few days later, he called me and said they backed out of the deal because they were concerned the Raiders were leaving Oakland. He told me, 'We think the Raiders are leaving and we can't be stuck with nothing.'"

On April 25, 1979, eight days after the A's drew an embarrassing crowd of 653, the Oakland Coliseum slapped an $11.5 million damage suit against Finley for not promoting the A's in the community. The Coliseum was seeking $10 million in punitive damages and $1.5 million in damages they claimed they lost since 1975. The suit contended that Finley breached his contract by violating the provision that he would "maintain an American League baseball team of the character and standing required by the major league rules for the conduct of professional major league baseball games and will endeavor in good faith to obtain the maximum occupancy of the stadium by the public."

The Coliseum's 1979 suit maintained that while A's attendance dropped 50 percent since the start of the 1975 season, American League attendance had increased by 35 percent. The suit also asserted that Finley did not advertise the A's and reduced his promotional literature, failing to sustain a ticket sales campaign throughout the year. In 1978, Finley "disdainfully rejected" a matching offer of $100,000 from Oakland officials to promote the A's, the suit contended. "It's hard to prove that you haven't promoted the team if you're calling newspapers every day and trying to pump your product," said John Hickey. "And he did do that. The point was that he had a bunch of lousy players and didn't want to pay anybody anything."

The lawsuit forced Finley to hire a director of promotions and group sales: twenty-two-year-old Ted Robinson, a 1978 Notre Dame graduate and a young broadcaster. Creating that position was only for allusion, Finley's response to the lawsuit charges. "Charlie hired me because he needed somebody on his staff directory that had the 'director of promotions' title," recalled Robinson. "Charlie told me I could do any promotion as long I didn't spend any money. My budget was zero. I was the last person hired by Finley. I was hired largely because of Finley's ongoing battles with the Oakland Coliseum over the lease. They finally sued him for failing to promote the team."

Matt Levine, a consultant contracted by the Coliseum board for the suit, was tasked with documenting what the standards of marketing were in Major League Baseball and contrasting them to the A's practices. He determined quickly the A's were at the bottom. "The A's, under Charlie Finley, were the most poorly marketed franchise in all of baseball," noted Levine.

Fellow owners were also pressing Finley. During the 1979 winter meetings in Toronto, American League owners voted on a $10,000 per date minimum for visiting clubs in large part because they were losing money coming to Oakland. Visiting clubs were rumored to be receiving only $2,992 per game in Oakland from the 20 percent cut of the gate. The new agreement was called the Finley Regulation.

The A's proposed move to Denver didn't completely die. Finley, MacPhail, Davis, and Lurie met again and agreed on a buyout proposal to present to Oakland officials. On January 2, 1980, the group submitted a formal proposal and request to the Coliseum board to release the A's from the remaining eight years of their contract. The Giants, the American League, Davis, and Finley each contributed $1 million to the $4 million lease buyout package that included indemnity conditions. The buyout was also contingent on Oakland officials dropping their suits. They refused.

On February 12, the Coliseum board announced the A's were staying in Oakland. "We have no alternative but to proceed with preparations for the A's home opener on April 10," said William Cunningham. A frustrated MacPhail subsequently withdrew the buyout offer. The A's were staying in Oakland. "The supervisors voted to accept the buyout, but the city council took no action when it met in executive session Monday," Cunningham said. "So that meant the Coliseum had to go by the City Council's previous vote, which was 8–0 in favor of keeping the A's in Oakland." The Coliseum board required city and county approval before accepting the $4 million lease buyout.

The book finally closed on Davis's agonizing three-year quest of trying to bring the A's to Denver. He was deeply frustrated that he promised Denver a baseball team and couldn't deliver. He prematurely announced the A's purchase. "Davis looked a little bit like one of the bad guys," remembered Fallick. "That ticked him off. He was sorry he ever started it because his reputation was tarnished from the negotiations and the deal that was never finalized. He made this promise to Denver and told them, 'You're getting a major-league baseball team.' And then he said, 'Well, maybe not.' The fans felt he broke his promise."

While the A's gathered the pieces for another season of existence, Oakland eventually lost the Raiders in 1982. After a fierce tangled web of antitrust litigation, a jury of six freed Davis to move his Raiders to Los Angeles. Davis won his suit against the NFL.

Another season of A's baseball would be played in Oakland in 1980 and a desperate Finley decided to change it up. Desperate to generate some excitement, Finley turned to the Miracle Man.

3

FOREVER YOUNG

He never got old to me, he just stayed forever young. I always thought of him as Billy the Kid. Stengel called him Billy the Brat sometimes. He played a kid's game and had a kid's name. That kept him young.
—Van Amburg, Billy Martin's classmate and a former news anchor, 1990

To understand what made Billy Martin tick, one must understand West Berkeley, the effects of the Great Depression, and Martin's indomitable mother, Jenny Salvini. On May 16, 1928, Alfred Manuel Martin Jr. was born inside a modest, green two-story Victorian, one-family home at 1632 Seventh Street in a racially diverse poor neighborhood in West Berkeley. To this day, the house towers over others on the street. A small address plate that reads "EST. 1876" is fastened at the top of the outside door entry of the second story. The house was originally on Sixth Street, but Jenny had it moved on rollers to Seventh. On the way there, the chimney fell off the house while turning a corner. The house was once a rest stop for Pony Express riders. They rested, drank whiskey, and watered-up their horses before heading to the next drop-off.

Billy was born in an upstairs bedroom and circumcised on the kitchen table. The family needed to wire the home with electricity before the doctor would deliver him. They were very poor, and the world was on the brink of the Great Depression, a decade after World War I. California prospered during the decade of the 1920s, but the stock market crashed in 1929 and ushered in the worst economic collapse in the history of America. Martin was born into resistance, tension, and poverty. "He was so poor back then that he would literally take mustard sandwiches to school," said Billy Martin Jr., Billy's second child. "He pulled bags out of the trash, took out the bread, and spread mustard between both slices. On his way to school, he took fruit from the neighbor's fruit trees to fill up his sack to make it look like he had a full bag. He had two pairs of pants and three shirts." Young Billy's mentality was to take before it was taken.

Jenny's mother, Raphaella, whom everyone in the household called "Nonna," helped raise and nurture Billy at home while others were working. Grandma Raphaella spoke no English and was very strict with her ten children. She was the reason everyone stopped calling him Alfred and started calling him "Billy." She called him "Bellis," short for *bellissimo,* the Italian word for beautiful. Once the neighborhood kids heard her calling him that, Bellis became Billy. He slept in the same bed with grandma until he was fifteen, a practice that was not uncommon during the depression. His sleep kicking became too much, so he stopped.

Martin didn't know much about his biological father growing up. "I don't even know what he did for a living," Billy once said. By the time Billy was born, Alfred Manuel Martin, Sr., twenty-six, was no longer in the picture. Alfred was of Portuguese descent from the Hawaiian island of Kauai. He met Jenny, twenty-six, in nearby Oakland. He was dark and over six feet tall with handsomely chiseled features and a bird-beak nose. Alfred got around. He hopped around town and enjoyed the East Bay nightlife. He was a Berkeley fisherman and musician. He fished at the wharf and toured local nightclubs. Jenny and Alfredo decided to get married. The marriage only lasted three months, enough time for the couple to conceive Martin.

The short marriage ended abruptly when Jenny caught Alfred cheating. According to Jenny's accounts, when she was three months pregnant with Billy, she got wind from a girlfriend that Alfred was cheating on her with a student at the nearby University of California. She was livid. Jenny spotted the mistress wearing the same watch she had gifted Alfred, roughed up the unwitting girl, and took back the timepiece. Then she went home and shattered Alfred's car windshield with a hammer before throwing him out of the house. After Jenny cut ties with Alfred, she started calling him "Jackass." She refused to say his name. She carried that resentment with her for the rest of her life. Alfred was Jenny's first love and his infidelity devastated her.

In a 1979 interview, Jenny described her bitter feelings toward Alfred to sportswriter Maury Allen: "I don't even like to talk about him. He was no good. He told everybody he left me. I threw him out. He was sleeping with the girls from the university . . . I don't even like to mention his name. I'll spit on his grave. I promised him that. He can count on it. I don't ever want his name mentioned."

Alfred died at Alameda Hospital on May 31, 1981, at the age of seventy-nine, while Billy was managing the A's. As Billy started developing some of Alfred's facial features, Jenny started telling him, "You look just like the jackass who broke my heart and left me." That took a toll on him. "She was really tough on him," said Billy Jr. "That makes it easier to understand why he never really felt like he was good enough in a weird away."

The hot-tempered Jenny, standing less than five feet tall, was an Italian firecracker. She was conditioned to be. Her father, thirty-two-year-old Nicola Salvini, an Italian fisherman, came to San Francisco, where his brother lived, on rafts from Italy in 1879. It was arranged that Nicola marry eighteen-year-old Raphaella, and they began producing their ten children. Jenny was strong-willed and would not take no for an answer. She was pugnacious. She stood up for herself and acted on impulse that sometimes led to violence. She was a rebel and fighter. "When I was younger, if anyone said anything bad 'bout me, I'd go up to 'em, ask 'em if they said it," Jenny said in 1981. "If they said 'yes,' I wouldn't listen to no more words. I'd punch 'em right in the mouth." "When I interviewed Billy, it was like talking to his mother," said Dave Newhouse, longtime *Oakland Tribune* columnist. "When I interviewed his mother, it was like talking to Billy. They were both fighters."

Raphaella later died on January 11, 1947 at age eight-six. Before immigrating to America, she was a native of the Province of Foggia, Italy. Billy never knew his grandfather. Nicola passed on May 24, 1924. He was seventy-seven.

Billy's second wife, Gretchen Martin, described her former mother-in-law's combative nature. "What can one say about someone else's mother?" Gretchen said in 1988. "She's extremely aggressive. He learned firsthand how that's done—I guess it's apparent I didn't like her at all. I think Billy was a self-made man. She didn't help him. She inadvertently did by making him want to achieve on his own. He had a lot to overcome and he had the foresight to realize it." Despite his mother's imperfections, Billy was fiercely loyal to her. Though she was hard on him, she charged him to always stick up for himself. "She had a huge influence on his life," said Jackie Moore, one of Billy's coaches in Texas and Oakland. "He went back and spent as much time with her as he possibly could, and that's not easy in baseball. He talked about her numerous times."

Mark Ibanez was a twenty-three-year-old weekend news anchor for KTVU, Oakland's longtime television station since 1958, when Billy first arrived to manage the A's in 1980. Ibanez was fairly new to the station and the industry, so he didn't land a lot of opportunity right away, but he persisted on running a feature story for the weekly newscast. Billy Ball was the craze of the Bay Area in 1980 and he persuaded the news director to let him put together a Mother's Day feature on Billy's mother. Ibanez recalled how he came up with the idea:

The Billy Ball phenomenon was going crazy. I had read an article in a local paper about Billy's mom and the news director liked the idea of doing a Mother's Day story on her. So I went over to her Berkeley home and she was a walking, talking sound bite. She was so uninhibited in front of the camera. She had a sailor's vocabulary and cursed many times during the interview. She cursed so much that we had to insert a censor beep every time she said a bad word.

But after reviewing the piece back at the station, Ibanez realized that something was missing—Billy. He needed to interview Billy—and fast:

So I arrived at the Coliseum on the Saturday before Mother's Day three hours before the game started at 1:00 p.m. I was intimidated because I'd heard so much about the great Billy Martin. I kept waiting, waiting and waiting until he finally showed up fifteen minutes before the game. Mother's Day was the next day, so I had to interview him. My cameraman and I finally ambushed him in the tunnel as he walked briskly by. I asked him, 'Billy, do you have a second for a quick interview?' and he replied, 'It's fifteen minutes until the game!' and kept walking. But when I told him the feature was on his mom for Mother's Day, he immediately turned around and gave me the biggest smile. I told him I only had two questions and he told me I could ask as many as I wanted about his mom. The interview showed the softest side of Billy you'd ever see. He was going to blow me off until I mentioned his mom.

Berkeley, on the east shore of San Francisco Bay, had been a destination for a wave of Italian immigrants beginning in the late nineteenth century. They were escaping poverty, natural disasters, disease, and violence brought on by the struggle for Italian unification and independence from foreign rule. Like immigrants from other countries, Italians sought economic opportunity and relief from social strife. They eyed the West Coast. California was appealing to many of them because of industrialized fishing opportunities. A majority of them were young Italian men who planned on working and sending money back to their homeland. They wanted to eventually return. Many immigrants began building communities and families in the Bay Area.

The Salvinis were among them, and they faced the difficulties common to many immigrants at the turn of the century, including language challenges and ethnic stereotyping. In general, however, Italians who emigrated to California enjoyed more freedom and acceptance than was true of immigrants in other parts of the country, primarily because of the ethnic diversity brought on by the gold rush of 1849.

Jenny was born in San Francisco on June 26, 1901, and her family eventually settled in the hardscrabble West Berkeley area around 1906. It's possible that the San Francisco earthquake of that year forced the Salvinis—along with other immigrant families—to cross the bay and settle at the Berkeley waterfront. Berkeley's population soared from 13,214 residents in 1900 to 56,036 in 1920. The Golden Gate Ferry Company began designing a pier that lured auto ferries to Berkeley. It became known as the Berkeley Pier.

Before giving birth to Billy, Jenny had a son, Francis "Tudo" Pisani, from a previously arranged marriage to Donato Pisani around 1918. Pisani was ten years older than Jenny. Raphaella ran a boarding house and arranged for her seventeen-year-old daughter to marry Pisani, one of her boarders. Arranged marriages were a part of Italian tradition during those days. Jenny never loved Pisani and promised her mother she would leave him as soon as she found another partner. Jenny hated authority, even if it came from her mother. The marriage was short-lived.

On May 7, 1921, the *Berkeley Daily Gazette* announced that Donato had left Berkeley for the "Alaska canneries on the ship *Star of France*." On December 2, 1921, the *Oakland Tribune* published a notice from Donato announcing he "will not be responsible for any debt contracted by my wife Jenny Pisani." They divorced in 1923 and Donato was granted custody of Francis. After a seven-year custody battle ensued, a judge granted her full control of Francis on August 8, 1930. A womanizer and gambler, Donato Pisani was later shot dead in Kansas City, according to Jenny's account.

About eight months after Billy was born, Jenny met John Thomas Downey, a handsome Berkeley truck driver from Toronto. He was bright, easygoing and hardworking. Everyone called him "Jack" and he was perfect for the tempestuous Jenny. They met on a Sausalito-bound ferry and married on November 5, 1929. Jack inherited Jenny's two sons, Francis and Billy, from her previous marriages and they gave birth to three more children, Joan, Pat, and Jack Jr. Jack raised Billy and became the father figure in his life. "My dad absolutely loved him," said Billy Jr. "He thought the world of him. He was fair to him and treated him like his own." Billy considered Jack his father. Jack was a positive role model to Billy. He was also the calming presence in a household full of fiery, emotional women. Billy was comfortable with him. When Jenny enforced household rules with him, he ran to Jack.

"She'd ride me because I wouldn't do my chores," Billy once said of them. "I'd be out playing baseball or basketball or football, and she'd get mad at me and say, 'Why don't you get a job like your dad.' But he'd just let me do what I wanted to do."

As in other parts of the country, the federal Works Progress Administration program offered a measure of relief to workers in the Bay Area during the Depression. Jack worked as a WPA handyman and carried the family's financial burdens on his shoulders. Jack was a tireless worker and made sure his family was fed, even if breakfast consisted of stale bread and coffee. "You'd be cocky too, if you were a WPA baby," Billy once said to a group of A's boosters. "Nobody gave you anything. You had to fight for everything you got." Those conditions made him into a battler, forced to hustle harder than others to survive. He battled like that everywhere. He hustled, scratched, and clawed for the bare minimum. "His early life was never easy for him," said Jackie Moore. "He was proud of it, and he should have been. Those circumstances would make anyone grow into a man quick."

Growing up, the beak-nosed Billy was insecure, abrasive, and suspicious. He didn't know his real name was Alfred until he attended Burbank Junior High. While the seventh graders were waiting to be assigned to their homeroom class, a teacher called for Alfred Manuel Martin. He figured there was another Martin boy in the room, so he ignored her. When he realized the teacher never called his name, he approached her and asked her why. "She asked me my street address, and when I told her, she said 'Your name is Alfred,'" Billy once recalled. He tried to convince her that his name was not Alfred, but she told him to go home and talk to his mother about it. "I said 'Mom, you're not going to believe what happened,'" Billy once remembered, "but the teacher said my real name is Alfred." He was confused and asked her why she never revealed his real name to him. "She said, 'Because I didn't want you to know you had the same name as that jackass, your father,'" Billy said.

Young Billy's home away from home was James Kenney Park, a two-square-block park located just down the street from his house, at the corner of Eighth and Virginia. Today, after a multimillion-dollar upgrade, Kenney Park features tennis, basketball and volleyball courts, baseball and soccer fields, along with a community center. But in the '30s and '40s, it was by no means an idyllic playground. It was a place where a young boy shouldn't go if he wasn't prepared to scuffle. Martin showed up and scuffled there.

"In Oakland, where I grew up, I had a pretty rough going," Billy told a reporter 1966. "I was little. I wanted to be a competitor, and I had to fight my way for a job all the time. I had to learn to fight or I would have been lost in the shuffle. It wasn't that I was a tough kid. I don't mean it that way, but I wanted to make the team. I didn't want to be shoved aside. So I fought my way past the bigger guys. I have been fighting all my life to make it."

The brassy Martin spent a lot of his early childhood and teenage years competing on Kenney Park's dusty fields. "West Berkeley was a blue-collar neighborhood back then and Billy was lucky he had talent as a ballplayer," said John Underhill of the Berkeley Historical Society. "He was in high school during the war years." He also sold towels there and hung out with the older players and learned from them. Billy brought his battling, brash, hard-nosed style of living with him when he played sports, and it worked. He was a ferocious competitor. Everyone called the 5-foot-2 sparkplug "Little Billy" on the field until he sprouted to 5-foot-10 by the time he graduated from Berkeley High. It was a significant growth spurt. Billy was a hyper, fast-handed ball stealer on Berkeley's basketball team. He idolized Augie Galan, another Berkeley-born big leaguer who grew up playing on local sandlots.

Young Billy played baseball, football, basketball and volleyball on Kenney's fields and courts. And he got used to defending himself. In his autobiography *Number 1,* published in 1980, Martin shared how World War II toughened his neighborhood and him. "A kid growing up in West Berkeley didn't have a choice in the matter. I have always said that I never started a fight in my whole life, and that was true even when I was a kid. But it was true then, as it is now, that I was taught never to back down if I found myself in a situation where I had to fight. It was either fight or stay away from the park. That was the choice, and I loved the park too much to stay away."

While the Salvinis of West Berkeley had a dull view of the shabby wooden house across the street from their living room window, not all of Berkeley was poor. Berkeley's privileged class in the affluent upper reaches enjoyed a spectacular view of the Golden Gate from Grizzly Peak Boulevard. The houses were designed and constructed with architectural excellence on the winding roads. From their porches on the Contra Costa Hills—now called the Berkeley Hills—rich Berkeleyans could peer over the poor flatlands of Berkeley and Oakland to watch San Francisco wake up every morning across the bay. The rich and educated lived in the Berkeley Hills. Immigrants and people of color were redlined—denied loans because of discrimination—and excluded from the remote area. "He saw signs on restaurants around town that read 'No Italians Allowed' and 'We Do Not Serve the Irish,'" said Billy Jr. "He lived that world."

Some of the privileged communities in the hills built gates to keep people of color out. Nestled in the hills was the University of California, Berkeley, the city's keystone that was attracting and producing some of the brightest minds in the country. Many of the privileged kids from the hills attended school with Billy, and he resented them.

"He didn't like people that had gone to college, especially from the University of California," said Brian Kingman, one of Billy's former A's pitchers. "He grew up in Berkeley and he just thought they were privileged, spoiled people."

4

CASEY'S BOY

Managers with hot tempers make the game more colorful. They take the dullness out of baseball. Things happen. There's excitement. The fans love it.
—C. L. "Brick" Laws, former Owner, Oakland Oaks, 1969

In April 1946, Billy's baseball career at Berkeley High came to an abrupt end. Berkeley, which played in the Alameda County Athletic League, had a fierce interleague rivalry with the Hayward High Farmers. Billy hated them. Hayward fans always made fun of his beak nose when he played on their diamond. So when, early in the season, the schools faced off in Hayward, tension was already at a high level. Adding to it was a rumor that Billy and Pete Hernandez, the Farmers' top pitcher, were going to fight after the game.

The buzz fueled the rivalry even more, and boosted attendance. Billy came into the game leading Berkeley in hitting with a .425 batting average. Hernandez started the game, fanned 12, and led the Farmers to a 6–2 victory. Billy, playing shortstop, cracked two hits in the game. As expected, Billy and Hernandez brawled after the game. Billy got the better of the pitcher, which prompted Berkeley's principal to kick him off the team. The incident worried Martin because he was afraid his growing reputation as a fighter would scare baseball scouts away. But he stayed on their radar.

Martin graduated from Berkeley High in June 1946. He worked at the Heinz pickle factory every summer until he started playing professional baseball. Billy's scrappiness, confidence, and aggressive style of play attracted the attention of New York Yankees scout Eddie Leishman, who signed him to play for their farm club in Idaho Falls for $200 a month. The eighteen-year-old joined the Idaho Falls Russets baseball club of the Class D Pioneer League. Billy, playing mostly at third base in Idaho Falls, batted .254 and committed 16 errors in only 32 games.

Billy was a part of an Oakland baseball renaissance in 1948, when he played second base for the Oakland Oaks. The hometown kid, Billy the Horn, as opponents called him, was the pride and joy of Oakland that season. The Oaks had purchased Martin from Idaho Halls in 1946, and Charles Dillon "Casey" Stengel, fifty-five, the new manager of the Oaks, invited Billy to spring training in Boyes Hot Springs, California, their spring headquarters. Stengel, a respected game strategist, had a three-year plan to bring a championship to Oakland.

C. L. "Brick" Laws, president and co-owner of the Oaks, offered "Ol' Case" the manager's job in 1945. He didn't think Stengel would take it. Stengel had managed the Kansas City Blues of the American Association to a seventh-place finish in 1945 and was seriously considering retirement. Stengel had struggled miserably as a major league manager in previous stints with the Brooklyn Dodgers (1934–36) and Boston Braves (1938–43). The fiery and colorful Stengel produced only one winning season during that span and never finished better than fifth. He was on the verge of walking away from the game.

After spending more than a month deciding, Stengel accepted the position and the $12,000 annual salary. Being near his Glendale, California, home was also a factor. He inherited the aging Oaks, who finished in fifth place in the standings with a 90–93 record in 1945. "The minute I saw him in the spring [1945] I had a feeling of security with Stengel," Laws told the *Oakland Tribune* in 1968. "I had a feeling he knew talent. He analyzed the situation, and told me it would take two, or maybe three years, and he'd bring the pennant to Oakland. He did it in three years."

Billy reported to Boyes Hot Springs in 1947 and played third base. Stengel, though, felt Billy needed more seasoning with their Class C club in the Arizona-Texas League. The third baseman posted torrid offensive numbers for the Phoenix Senators. He won the Texas League batting crown with a scorching .392 batting average. By September of 1947, the brash Billy, considered a can't-miss prospect, was playing for Stengel in Oakland. Billy was obsessed with playing and pressured his manager. He hated when Stengel platooned him. He once replaced infielder Dario Lodigiani, Stengel's second baseman before he arrived, and warned him, "You'll never get your job back, Lodigiani."

Stengel fell for Billy's brashness and grit, while Martin came to admire Stengel's managerial style. Stengel was a master psychologist who knew how to motivate his players. In Martin's case, Stengel gave Billy confidence and made him believe in himself. A relative youngster on a team of older players, Billy soon became known as "Casey's boy." Managing an aging Oakland roster that was nicknamed the "Nine Old Men," Stengel soon began platooning players in order to keep them fresh. He was known for using 15 to 20 players each game and using a pitcher for only two or three innings.

Standing 5-foot-10, the twenty-year-old Billy played second base and batted .277 for the Oaks in 1948. He played with explosion and a ferocious drive to win. "He played up and down the California coast, so people were very aware of him," said Bob Lacey, who later pitched for Billy in Oakland. "He was a good player."

Martin also remembered one of the lessons he'd learned in Kenney Park: to always be ready for a fight. Dave Newhouse, who covered Billy later as a columnist, recalled seeing the Oaks play the Hollywood Stars in Oakland as a boy in 1948. The game, the first of a Sunday doubleheader, featured a fight between Billy and Lou Stringer of the Stars, another second baseman. "Billy was on first base and Stringer taunted him to try to steal second base. He was calling Billy 'Horn.' So Billy tries to steal second and does one of those popup slides. He came straight up, got on top of Stringer, and must've hit him twenty times. He wasn't strong enough to knock him out. Billy was feisty, but he wasn't a big guy. But he loved to fight." They finally pulled him off Stringer and Casey walked Martin off the field. The umpire ruled Billy out on the play.

The Oakland Baseball Park, the home field of the Oaks from 1913 to 1955 with a cozy capacity of 13,000, was in Emeryville—between Oakland and Berkeley—a few blocks from the original Trader Vic's, now a chain of Tiki bars. In 1945, Americans were hungry for entertainment after the depression and World War II, and the Oaks helped fit the bill. Stengel's Oaks, who finished with a record of 114–74 in 1948, sparked civic pride and brought Oakland its first Pacific Coast League championship since 1927. Thanks to a late-season charge, the team finished two games ahead of their cross-bay rivals, the San Francisco Seals (the team that gave Joe DiMaggio his pro start in 1932). Deciding to manage the Oaks breathed new life into Stengel's managerial career. When the season culminated, Stengel signed a two-year deal to manage the 1949 Yankees. Over the next twelve years, Stengel led the Yankees on an unprecedented run, capturing ten pennants and seven World Series titles.

Stengel brought Martin and Jackie Jensen, an outfielder, to New York following the 1949 season when the Yankees purchased them from the Oaks. "That boy played for me in Oakland last year," Stengel told the *Oakland Tribune* in 1949 about Billy. "Helped me win a pennant, but do you know I almost lost him. He was playing in the all-star high school game out there in 1946 and I was supposed to pick out the best player.

"I didn't even notice Martin until my trainer, Red Adams, pointed him out. Everybody liked a kid by the name of Arnerich, but Red tells me Martin is the best infielder of the lot. So I hit some balls to him and I find that Red knows what he is talking about."

The Yankees were a team in transition and Billy became of one Stengel's loyal team leaders. "Casey felt the Yankees needed that spark that my father provided," said Billy Martin Jr. Martin, who was making $9,000 with the Oaks, made only $7,500 with the Yankees. He joined the Bronx Bombers in the second year of their run of five consecutive World Series championships from 1949 to '53. It was in New York where the young Billy was baptized in the Yankee way. He soon befriended teammates DiMaggio, Mickey Mantle, Yogi Berra, and Whitey Ford, and a lifelong addiction to the Yankees developed. Playing mostly second base, Martin batted .250 in only 34 games in 1950. After the season, he married his first wife, Lois Elaine Berndt, eighteen, at St. Ambrose Catholic Church in Berkeley on October 4.

A month later, Billy was drafted and served in the army at Fort Ord, California, beginning in November 1950, but was granted a dependency discharge at his request in April 1951. Martin was earning $75 a month in the army and claimed he couldn't fully support his family back home unless he returned to earning the salary his former employer, the Yankees, was paying him. Billy's only appearance in the 1951 World Series against the New York Giants was as a pinch-runner in the eighth inning of Game 2. He scored the final run in the Yankees' 3–1 victory that evened the Series.

By 1952, Billy, wearing uniform number 1, was the Yankees' permanent second baseman. It was during the '52 World Series that he began demonstrating a flair for the dramatic. Playing second base, his hustling, series-saving catch of Jackie Robinson's bases-loaded, wind-pushed pop up on the infield in the seventh inning, finished off the Brooklyn Dodgers at Ebbets Field in seven games. Billy's catch helped the Yankees preserve a 4–2 victory and win their fourth straight World Series crown.

The following year, Martin helped the Yankees win their fifth straight world championship, again against the Dodgers, but this time with his bat. Batting .500, Billy tied the all-time record for hits in a World Series with 12.

On the field, Martin and the Yankees were winning championships. Off the field, Billy and Mickey Mantle took full advantage of New York nightlife.

But the good times were interrupted in 1954 when he was called into the service again, after he was reclassified to 1-A by his draft board. Billy served in the army for twenty-two months. Private Martin served as a play-er-manager on a team comprised of soldiers. "He was pissed because when they drafted him, they didn't send him to the Korean War," said Billy Jr. "They had him run their baseball team in Fort Collins. He's running and coaching a military baseball team. He was furious. He couldn't believe they took him from the Yankees to do that."

The Yankees were without Billy for the entire 1954 season, and didn't make the World Series, snapping a run of five straight World Series titles. He played briefly for the Yankees on terminal furlough in September 1955 but received his official army discharge in October. Playing mostly second base, Billy batted .300 in only 20 games in his September return. Martin then posted a .320 average with eight hits as the Yankees dropped the World Series to the Dodgers in seven games.

After sparking the Yankees to another World Series in 1956 as New York defeated Brooklyn to avenge their 1955 defeat, the next season marked a turning point in Billy's career. On May 16, 1957, he and teammates Hank Bauer, Mickey Mantle, Johnny Kucks, Whitey Ford, and Yogi Berra were celebrating his twenty-ninth birthday at Copacabana nightclub in New York City. A delicatessen owner in the nightclub claimed Bauer assaulted him, but the Yankees front office zeroed in on Billy, who'd long been considered a bad influence on Mantle. Even Stengel, his baseball father and protector, couldn't save him. All the players were fined as a result of the incident, but George Weiss, the Yankees general manager, traded Billy to the Kansas City A's at the July 15 trade deadline.

As a player, Martin became a journeyman after leaving the Yankees, bouncing from six teams in five years with stops in Kansas City, Detroit, Cleveland, Cincinnati, Milwaukee, and Minnesota. After playing on six pennant winners in New York, Martin never participated in the postseason as a player again. "He was never the same player after he was traded," said Billy Jr. "He bounced around from team to team every year almost."

Billy finally found some stability with an organization only after he retired from baseball as a player at age thirty-three in 1962. The Twins released Billy in the spring, but they offered him—at the urging of manager Sam Mele—an opportunity to stay in the organization as a scout and work in a public relations capacity in the front office. Becoming a scout was Martin's entry into the world of baseball management. He also served as a pitchman for Grain Belt, a local brewery. Billy, who served as the Midwest supervisor of scouts, purchased a home in Minneapolis and settled in the area with second wife Gretchen, who gave birth to his second child, Billy Jr., in 1964. (Kelly Ann, his daughter from his previous marriage, was born in 1953.) Legendary baseball scout Dick Wiencek was also a scout supervisor for the Twins in 1962, on the West Coast. The bond proved long-lasting. Billy would later bring Wiencek to Oakland to run the A's farm system.

In Minnesota, more doors opened for Martin. Calvin Griffith, the Twins' owner, brought him in as a third base coach and to work with young infielders, notably young shortstop Zoilo Versalles. Bringing the aggressive Billy on the field in 1964, Griffith felt, would energize his club's sluggish play. Reclaiming No. 1, the same number he wore during most of his playing career, he brought a running mentality to the Twins. Rod Carew, an eighteen-year-old second baseman in the Twins organization who later won the American League Rookie of the Year in 1967, credited Billy for shaping his game early on. "Billy convinced me that if I wanted to hit homers, and I could have hit twenty or more a season, my average would suffer, so in 1969, I stopped trying to jack everything out of the ball park and won my first batting title." Carew went on to win seven batting titles, hit .328 for his career, and was an eighteen-time All-Star selection. He was inducted into the Baseball Hall of Fame in 1991.

By 1967, rumors surfaced that Billy, thirty-nine, was a candidate to become Charlie Finley's next manager. Finley was moving his Kansas City A's to Oakland. Finley had just fired Alvin Dark and asked Griffith's permission to interview Billy. While the A's job was attractive to Billy, born and raised only ten miles from Oakland, he was well aware of Finley's compulsive habit of changing managers. He shared his reluctance to the Associated Press in 1967. "The deal would have to be pretty good to go with Finley because he has been known to change his mind on managers at the slightest provocation."

Although the controversial Billy could shake up a team, there were still some who thought he was too explosive to be a manager. There was no question of his having a keen baseball mind, but his temperament was a red flag. In 1966, Billy had tangled with Howard Fox, the Twins' traveling secretary and one of Griffith's closest friends, in the lobby of the Statler-Hilton Hotel. The fight left Fox with a bloody nose. Billy and Finley never joined forces in 1967 as Finley never followed through. "If Finley doesn't take me now, he'll never get me," Billy said at the time. Even though he wouldn't be hired by Finley until 1980, Billy was always on his radar as a managerial prospect.

Finley hired Bob Kennedy to manage the A's in 1968, the team's first season in Oakland. Billy, seeking managerial experience, took over as pilot of the Denver Bears, the Twins' Triple-A affiliate in the Pacific Coast League. Having spent more than three seasons as a third-base coach in the major leagues, Martin felt the move down to gain experience would help his chances to manage one day in the majors. But it took some convincing. "He didn't want to do it because he was afraid he might never get back up," Billy Jr. recalled. "My mother kept convincing him that it was the right move." Gretchen was very business savvy and Billy respected her advice, most of the time.

Billy inherited a Denver team that was 8–22 when he took reigns on May 26, 1968. One of Billy's veteran arms on the Bears' staff was forty-six-year-old closer Art Fowler, who later became his personal pitching coach and drinking confidant wherever he managed in the big leagues. The ancient Fowler, a grandfather at the time and also the Bears' pitching coach, had a 1.93 earned run average that season. Under Billy's leadership, the Bears finished their final 115 games with a 65–50 record, a .565 winning percentage. They ended the season in fourth place with an overall record of 73–72. Creating a winning culture like the one he cultivated in Denver would become Martin's trademark with every team he inherited. He won immediately. The criticism, though, was the winning climate never lasted long. "The expiration date on Billy was always short wherever he managed," said Randy Galloway, who covered him for the *Dallas Morning News.*

Billy was ejected from eight games that season with the Bears, but the consensus was that he had mellowed. (He later admitted that his biggest challenge that season was "getting the umpires to like me.") Griffith was convinced. After firing manager Cal Ermer in September, Griffith hired Billy on October 11, 1968. He became the manager of the 1969 Twins, inheriting a seventh-place club that finished with a 79–83 record the previous season. The public and media had been pushing hard for the Twins to hire Billy, who signed a one-year deal for an estimated $35,000. Griffith acknowledged the grassroots and media campaign waged on Martin's behalf during the press conference welcoming him. "You people here in the news media certainly helped the decision. I'd never seen such a campaign in my life about one personality," Griffith told reporters. "I say personality because Billy is a personality. He's one of the better known men in baseball, and I feel that under Billy's guidance and leadership, we can produce a winning team."

Early on, Martin borrowed heavily from Casey Stengel's managerial playbook, and it paid off. Martin led the Twins to the very first American League West Division title in 1969. His popularity soared in the Twin Cities. But there was front office tension with Billy and reports of clubhouse unrest. He publicly criticized Sherry Robertson, the team's farm director and Griffith's brother, in May about a minor-league roster move. He later apologized to team officials for airing his complaints to the press and agreed to vet all concerns through Griffith first.

On August 7, the unrest turned physical. After a Twins game against the Tigers, Billy roughed up Dave Boswell, a Minnesota pitcher, outside a downtown Detroit bar. Most accounts contend that Boswell attacked outfielder Bob Allison before Billy stepped in to help. As Martin told the Associated Press, his "help" consisted of "about five or six punches to the stomach, a couple to the head, and when he came off the wall, I hit him again. He was out before he hit the ground." Boswell required stitches. Griffith fined Boswell for his involvement and had warned Billy about fraternizing at the same bars the players frequented. Griffith also did not approve of the high-stake poker games Billy was allowing on team flights. Griffith's concerns over Billy breaking policy and guidelines were growing, all while Billy was garnering a rabid Minneapolis following.

Ultimately, the owner ran out of patience. Griffith announced on October 13, 1969 that the popular Billy was fired, despite his leading the club to a 97–65 record and a division title as a rookie manager. "You know Billy can go into a crowd and charm the hell out of you. But he ignored me," Griffith told reporters. In the nine years that Billy was in the Twins organization, fans connected with his fiery personality. Griffith's decision to let Billy go was unpopular and fans scheduled boycotts.

The following year, 1970, marked the first time in twenty-four years Billy was out of baseball. He stayed in Minneapolis working as a radio announcer at KDWB, a local rock radio station. He maintained business ties through the station serving as a special assistant to the president, Victor Armstrong. The local brewery kept him busy making public appearances. By June, Billy was again rumored to be Finley's next manager in Oakland. Finley flirted with hiring Billy when the A's were struggling under skipper John McNamara. But Finley allowed McNamara to finish the season, and Billy signed a two-year contract with the Detroit Tigers on October 2, 1970, earning $60,000 annually. That same day, Finley hired Dick Williams to replace McNamara as the A's new skipper. Williams would go on to lead the A's to three consecutive postseason appearances that included two World Series titles.

In Detroit, the flamboyant Billy joined a notoriously conservative, close-knit front office and inherited an aging club that had finished the '70 season 79–83. Several players from the Tigers' 1968 championship team were still on the roster. Jim Campbell, the general manager, thought his team needed a kick and turned to Billy. Billy sparked the Tigers to 91 wins and a second-place finish in 1971 and, as in Minnesota, fans quickly embraced the fiery skipper. Martin led the Tigers to the American League Championship Series in 1972 but lost to Finley's A's in five games. By 1973, the Tigers' image-conscious front office clashed with Billy, who had criticized the farm system to the press for not producing enough stars to replace the aging veterans on the club. Billy was a hard loser. Some players complained of a tense clubhouse under Billy. Some players loved him. Some hated him.

American League president Joe Cronin had suspended him for ordering his pitchers to throw spitballs in a late August game, but before Martin served his three-game suspension, Campbell—after sharing concerns with Billy a week before—fired him on September 2, 1973. Billy used the spitball order to bring attention to the spitballs Gaylord Perry was throwing for the Indians during a recent Tigers loss. Martin had one year left on his contract. Campbell contended that "from foul line to foul line, Billy did a good job." His showmanship was too much for them outside the lines. "We can't have people working for us making derogatory remarks about the commissioner and the president of the American League," Campbell told reporters after firing Billy. "Frankly, we don't do business that way."

Billy left the Tigers with a winning record of 248-204 in almost three full seasons, including a division title in 1972. At the time of his firing, the team's record was 71–63. The Tigers slumped after Billy left, enduring four consecutive losing seasons from 1974 to '77.

Martin's employment prospects suffered no such slump. After Campbell let him go, Billy found work less than a week later when Bob Short, owner of the Texas Rangers, fired Whitey Herzog on September 7. Short, who made millions from his trucking empire, hired Billy the next day, inking him to a five-year deal reportedly worth $65,000 annually. Short, who was a Billy Martin enthusiast, met him when he was owner of the NBA's Minneapolis Lakers. Billy and Short had established a friendship that began in Minnesota. Billy campaigned for Short when Short ran for governor of Minnesota in 1970.

Short owned the Washington Senators and moved them to the Dallas-Fort Worth area after the 1971 season, renaming the team the Texas Rangers. Billy took over the worst team in baseball. When he became manager, the Rangers were 48–91 and trailed the first-place A's by 33 1/2 games. Only 686,085 fans came through the turnstiles at Arlington Stadium to watch the 1973 Rangers. "When the franchise moved here in 1972, nobody showed up," remembered Randy Galloway. "Attendance was bottoming out for two years. They had a horrible team. It was an awful year." It was a baseball disaster designed for Billy, who was building a reputation for healing sick clubs.

Reviving the placid Rangers would be Billy's biggest challenge as a manager. "Martin is the best manager I've seen," Bob Short told reporters. "If my mother were the manager and I had a chance to hire him, I would fire my mother." The Rangers finished the season with a 57–105 record, 37 games out of first.

Short sold the club six months later for $9.6 million and the assumption of $1 million in debt, in early April, to Brad Corbett, a thirty-six-year-old plastic pipe manufacturing magnate from Fort Worth. The Rangers were now in the hands of local ownership. Billy was a hit in Texas and fell in love with the country-and-western culture. He started wearing boots and hats with a looped mustache. "He loved it," said Galloway. "He went totally western until the day he died."

As in Denver, Minnesota, and Detroit, Billy almost immediately breathed life into the organization, leading the Rangers to a second-place finish in 1974 with a record of 84–76. Dubbed "Billy's Turnaround Gang," the team brought 1,193,902 fans through the turnstiles in 1974, and this was in football country. The Rangers' turnaround earned Martin American League Manager of the Year honors, and he became the king of Dallas-Fort Worth. "They challenged the mighty A's down to the last two weeks of the season," recalled Galloway. "It was a shocking season. Billy had a terrific year. He built the foundation for the franchise. It was great short-term success and proved that fans would come. They showed up. That ballpark was as loud as it ever was. That was all Billy, and boy, did the fans love Billy. Baseball took off in Texas."

Martin's son recalled that seeing how his father resurrected Texas baseball in 1974 helped him appreciate his father's gifts as a manager. "I was old enough to realize how much of a difference he made to a team," said Billy Jr. "Even though that was the only team he managed that he didn't take to the postseason, it was the first time I realized how good he was."

With the instant success Billy brought to the organization, some younger players thrived and gained recognition. Jeff Burroughs, a twenty-three-year-old, power-hitting outfielder, won the American League's Most Valuable Player crown. First baseman Mike Hargrove, twenty-four, won the AL Rookie of the Year Award and Ferguson Jenkins, who boasted a 25–12 record on the mound for the Rangers, was named Comeback Player of the Year.

But the autonomy that Short gave Billy when he hired him disappeared when Corbett took control. The magic left the building in 1975 and key players underperformed. The Rangers never could generate the same momentum they did in '74. The adrenaline rush from the 1974 season seemed to suck everything completely out of them under Billy's intensity to win. "The team got stuck in the same ditch," said Galloway. Nothing was left in '75. In July, Billy insisted on signing twenty-nine-year-old catcher Tom

Egan, who was recently released by the California Angels. Rangers GM Dan O'Brien refused to sign him, a decision Corbett supported. Billy preferred older players on the roster and aired his anger to reporters. "He [Corbett] knows as much about baseball as I know about pipe," Martin told reporters. "One year in baseball and he's already a genius." The end for Billy in Texas was near.

According to Billy Jr., it was a disagreement over the seventh-inning stretch song at Arlington Stadium that helped lead to his father's dismissal. Billy insisted on John Denver's smash hit "Thank God I'm a Country Boy." It electrified the stadium when fans stomped their feet. Corbett preferred "Take Me Out to the Ballgame." "That didn't fire anyone up," said Billy Jr. "Dad told them to play the Denver song and then Corbett would run in there and tell them no. That was kind of the last straw between them because they really got along. They really liked each other."

Corbett fired Billy on July 21, 1975. The fourth-place Rangers were 44–51. The firing, announced after a Monday night home win against Boston, left a teary-eyed, shirtless Billy sulking in the clubhouse. It couldn't have come as a complete surprise. Days before, he and Corbett had engaged in a loud confrontation about the club's future. For two days and nights after the argument, Billy stayed at the ballpark, operating on little sleep. He found out he was fired from Frank Lucchesi, his third-base coach. The front office told Lucchesi they were firing Martin the night before and asked him if he would take over as skipper. He accepted. "I'm happy about one thing," Billy said after being fired. "I brought Texas a winner . . . I brought them a million fans and I brought them real major-league baseball."

Three stops into his career as a manager, Billy was earning a reputation as a dugout genius, albeit one who was high maintenance. He wanted to be involved in all baseball decisions. Some owners felt the wins Billy brought weren't worth the headaches. Other front office officials, however, thought they could still handle Billy. "As good as he was as a manager—among the best ever—he could wear people out," said Galloway. When owners hired

Martin, they knew he was going to pour out his soul to win immediately and attract fans. He was a force—but a force that didn't last long in one city. "Billy's problem was that as well as he got along with players, he did not get along well with people who he felt knew less about the game than he did, and that included both owners and general managers," said Peter Golenbock, Billy's co-author on his autobiography and author of a Martin biography. "It got him in very deep trouble."

Yankees owner George Steinbrenner thought hiring Billy was worth the risk. He hired him twelve days later, on August 2, 1975, replacing Bill Virdon. Billy took over the Yankees on Old-Timers' Day in front of a crowd of 43,968. The 53–51 Yankees were a major disappointment that season. They had acquired Catfish Hunter and slugger Bobby Bonds in the offseason to take them over the top. While both performed well, injuries to key players and pitching slumps mired the Yankees at two games above .500, which didn't sit well with the team's mercurial owner. Dampening the fans' enthusiasm even further in 1975 was the fact that they were playing home games at Shea Stadium because extensive renovations were being done to Yankee Stadium. Billy was brought in to bring excitement and fire up the veteran club comprised of the likes of Thurman Munson, Graig Nettles, Chris Chambliss, Sandy Alomar, Roy White, Rudy May, Sparky Lyle, Pat Dobson, Hunter, and Bonds.

The front office realized that Martin had a number of things going for him in New York. First, he was closely connected to Yankee history and tradition, having spent most of his playing career with the team during the glory years in the 1950s. In addition, the brass figured that Billy's reputation as a battler would connect well with New York's working class. He was rejoining the same organization that broke his heart and sent him packing eighteen years before—after the Copacabana nightclub incident in 1957. But a new front office was in place. Billy's life had changed when Stengel brought him to New York in 1950. His playing career tumbled into irrelevance once he left the Yankees. Gabe Paul, the Yankees president, wanted to hire Billy badly as soon as Texas fired him. Of all teams, the Yankees knew his reputation well, but were convinced they could handle the firebrand. The Yankees finished the season 30–26 under Billy with an overall record of 83–77, enough for third place in the standings.

In 1976, things started looking up. Bolstered by some key offseason acquisitions that included spark plugs Willie Randolph and Mickey Rivers and a move back to the refurbished Yankee Stadium, Billy led the Yankees to a regular season record of 97–62 and the AL East championship. He'd brought Yogi Berra in as coach, reminding fans of the team's dominance in the 1950s. Against the AL West champion Kansas City Royals, Chambliss hit a dramatic leadoff home run in the bottom of the ninth in the deciding Game 5 of the League Championship Series, sending the Yankees back to the World Series. In his first full season as the Yankees' manager, Martin had led the team to their thirtieth pennant in team history and first since 1964. Munson, the team captain, was named the American League's Most Valuable Player in 1976. "To me, personally seeing it [the pennant] come back to New York means more to me than anything I've done in my career," Billy said after advancing to the World Series. "Now I think I know how Casey Stengel felt back then." Led by eventual Hall-of-Famers Johnny Bench, Joe Morgan, Tony Perez, and manager Sparky Anderson, the "Big Red Machine" Cincinnati Reds completed a four-game sweep of the Yankees in the World Series, but Billy had become the toast of New York. He was recognized everywhere.

The Yankees, having signed prolific slugger Reggie Jackson to a massive five-year, $3 million contract, made the jump in 1977 when they won the World Series over the Los Angeles Dodgers in six games. It was the Yankees' first world championship since 1962 and Billy's first and only as a manager. The addition of Jackson, the brashness, ego and stardom—and his relationship with Steinbrenner—brought clubhouse tension that required constant mediation. Jackson was baseball's richest free agent.

As the wins mounted, so did the conflicts. Billy's exploding popularity was threatening to the front office and he clashed with the meddling

Steinbrenner. Fans loved him, but they didn't live with him. Billy resented Steinbrenner's special treatment of Jackson and his extravagant offseason courtship to lure him to New York. Billy was drinking heavily and always rumored to being on the chopping block.

The tension manifested on national television in the sixth inning of a nationally televised Saturday afternoon game at Boston's Fenway Park on June 18 when Billy and Jackson nearly tangled in the visitor's dugout. Billy had removed Jackson from the game for not hustling on a ball that dropped in right field, resulting in a heated confrontation when Jackson returned to the dugout. Coaches Elston Howard and Yogi Berra restrained Billy from Jackson. Billy had sent Paul Blair to right to replace Jackson, who was angry and humiliated for being pulled. Some scribes called the Yankees "Team Turmoil." Billy's relationship with the Yankees' front office had soured, but he led the Yankees to 100 wins in 1977. Billy toughened them. Jackson's World Series heroics that season (he hit three home runs in Game 6 on three consecutive pitches off three different pitchers) proved why he was the difference maker on a club swept in the World Series a season before. "There was no love lost between Billy and Reggie," said Ray Negron, a former Yankees clubhouse attendant. "There was legitimate hate there. It had nothing to do with Reggie being black."

On July 17, 1978, with the Yankees and Royals tied 5–5 in the bottom of the 10th, Billy ordered Jackson to bunt after Munson led off with a single. Jackson took the first pitch inside for a ball, and Martin took off the bunt sign. The expectation was for Jackson to swing away, but he bunted again on a two-strike pitch, popping out to the catcher. Billy was livid and suspended Jackson for five games without pay for his insubordination. Billy's stormy relationship with Jackson was worsening and the feud had come to a head.

"There were always two or three players on a team who despised Billy," said Golenbock. "They were almost always substitutes or egomaniacs—the narcissists who wanted to be the stars where, of course, Billy wanted to be the star."

The final straw came at O'Hare Airport in Chicago when Billy told Murray Chass of the *New York Times* and Henry Hecht of the *New York Post* that Steinbrenner and Jackson deserved each other. "One's a born liar, the other's convicted!" he told them. His remarks referred to Steinbrenner's conviction for illegal political contributions in 1974.

Steinbrenner, enraged, sent Al Rosen, the Yankees' president, to Kansas City to fire Billy. Judge Eddie Sapir, Billy's attorney and close friend, maintains that he persuaded Martin to resign for health reasons before Rosen arrived, which would have nullified the three years remaining on the manager's contract. The next day, on July 24, Billy, stressed, fragile and wearing dark sunglasses, tearfully announced his resignation at a press conference in the lobby of the Crown Center Hotel in Kansas City. He'd seen the writing on the wall and the walls were closing in on him. "He was so distraught at the press conference," said Negron. "If he had a gun there, he would have shot himself. It was like someone had died." "I owe it to my health to resign," Billy said. "I'm sorry about some things that were printed. I did not say them. I want to thank my coaches, the players and the news media for everything."

Negron met with Billy at his New Jersey apartment when he returned from Kansas City and stood by a somber Billy the entire night. Instead of watching the Yankees finish the series in Kansas City on television, they watched a *National Geographic* program. "All he did was cry and cry," said Negron. "In the middle of the crying, he kept on saying, 'I don't hate Reggie. I don't hate Reggie.'" Rosen replaced Billy with easygoing Bob Lemon, who had been fired by the White Sox in late June.

Billy's departure was complicated by the fact that Yankee fans adored him. They flooded the phone lines at the Yankee offices to protest, persuading Steinbrenner—five days later—to publicly announce on July 29 during the Old-Timers' Day festivities his plan to bring Billy back to manage the team after the next full season. Fans showered Billy with a five-minute ovation when public address announcer Bob Sheppard introduced him at Yankee Stadium as the Yankees manager for 1980. As much as Billy was known for fighting for his players, fans fought for him. Front offices always needed to consider his popularity before cutting ties. "In my gut, it wasn't right that he had to leave," Steinbrenner said. "After he resigned that Monday, I knew the next day that I had to bring him back. I don't want him to change out on the field; I want him to change in his public behavior, and I think he has." Negron remembers sneaking Billy into Yankee Stadium on Old-Timers' Day. "We hid him in this storage room," said Negron. "There [were] already rumors in the clubhouse before the game that he was coming back." Steinbrenner would bring Billy back to manage a total of four times.

Billy returned sooner than anticipated. In 1979, Steinbrenner rehired him on June 18, when his underachieving, fourth-place Yankees needed a jolt after struggling and lacking fire under manager Bob Lemon. The Yankees were 34–31 when Billy took over. All-Star closer Rich "Goose" Gossage was sidelined most of the season after tearing ligaments in his thumb during a clubhouse scuffle with Cliff Johnson on April 19. Lemon's heart was heavy from the death of his son, twenty-six-year-old Jerry Lemon, who was killed in an auto accident in Phoenix, Arizona, days after the Yankees won the '78 World Series. Lemon had become too emotionally detached to manage. "He never got over that," said Negron. "There was a very heavy pain going through his heart. Steinbrenner kept him on the job to try and forget, but it wasn't working.

"Billy called me when he got to New York. The first call he made was to me. He asked me if I was going to see the 'big guy,' Reggie. I told him I was on my way in a few minutes. He said, 'Okay, please tell him that George is bringing me back early. Let him know that he's my right fielder and he will be batting cleanup every day. He doesn't have to worry about DHing.'"

The shocking death of team captain Thurman Munson on August 2 in a plane crash devastated the Yankees and destroyed their desire to finish the season. The Yankees, 55-40 under Billy, finished the 1979 season in fourth place with a record of 89-71. Billy was ready to manage them in 1980 as planned. Plans changed a few weeks later, though, when on October 23,

Billy scuffled with fifty-two-year-old Joseph Cooper, a traveling marshmallow salesman from Illinois, during a lobby tussle at the L'Hotel De France in Bloomington, Minnesota. Cooper needed twenty stitches in his upper lip. Both had been drinking in the hotel bar before the fight.

Eleven months earlier, on November 11, 1978, Billy punched Ray Hagar, a sportswriter for the *Reno Evening Gazette*, in Reno, Nevada. Billy asked to see his notes. Hagar refused. Hagar ended up with a black eye and three chipped teeth. He marveled how quickly Billy's mood changed. After Billy offered Hagar a public apology, the sportswriter dropped criminal charges against him.

Steinbrenner, after agonizing and feeling pressure on what to do with Billy, fired him on October 29, 1979. He felt Billy needed a break from baseball and hired Dick Howser as his replacement. Steinbrenner's influential circle was whispering in his ear. In the book, *The Last Yankee,* written by David Falkner, the image-conscious Steinbrenner shared his thoughts: "I was afraid for Billy. I had to get him away from people, away from bars, away from this kind of thing. I was worried some guy would pull a gun or a knife on him. I didn't want that for Billy or his family. There was one other thing that made up my mind quickly. When Billy hit this guy, he fell down inches away from one of those huge metal andirons. If the guy hits his head on that, he's dead. Wouldn't that be something, the manager of the Yankees on trial for murder?"

Commissioner Bowie Kuhn, meanwhile, started investigating Billy's alleged October assault on Cooper. Considering the severe nature of the injuries of Billy's victims, it was being speculated that Kuhn could end up banning him from the game. Sapir asked Steinbrenner to wait until Kuhn's investigation was completed before deciding on Billy's fate. Steinbrenner didn't listen. "There was not a more intelligent baseball man in world than Billy Martin as far as George was concerned," Negron said. "There were two Billy Martins. The baseball genius and the troubled soul."

Billy departed from the Yankees scorned, scarred, and badly hurt. The following month, in January 1980, Billy had told reporters that as long as he was still hurting, he wouldn't return to the game. Owning several country -and-western wear shops for men and women kept him busy away from the game. He also became a feature attraction on the college lecture circuit. He lived in Dallas near his buddy Mickey Mantle and planned on focusing on family and golf. He traveled to Canton, Ohio, on Christmas Day to visit Thurman Munson's widow, Diane, and her three children. He was also attending Mass every Sunday and professing his Christianity.

"I've never been the kind of guy to pick up a phone and ask for a job," said Billy said in December 1979. "Sure, I'd like to manage again, but I'm not ready for it right now."

5

THE ODD COUPLE

The Oakland A's have been a bad team for three years. Their gate appeal is zilch. What can Finley do short of selling the team to someone locally who might promote it? Hire Billy Martin.
—Dave Newhouse, *Oakland Tribune,* February 1980

Toward the end of the 1979 season, A's catcher Mike Heath had a hunch Billy Martin would be returning west to manage the Oakland A's in 1980. Heath bumped into Martin in September at the Edgewater Hyatt House in Oakland, the hotel headquarters for visiting American League clubs playing the A's at the time. The Hyatt House was also a popular hangout of the Raiders. Heath had fond memories of playing for Billy's Yankees when he was a rookie in 1978. He revered Billy.

In 1978, the Yankees had called up Heath from the Double-A West Haven (Connecticut) Yankees because catcher Thurman Munson was battling sore knees. The team was in fourth place in July, although they maintained a winning record. Steinbrenner had made a flurry of lineup and position changes to shake the defending world champions back into contention. Widely regarded as the heir apparent to the aging Munson, Heath became the Yankees full-time catcher and Munson played right field to rest his knees.

He was in awe when he first stepped inside the clubhouse at Yankee Stadium as a twenty-three-year-old rookie catcher from Tampa, Florida. Sitting at his locker, Heath looked around and marveled at famous teammates surrounding him such as Reggie Jackson, Ron Guidry, and Catfish Hunter. His mood changed, though, when he overheard someone yelling down the hallway that the Yankees needed more pitching and not a rookie catcher. Nervous and rattled, Heath received a boost of confidence when Billy appeared by his locker and assured him by his locker that he was needed and would be staying put. "If Billy Martin was alive today, I'd love to be playing for him," said Heath. "I respected him that much. He was hard on catchers, but he was teaching you the game. He was probably my favorite manager. Billy taught me a lot about the game. He taught me how to go about my business."

Despite Martin's reassuring words, the Yankees still packaged Heath in a deal to the Rangers after the season. The Yankees netted pitcher Dave Righetti and three other players in return, two of whom were also pitchers. The Rangers had planned on using Heath as a backup catcher to Jim Sundberg, but since Sunberg played around 150 games a season and Heath did not want to be a backup, Heath asked them to send him down to their Triple-A club in Tucson.

At the time, Heath was one of the top catching prospects in baseball. The Rangers agreed to send him down and used his last option, which froze him. That meant he needed to first clear waivers before coming to the big leagues. The Rangers traded him to the A's. Heath was playing against the A's Triple-A affiliate in Ogden, Utah, on June 15, 1979, when he got word that he was coming to Oakland and switching clubhouses. "I walked into the clubhouse and all my stuff was packed," remembered Heath. "They told me I was traded and to report to the next clubhouse. The A's didn't know what they were going to do with me, but they had to call me up to the big leagues since I ran out of options."

Heath was anxious to see what was in store for him in Oakland and surprised and excited to see Billy again at the Edgewater Hyatt House. "I told him that I really respected him and that I loved playing for him in New York," said Heath. "He was my type of manager. At that point, I figured he was doing some scouting." Billy remembered Heath and hinted that he would be managing the Oakland A's soon. "You're going to be playing for me sooner than you think," Martin told him. Heath couldn't wait.

After the A's move to Denver derailed again just days before spring training started, Finley needed to hire a manager quickly for the 1980 season. In February, reports circulated that Finley was interested in hiring Billy. Steinbrenner had fired him in October, but he still had two years left on his contract with the Yankees through 1981. Finley could not sign Martin while he was under contract with Steinbrenner. They needed to come up with a resolution to free Martin, but Steinbrenner was leery of doing business with Finley.

The tension between the two owners dated back to 1973, when Steinbrenner pursued A's manager Dick Williams, who had just led Oakland to its second straight championship. Williams had grown tired of Finley's interference and resigned as manger with two years left on his contract. Nonetheless, Williams signed a three-year pact with the Yankees on December 13, 1973. Finley vowed to take legal action for the Yankees signing his property and demanded two top prospects in return.

The deal fell through quickly, however, when American League president Joe Cronin ruled that Finley's contract with Williams was binding and blocked him from signing with the Yankees. Williams, who had vowed that he would not return to Oakland, ended up signing to manage the California Angels in June 1974 after they fired Bobby Winkles. Finley hired Alvin Dark to replace Williams and the Yankees tapped Bill Virdon to replace Ralph Houk as their next manager. Steinbrenner, who was a part of the group that purchased the Yankees from CBS for $10 million in 1973, never forgot how Finley blocked him from signing the best manager in baseball.

In 1980, the roles were reversed. In addition to his lingering resentment over the Williams incident, Steinbrenner suspected that Finley would try to sucker him into paying most of Billy's Oakland salary. The A's owner had pulled off the maneuver before. After hiring Chuck Tanner as manager in 1976, Finley got the Chicago White Sox—the team that had fired Tanner—to pay half of his $60,000 annual salary.

So Steinbrenner had questions: "One, is Finley willing to pay the full load . . . and can he pay Billy?" Steinbrenner asked a group of reporters. "I'm not asking compensation as Finley did when we tried to hire Dick Williams. But I don't know if he would expect us to pay part of Billy's salary. I'm not talking with Finley. I'm only talking with Billy's lawyer and with [American League president] Lee MacPhail. I'm more interested in Billy than in Finley. But it would seem strange if the man who held us up for Dick Williams and held the Pirates up for Chuck Tanner wanted us to pick up part of Billy's salary."

MacPhail scheduled a special hearing for March 6 to rule on whether the Yankees would still be partly responsible for the balance of Billy's salary if he signed with another club. There were also rumblings that the Mets were interested in hiring him. Steinbrenner hoped to avoid the hearing and met with Eddie Sapir, Billy's attorney, in Tampa, in mid-February to discuss an amicable termination of Billy's contract. They agreed on a $150,000 settlement and Billy was free to sign with the A's. Billy had an option of staying with the Yankees in an executive capacity to fulfill the remaining two years on the contract with no salary reduction if he couldn't agree on a deal with Finley.

"George was concerned for Billy but didn't want to be paying for Oakland's manager and bail Finley out," said Sapir. "He wanted Billy to have a job and knew he would be going home. So I arranged a settlement with Steinbrenner to resolve the remaining years on Billy's contract with the Yankees. That opened the door for Oakland."

Billy had been on Finley's radar a decade before. In 1970, he was interested in hiring Martin to replace John McNamara as the A's manager during the All-Star break. Finley knew Billy would be available after the Twins had fired him as manager the previous October, even though he dramatically turned the club around that season and led them to the playoffs before losing three straight to Baltimore in the American League Championship Series. Enraged Twins fans drove around town protesting with chants of "Bring Billy Back" bumper stickers. During an NFL game in October between the Detroit Lions and Minnesota Vikings in a crammed Metropolitan Stadium in Bloomington, Minnesota, a plane slowly flew over the stadium towing a banner that said, BRING BILLY BACK. Finley phoned Calvin Griffith, the Twins' owner, to inquire about Martin. Griffith reportedly warned Finley not to hire Billy. "Don't do it," Griffith advised him. "You'll be taking an awful chance."

Billy ended up signing a two-year deal in October 1970 to manage the Tigers. During the press conference introducing Martin in Detroit, a reporter asked him how close he was to signing with the A's and replacing McNamara. "As close as I am standing to you," Martin replied. Years later, Billy told Ron Bergman of the *Oakland Tribune* his side of the story on almost becoming the A's manager as early as 1970. "He tried to hire me when the A's were losing, Then he told me his wife had said it would be bad to fire John McNamara during the season, so Finley suggested I wait until the end of the season. He was supposed to send me film and reports on his players, and he never did. Finally, I sent him a letter and told him no way. I had tried to reach him by phone, but he never answered my messages. When I sent him the letter, he phoned and asked me, 'What's wrong, Billy? Do you want more money?' I told him there was no way he could buy me."

While Billy was a coach for the Twins in 1966, he was monitoring the construction of the Oakland Coliseum, his home area's new sports complex, from Minnesota. He was bragging about the future of big-league baseball in Oakland. He was not a manager yet and the A's were still in Kansas City. He would have loved to manage Oakland's first major-league baseball team: "The Oakland job would be a natural, but I would only manage under certain conditions. It would have to be a team I could mold into my type of club. It wouldn't necessarily have to be a running ballclub, but one made up of guys I'd like to play and not those the front office told me to play. One thing's for sure. Any team would go over in the Oakland Stadium—even Kansas City. The Giants would really be hurting once the Oakland team got its public relations going. The Twins sent their players out during the off-season, and they were largely responsible for killing baseball in Milwaukee. Who really wants to watch a game at cold, windy Candlestick Park when they can be more comfortable sitting in the East Bay? I'd be interested in managing in Oakland. Who wouldn't want to manage in his home area?"

Finley's personal affairs also affected the negotiations and the future of the team. On January 3, 1980, Joseph County, Indiana, Judge John Montgomery ordered Finley to pay his former wife, Shirley, $2 million in the final settlement in a divorce case that had been ongoing since 1974. They had married in 1941. Shirley was also awarded one of their three farms and $967,000 from a family fund and insurance policy. Shirley and Finley both maintained control of their stock of the A's. Finley had 31 percent of the A's; Shirley, 29 percent; and the remaining 40 percent was split among their four children. The settlement ended an order that any sale of the A's needed court approval. The family was prepared to sell. Finley dropped his $200 California business license and the A's closed and cleaned out their offices four days later, leaving everyone in the dark about the A's future in Oakland.

Once Billy found out that he was free to sign with the A's, he sent Sapir to Chicago to meet with his agent, Doug Newton, and negotiate a deal with Finley to bring him to Oakland. John Hickey, a longtime A's beat writer, explained Finley's decision to bring on Billy. "Finley wanted to make a splash and he couldn't by recreating the A's teams of the early '70s any longer. So he went out and got the biggest showman he could get and that was Billy Martin. It was a big story. He didn't have the players and the franchise didn't have a face or personality. I think he was also thinking, 'If I could build this up, I can sell this team and I'll get more for it.' I'm sure that wasn't his only consideration, but that's certainly how it played out. There hadn't been anyone like him in the Bay Area on either team. Billy was a personality. They didn't have marquee player. Prior to that point, he had a really checkered career."

To all appearances, it was an odd match. Many wondered why Billy wanted to manage the lowly A's, a team that had finished the 1979 season at 54–108 with a home attendance that was the worst in the major leagues (306,763). Considering Finley's track record of micromanaging his managers, some couldn't understand why he was pursuing the independent, rebellious, hotheaded Martin, whose clashes with front office brass were legendary. Billy would never tolerate Finley's in-game dugout calls. Given the A's were for sale, there was whispers that Finley was negotiating with a local group to keep them in Oakland, but first needed to deliver Billy to enhance the marketing appeal for his celebrated homecoming. Billy's return became the best star power Finley had to offer.

Even if the A's move to Denver were approved, Billy would have still been the ideal candidate for the job. He landed his first gig as a manager in the Twins organization with the Denver Bears in 1968 before managing the big club the next year. He was a fan favorite in Denver during his time there. "Billy had a great track record of turning teams around," said Bruce Jenkins, columnist for the *San Francisco Chronicle.* "The A's were exactly that kind of a team. He was a Berkeley guy and played for the Oakland Oaks. Finley did have a genius for marketing and ways to stir up the public and this was one of his masterstrokes."

Finley's public position was that he was the one helping Billy, a beleaguered manager who needed another chance. "His attitude toward Billy was, 'Look, man, I'm doing you a favor. You're out of baseball. So we're not going to get into these big negotiations about pay,'" remembered Sapir. "He figured it might be a good opportunity for Billy. It was his home. The opportunity was right for us at the time and the team was for sale. Finley was a shrewd operator." Billy was initially seeking a three-year deal but settled on two. "We realized that Finley was trying to hire Billy to manage because the team was for sale and he would enhance the value of the franchise," said Sapir. "Billy was looking for a job and going back home was good. It also gave him an opportunity to stay there when the team was sold."

The fifty-one-year-old Martin and Finley agreed on a two-year contract worth $250,000. Finley paid Jim Marshall $34,000 in 1979. "We didn't need a long-term deal because we knew Finley was going to sell it," recalled Sapir. "The settlement money from Steinbrenner was enough to keep him happy during his two-year deal in Oakland. He would be going home, to the Bay Area, to his family, friends. The potential outweighed how much Finley paid him."

On February 21, Billy flew to Chicago for a press conference introducing him as A's manager with Finley, who didn't attend a single A's home game in 1979, present inside an eighth-floor suite at the Drake Hotel. "Finley was on his way out and I think Billy told him, 'Look, get me back home for a bit and I'll help you bring this franchise up,'" said Mickey Klutts, former A's infielder who played for Martin in Oakland. "I think Billy, after his stints in New York, was looking for a team to build. I don't imagine Finley paid him much, but Billy was never in dire need of money. He wanted go home and build up the Oakland A's."

The press conference was held in Chicago because Finley had dropped his California business license. A's catcher Jim Essian had recently tried to call the A's office in December, but their number was disconnected. "Ladies and gentlemen, the Oakland A's have a new manager," Finley told the reporters gathered in the suite. After a brief pause, Finley looked at Billy and told him, "Billy, welcome to Chicago!" Finley continued to talk to Martin in front of the reporters. "Billy, I know damn well you're going to be a tremendous help, not only to the fans in Oakland but to me."

Part of the agreement between Finley and his new manager was that Martin would have full autonomy on the field. Billy stressed that he would run a tight clubhouse and players would be required to wear suits and ties on planes like other major leaguers. Not only was he was up for the challenge professionally, his personal history helped fuel his desire to bring baseball fever back to Oakland. After all, his ticket to the major leagues and the Yankees came from starring for the Oakland Oaks. "I think I can get the fans to come back in Oakland," Billy told the audience. "They like exciting baseball, and that's my style of managing. I'm happy to be here. Charlie made me a wonderful offer and I'm pleased with the opportunity to keep baseball in Oakland, which is my hometown.

"I'm not going for fourth or third or second place. I'm going for the top. I don't know how long it will take. This is definitely a challenge. But when I took the Texas job for my friend Bob Short, he had a chance of the team going down the drink. We finished second and drew 1.2 million. I've got one rule. It doesn't take any ability to hustle. The first time a guy doesn't run a ball out, I'll tell him I'm going to do to him what he's doing to me—embarrass him. I still go to church every Sunday. I still believe in Jesus Christ. I'm the same old Billy Martin."

The same old Billy Martin set about trying to enlist some of his baseball friends for key positions, including some A-listers. He offered Mickey Mantle the job of hitting coaching. But Mantle, a successful insurance executive in Dallas at the time, turned him down. He succeeded in bringing Art Fowler and Clete Boyer on board.

Dave Newhouse, longtime Bay Area columnist, described what Billy's return to Oakland meant: "He was coming home and it would be the chance he needed. After only 306,763 fans came to watch the A's the entire season in 1979, Oakland needed it. He would juice the area. It was his homecoming. Love or hate him, you followed him and came to watch him because you never knew what he was going to do. He was a show. He was the A's Barnum & Bailey with those white shoes. If they were going to compete with San Francisco across the bay, they had to do something. It was a shot in the arm for Oakland and a shot in the arm for him."

Newhouse's view reflected the fans' perspective. As for A's players, most looked forward to Billy's leadership and discipline. The team had lacked accountability in 1979. Some players did not respect Marshall and seemed to play hard only when they felt like it. Injury-prone Shortstop Mario Guerrero played when he wanted and hung out in his street clothes in the runway next to the dugout during games. He talked to fans when he wasn't bouncing a ball off the concrete. He lost all interest in playing for the A's.

Outfielder Miguel Dilone was another A's player who used to hang out in the runway and talk to fans during games. Before a Sunday doubleheader in Oakland against the Rangers on June 24, Marshall warned players to watch the game only from the dugout. An angry Dilone thought that Marshall was singling him out and confronted him in the dugout with a bat in his hand after the team meeting. A's coach Jim Saul had to step between them. Dilone was immediately sent down to Triple-A Odgen and the Cubs later purchased his contract. "The whole atmosphere in Oakland is bad," Dilone said after he left. "Guys stay home on trips there. They say they have headaches." A's outfielder Glenn Burke also left the club in early June without any warning. He said he was done with baseball. "Marshall had a very young team and he was an old-school guy," recalled Hickey. "He would never go out and argue a call. His message to his players was, 'You're young and this is how baseball works. After you're here for three or four years, then you'll have the right to stand up and fight for yourself. Until you've proven yourself, you're a second-class citizen, basically.'"

Pitcher Steve McCatty emphasized that Billy's arrival brought back the fight and swagger of the swingin' A's of the early '70s. "Billy was the epitome of what the A's had been in the past," said McCatty. "That was Billy growing up. He wasn't the best player, but he fought his way through it. It was the perfect fit for our organization." Mike Norris, who pitched for Billy from 1980 to '82, remembered how excited he was to have a proven manager with a winning track record. The announcement that Billy would manage his hometown team was a rare Finley splash for the remaining interested A's fans. "We were going to have a proven, winning major-league manager," said Norris. "He had just left the Yankees and did a pretty good job there."

Many around baseball wondered how the combustible pairing of Finley and Billy would play out. It was an affair of convenience. Finley ran through fourteen different managers in the previous nineteen years and hiring Billy was his fifth managerial change in four seasons. Billy was always considered aspirin. Not medicine. A short-term fix. But he always had a penchant for resurrecting a club. Reggie Jackson, who won World Series championships playing for Billy and Finley, was asked about the polarizing figures joining forces in Oakland. "I don't know. Both gentlemen are unpredictable."

There were early signs that suggested the pairing of Martin and Finley might be combustible. Ray Negron, Billy's friend and Yankees clubhouse attendant, said he almost joined Billy in Oakland. "When he got the job in Oakland, he asked me if I wanted to go with him," said Negron. "I told him 'yes,' but Doug Newton, Billy's agent, told him he didn't think it was a good idea. Billy called me and told me to stay with George because if he got fired in Oakland, I may not be able to get back to the Yankees."

But in early 1980, Billy needed to get right to work. The A's were scheduled to open spring training camp in Scottsdale, Arizona, the next day. It was a team in need of life and direction. The players needed confidence and discipline. Oakland needed baseball fever. And the owner was expressing optimism. "We could be the surprise team of 1980," Finley said. "All we need is leadership."

6

BILLY BALL

Billy baseball. If it were a fever, the A's would be an epidemic. There's another name for it. Confidence.
—RALPH WILEY, *OAKLAND TRIBUNE*, MARCH 23, 1980

BILLY STRUTTED INTO SCOTTSDALE FOR SPRING TRAINING WEARING his signature western garb—wide-brimmed cowboy hat, leather jacket, pointy-toed boots, and tinted glasses—arriving at the recently renovated Scottsdale Stadium to manage the 1980 A's. The A's spring training facility from 1979 to 1981 had recently undergone $250,000 worth of improvements that included new offices, air-conditioned locker rooms, concession stands and showers in addition to 4,300 new seats. Billy's office inside Scottsdale Stadium dwarfed the manager's office at the Oakland Coliseum.

The A's managerial vacancy may have been the least appealing in all of baseball, but the circumstances and timing seemed heaven-sent for Billy. He was energized and excited. For the first time in five years, Martin was free of distractions and stress that came from managing in New York. The pressure had caused him to lose weight, and drinking compounded his anxiety. Billy needed focus and his health back, and he knew that coming home was the perfect opportunity. His mother, Jenny, lived in the same house on Seventh Street in nearby West Berkeley and was still married to Jack Downey. "Being back home in Oakland was a great situation for him and he took advantage of it every opportunity," said Jackie Moore, one of Martin's coaches. He was happy to be home and confident he would bring excitement back in Oakland. "I'm back in my hometown," Billy told the media in spring training. "I'm close to my mother, who's seventy-nine now. I grew up in Berkeley, I played minor league ball in Oakland, I know the Bay Area, I know they're good baseball fans. I think we can live with the Giants there, I think we can draw 1.2 million, maybe 1.3 million a year."

Martin made sure to embrace his new opportunity. He munched hard-boiled eggs for breakfast in an effort to eat healthier, inhaled Scottsdale's fresh spring air, and gave thanks for a new lease. But some things remained unchanged. He frequented the Pink Pony Steakhouse, Old Town Scottsdale's popular dining and drinking establishment that was crammed with baseball figures and fans during spring training. There, Billy held court with a few writers and laughed with old baseball friends. "So it is that Billy Martin is going home again to Oakland. He is going home to manage the A's. And now he hopes to finish his career there, just up the freeway from Berkeley, where he was born and raised. Billy tells you, it is a changed place. They have torn down the Victorian homes of his youth and replaced them with high-rises . . . He is going back to it and he does not want to disgrace it," wrote David Israel of the *New York Times* on March 13, 1980.

Billy fastened on his new white A's cap and pulled up his double-knits. The flashy green-and-gold A's colors were a departure from the Yankees' staid pinstripes, but one element remained the same: he wore uniform number 1. And number 1 knew he needed to build the confidence of the young A's and show them how to win. He set the tone right away on the first morning of spring training, addressing his new players in the locker room of Scottsdale Stadium. His intensity inspired some players and intimidated others. He guaranteed them a winning season. Jeff Newman, the A's catcher, remembered. "Billy looked at us and said, 'Boys, we're going to win. I'm going to teach you and show you how to win.' We looked around and saw mostly the same guys who lost 108 games last season."

It didn't take long for Billy to establish his authority, which had eroded under Jim Marshall, the A's manager in 1979. Billy immediately announced a midnight curfew before day games and mandated that players wore coats and ties on travel days. The team instantly recognized the new leadership style. "When Billy came on, he wasn't going to stand for any of that stuff," recalled former A's beat writer Kit Stier. "He installed discipline in them right away. Not that he was the most disciplined man himself, but he knew how to run a baseball team. He already managed at other places and had been a winner. He made baseball fun for them again. But he was severely limited in what he had in terms of a roster."

A's outfielder Tony Armas got off to a bad start with his new manager. He was late reporting to spring training on March 1 and Billy threatened to fine him if didn't arrive by March 4. Armas had been late for spring training the previous season, too, which he blamed on visa problems in his native Venezuela, where he'd played winter ball. Martin didn't buy the excuse. Everyone else arrived to camp on time. Billy suspected that many players who played winter ball "take a vacation on us when spring training starts." Billy announced that any late-arriving A's winter-league players would not be granted permission to play the following winter. Billy changed his mind about fining Armas when he finally arrived, but he warned him to call next time. Armas showed up at spring training on time in 1981.

Bob Lacey, an A's reliever in 1980, recalled that Martin sometimes embarrassed players in an effort to keep control. "He was the best manager I've ever played for, but Bronco Billy would ride the wild player on the team to calm him down so other horses in the stall would see and fall back," said Lacey.

Billy bumped heads with Mike Norris on the first day of spring training. The twenty-five-year-old right-handed starter was the longest tenured A's player on the club, having signed in 1973. Part of Billy's introductory speech included a warning to the players about turning on him. "You ballplayers will screw over managers and coaches," Billy told his new players. "If you fuck me, I'll fuck back harder." Norris looked around and noticed that some of his younger teammates were horrified after hearing Billy's threat. They all knew that their new manager was fearless, bold, and crazy enough to bench Reggie Jackson on national television in 1977. The locker room was silent and Norris, finding humor in the players' reaction, laughed out loud. Billy shifted his attention to Norris, and told him to meet him in his office immediately after the meeting. Norris couldn't believe he was already in Billy's doghouse before touching the field for his workout. Billy asked him why he laughed and interrupted his speech in the locker room. "I told him that what he said scared the shit out of everybody," explained Norris. "Then he asked me why I wasn't scared, and I told him because I wasn't going to fuck him over. We were cool from then on and I think he respected me because he knew I wasn't afraid of him."

Finley and Billy began piecing together the organization. On March 6, Finley hired twenty-nine-year-old Walt Jocketty as the A's new farm director, replacing Norm Koselke. Koselke never had a background in baseball and spent a lot of time driving players around. "I was scared to death when I got there," Jocketty told reporters in 1994. "I had no scouts. I had four managers. No pitching coaches, no instructor, no secretary. Nothing. I had to type all the contracts."

Up in the majors, Clete Boyer left the Braves organization as a minor-league instructor to become Billy's third-base coach. Martin's decision to bring Boyer back was partly to help him receive his pension benefits. Billy planned on grooming Boyer to be his Oakland successor. Boyer admired Billy's fearlessness. Like Billy, Boyer had his share of late-night bar scuffles. Boyer would be in Billy's inner circle on and off the field. Coaches Lee Walls and George Mitterwald were holdovers from 1979. Fowler replaced Lee Stange as pitching coach.

Billy was making new hires off the field as well. To fill the role of traveling secretary and public relations director, he brought twenty-eight-year-old Mickey Morabito over from the Yankees on March 25. Morabito had started as a batboy for the Yankees in 1970 and eventually became the team's director of public relations. He was also a longtime friend of Martin's and helped him survive the enormous media scrutiny in New York. For the A's, Morabito inherited the task of restoring community relations and coordinating team travel.

Whether they'd be traveling back to the Bay Area had been the subject of some speculation. A rumor was circulating in early spring that the A's never made flight arraignments to return to Oakland to begin the season. This fueled suspicion that Finley expected to sell the team any day. Martin, meanwhile, ignored the rumors and began teaching the young A's the fundamentals and instilling them with confidence. "It started in 1980," former A's outfielder Mike Davis said in 2004. "Billy came to spring training and started building confidence in us and letting us know we could compete at the big-league level. We put together a great spring and were on top of the cactus league. He did that to build confidence in us."

A's players bought into Billy's winning style right away. They finally had an established, winning manager with a name. "This is the first time I've felt like I was in the big leagues since I broke in," Norris told Stephanie Salter of the *San Francisco Examiner* during spring training. "Nobody before has given us a total awareness of defense. Things like pickoff fundamentals; working on them makes a guy confident enough to call the pickoff play, and confidence is what you've got to have—especially as a pitcher. I've learned more in five weeks than I have in five years."

Billy identified with the bunch of unknown players. He was an underdog himself, scrapping and clawing to survive in life and reach the big leagues. Billy inspired them to believe in themselves. "We needed a no-nonsense manager to make us believe in ourselves," said former A's catcher Mike

Heath. "We loved Billy. He demanded from us and knew how good we could be."

In 1980, there was nowhere to go but up for the Oakland A's. In addition to finishing in last place in the American League West in 1979, thirty-four games behind the first-place Angels, the A's finished at the bottom of almost every major team category. Their team batting average of .239 and fielding percentage of .972 were last in the American League. Their 4.74 ERA was the second highest in the big leagues and they finished last in runs scored with 573. After the dismal '79 season, Martin's main challenge was to convince his players to forget it and move ahead. "Billy was at his best coming into a situation like the A's were in, and they were ripe for this charismatic, mercurial leader who was crazy in love with the game of baseball," said Salter.

Billy forced the club to divorce themselves from 1979 and made them believe they could win. "From day one, Billy inspired us to get out of our doldrums of '78 and '79," recalled former A's catcher Jim Essian, who played for them from 1978 to '80 and in '84. "His enthusiasm and ability to inspire us was remarkable. He told us we could win. He sparked us. Throughout the spring, he brought aggressiveness. He loved to put pressure on the defense."

Catcher Jeff Newman said Billy's confidence was contagious and motivated players. "He had so much confidence in the team and his ability to manage, it spilled onto us," said Newman. "We believed it and went out and played hard for the man. It was fun. Those days of Billy Ball were fun times. You have to give him a lot of credit for coming in and being a very positive person, showing and telling us we were going to win."

A's players circled around Billy on the infield dirt and he yelled, "You don't have to have great speed to steal home. You have to have the right pitcher." That awakened the A's slower runners. The perfect conditions mattered more than speed of a runner for the steal of home, emphasized Billy. "Any time a pitcher winds up, we'll go," Billy yelled again.

Stealing home was stealing a run. Daring, aggressive, and unpredictable baserunning was a part of Billy's theory that rattled opposing managers. In

1969, when Billy managed the Twins, he passed on his secret formula for stealing home to Rod Carew. Carew swiped home an astonishing seven times that season, tying Pete Reiser's 1946 major-league record. "Billy worked with me for hours reading pitchers to become more aggressive," recalled Carew. "Many of those hours we concentrated on stealing home. Few guys ever stole home. We worked on timing to the split second."

Billy preached aggressive baserunning throughout spring training. All his players were expected to take risks on the basepaths, not just speedsters like Rickey Henderson or Dwayne Murphy. Billy convinced them how they could go from first to third on a bunt. A's players lacked confidence and the fundamentals. He was teaching them things they'd never learned before. "It's going to get better," Billy told reporters. "Most of these kids have never been taught any fundamentals. We're going to keep working on them until we get it right. We'll come out before games and work on them. The players are all excited. That's half the battle right there."

A lively crowd of 2,980 filled Scottsdale Stadium to watch the Billy Martin–charged A's exhibition opener on March 13. Billy's A's spring debut created buzz. It was the team's biggest spring-training crowd since they moved their spring headquarters. The crowd was buzzing with chants of "Billy, Billy, Billy" before the game. It was a promising turnout considering the A's only averaged 3,787 fans per home game during the regular season at the Coliseum in 1979. The A's didn't disappoint the energetic fans. Billy tapped twenty-four-year-old right-hander Matt Keough to start the exhibition opener. Billy was fond of Keough. While Billy was managing the Yankees in 1978, he selected Keough to represent the A's in the All-Star Game in San Diego. Keough, Brian Kingman, and Steve McCatty tossed three scoreless innings apiece to shut out the Milwaukee Brewers 5–0. Tony Armas, now out of the doghouse for arriving late, collected four hits, including a home run and double to carry the offense. "Billy got us ready to run the bases and make the proper plays on the very first day," said Bob Lacey. The resourceful Billy emphasized stealing, hit and runs, bunting, outfield throws, and pickoff plays throughout camp.

Columnist Ray Ratto, who covered the team for the *San Francisco Examiner,* noticed a new energy that Billy had brought to spring training. "From spring training on, they just seemed like a team with purpose, which they hadn't had in the previous three years," said Ratto. "Spring training in 1980 crackled with energy they hadn't had since the World Series years. It had an edge to it."

Opposing teams began recognizing that every A's player was a stolen base threat. On Friday, March 21, while the A's were nursing a 1–0 lead over the Mariners in the top of the sixth in Tempe, catcher Jim Essian led off with a double and made it to third-base on a sacrifice. As Mariners pitcher Glenn Abbott peered in for the sign, Essian, the slowest A's player, suddenly broke from third-base and dashed home, shocking everyone. A rattled Abbott noticed Essian trucking home and threw wildly to his catcher, allowing Essian to steal home easily to seal a 2–0 victory. The slow-footed Essian didn't have any stolen bases the previous season and had amassed a career total of five since 1973. His teammates emerged from the dugout to celebrate with him. "He wanted us to be aggressive and gave me permission to steal home, so I did," recalled Essian. A's players were put on notice to stay alert at all times for the steal sign from A's third-base coach Boyer. The A's were showcasing a fresh, exciting and entertaining brand of baseball. "It was Billy's way of showing them that it could be done," said John Hickey. "There was nobody on the planet more shocked of stealing home than Jim Essian."

Watching Essian's steal of home from the press box in Tempe was Ralph Wiley, a twenty-seven-year-old columnist for the *Oakland Tribune.* He flew to Scottsdale to visit the A's camp for the weekend and watch them play under Billy. The *Tribune* hired the Tennessee native in 1975 as a copy editor from Knoxville College, where he worked in journalism at the *Knoxville Spectrum.* The quick-learning and inquisitive Wiley climbed the ladder fast at the *Tribune.* He covered prep sports, the city beat, and the Giants before headlining as a regular sports columnist for the newspaper in 1979. He was a provocative writer and brilliant wordsmith that earned him the nickname "the Wiz" from his peers in the press box. Wiley also covered some legendary boxing cards. That weekend, Wiley decided to write a column about the A's new aggressive style of play that included stealing home and suicide squeezes.

Wiley's challenge was how to best capture the forceful style of play he was seeing from what he had first described as "survival ball." The A's were becoming the epitome of Billy's scrappy nature in only three weeks of spring training. Wiley submitted his column to a novice desk copy editor, having settled on "Billy Ball" to describe the new daring A's. The column was scheduled to run on Sunday, March 23. But the editor told Wiley that "Billy Ball" sounded corny and he was removing it from the column in favor of "the style of baseball played by Billy Martin." Wiley insisted that it be kept in. The editor complied and "Billy Ball" appeared in Wiley's Sunday column. "Billy Baseball" perfectly headlined Wiley's piece:

"The A's are even much more fun on the field. Billy baseball is stealing and bunting at the same time, hoping the third-baseman fields the bunt and the shortstop covers second, enabling the runner to possibly gain third-base, or at least make threatening gestures.

Billy baseball is stealing home. Billy ball says a squeeze play a day keep the shutouts away. The A's have tried the squeeze six times this spring. It has only worked three times, but it has never failed to be exciting for the people in the seats, which is the very best part of it."

Triggered by the A's success on the field and centered on Billy's showmanship, "Billy Ball" became a national phenomenon and changed Wiley's life and elevated his career in journalism. It was only spring training and "Billy Ball" started floating around. "It had a great name and captured the situation perfectly," said Dave Newhouse. "It became history and became necessary."

The A's boasted a promising Cactus League record of 12–7 under Billy, who announced a starting rotation of Langford, Norris, Kingman, McCatty, and Keough. Keough, who was 2–17 with a 5.04 ERA in 1979, finished the spring with a record of 4–0 with a stellar 2.00 ERA. The pitching staff led the Cactus League with an ERA of 2.89. Billy was impressed with his five young starting pitchers. He had seen them develop across the diamond while managing the Yankees. Billy's main concern leaving spring training was his shaky infield defense. As a former second baseman himself, Martin had no tolerance for defensive mental lapses. "We need to shore up our defense in the infield," Billy said. "We've got good pitching from what I've seen. But pitching doesn't make defense. Defense makes pitching."

In Oakland, Martin didn't have the power hitters he had in New York, or the short porch in Yankee Stadium's right field. He believed that being assertive on the bases, pressuring the defense, was the A's only hope to manufacture enough runs to compete. But his players needed to move as ordered. The A's stole home three times during spring training. "Our job was to move guys over," remembered infielder Mickey Klutts. "We had to put pressure on the basepaths. We wanted other teams to make mistakes. He was all about putting pressure on the defense. He called an awful lot of hit and runs. We were an American League team that bunted guys over."

Back in Oakland, the news of Billy's arrival spurred ticket sales, despite the lingering uncertainty over where the A's would play in 1980. Some of the older locals, remembering Billy starring for the Oakland Oaks in the 1940s, wanted to come and celebrate his East Bay return. The story of a local boy returning home to rescue a dying franchise piqued local interest. The A's also benefited from the Raiders' plans to leave Oakland. Heartbroken and angry local Raiders fans turned their attention to the A's. It was Martin's job to make sure his players didn't disappoint.

7

THE RENAISSANCE

Being a part of that atmosphere that season was like nothing else I covered in sports. The crowds kept growing and growing. It was lightning in a bottle. It was the perfect intersection of Billy having something to prove, Charlie giving him the go-ahead, and the young players emerging.

— STEPHANIE SALTER, FORMER BAY AREA COLUMNIST, 2018

A PLAYERS' STRIKE CANCELED THE FINAL EIGHT DAYS OF THE SPRING exhibition schedule in 1980. In total, 92 exhibition games were canceled in Arizona and Florida. By striking, the players pressured the owners to finalize the new four-year collective bargaining agreement. Discontent was brewing. Not enough progress was being made on the basic agreement, according to the players, and they needed to send a message to the owners. Marvin Miller, the executive director of the Major League Baseball Players Association, claimed the last twenty weeks of negotiations had been unproductive and the owners, demanding and unreasonable, were the villains provoking a strike. The owners had purchased strike insurance in advance. Some owners were still resentful about the birth of free agency.

The major deal breaker at the table was the proposal by the owners to beef up compensation for teams losing players to free agency. Owners wanted clubs who signed free agents to hand over a major-league roster player in return. The players rejected their proposal. They insisted that would cripple the lucrative free agent market they had fought hard for. That would mean "tens of millions of dollars out of the hands of the players," Miller asserted.

Under their current system, a club losing a free agent netted a June amateur draft choice from the signing club. Considering the uncertainty of draft picks, owners demanded more comparable major-league talent in return that could help make up for losing prime talent to free agency. While most of their bargaining differences were resolvable, both sides were not coming any closer on agreeing to free agent compensation. The stumbling block was stalling negotiations and frustrating both sides. Neither side was budging and the discussions had turned sour. On April 1, the players asserted themselves and walked out. Players were only paid when the season started. So the canceled exhibition games only affected the wallets of the owners.

Although the players promised to resume play on April 9, Opening Day, they set a strike date of May 23, if an agreement was not reached. The strike threatened regular season games. The players threatened a strike just before Memorial Day weekend because it was baseball's most attended period of the season. Kids were out of school and the weather warmed up.

Most A's players stayed in shape by working out at Scottsdale Stadium during the strike week leading to opening night in Oakland on April 10. By that time, the A's still didn't have a radio contract to broadcast their games. Many radio stations questioned the A's financial stability and were skeptical of their ability to attract local advertisers. They also never sensed any long-term commitment from Finley. Talks of the team moving and the threat of a possible midseason strike scared stations away. The A's were the only major-league team without a radio flagship to begin the season. KXRX, a San Jose–based, 10,000-watt radio station, was the A's flagship in 1979. Finley ran through flagship stations like he did with managers.

The A's had unfinished business with the Angels. Billy had predicted during spring training that the A's would finish higher in the standings than the high-powered Angels, the defending division champs. It was a bold prediction. After all, Finley hadn't bothered to make any roster improvements during the winter and Martin was managing essentially the same group who lost 108 games the previous season. Las Vegas oddsmakers had listed the A's a 500-to-1 shot to win the pennant. Bobby Grich, the Angels' All-Star second baseman, got wind of Billy's brazen prediction and told the *Los Angeles Times,* "It shows the kind of deteriorating effect alcohol can have on your mind."

Many A's players already held a grudge against the Angels for humiliating them during a Fourth of July 17–6 rout the previous season. The Angels scored ten runs on only four hits in the eighth inning, sending sixteen batters to the plate. A's players felt the Angels showed them up with a big lead. The A's remembered and wanted revenge badly. "They embarrassed us and rubbed it in," recalled Steve McCatty. "They hit-and-run on us when they were way ahead and I was thinking, 'You got to be kidding me.' I think we ended up getting in three fights with them in 1980." The bad blood between the A's and Angels intensified during the season.

The anticipation surrounding the A's carried into the club's 13th season in Oakland. An enthusiastic Opening Night crowd of 24,415 witnessed Billy's homecoming. The excitement and anticipation in the air at the Oakland Coliseum that Thursday evening as the A's faced the Minnesota Twins was strange given the franchise was left for dead just a few months before. The second deck, for example, seldom opened, was filled with buzzing fans in green and gold. The crowd was the A's largest since they drew 36,463 on half-price night on June 5, 1978. They drew only 10,387 on Opening Night in 1979. Billy's family and friends were there for his homecoming. He reserved ten suites for them to celebrate and watch the game. "Billy was a local boy," said former A's reliever Dave Heaverlo. "It was a local kid coming home and turning things around."

The uptick in attendance from the previous year included the team's owner, who hadn't watched his team play live in Oakland since 1978. For the '80 opener, Finley watched the game from his box. But other things hadn't changed. Because the A's still hadn't found a new flagship radio station, Red Rush and Hal Ramey, the A's radio broadcasting tandem from 1979, sat in the press box and kept score. Finley had hired and fired Rush three times. Ramey was waiting to see if he was in Finley's plans for 1980. Longtime A's radio play-by-play announcer Monte Moore left the radio booth in 1977 and there were no stable A's radio voices until Bill King and Lon Simmons arrived in 1981. "Around the late '70s, there was almost a new guy every year," said Hal Ramey. "The change of A's announcers was not unusual in those days."

At the direction of Billy, Matt Keough, A's starting pitcher the next game, sat in the stands behind home plate to study Twins' hitters. This was in keeping with Martin's unorthodox idea of letting his next day's starting pitchers sit behind the plate and have a few beers while they scouted opponents for their game. Players were only too happy to oblige.

Billy's mother, now known as Joan, was sitting behind the A's dugout. Finley, the clever promoter himself, asked her to throw out the ceremonial first pitch before the game. "I don't know if she can even throw a ball," Billy said before the game. "I do know, however, she can throw pots and pans. Forks, too. She stuck one in my head one day." Joan was proudly wearing a shiny Kelly green A's warm-up jacket and cap when she threw a one-hopper to the plate. Joan planted a kiss on Finley's cheek and thanked him for bringing her son home.

Billy received a warm reception from his hometown crowd in Oakland, a city that had built a reputation for embracing and celebrating its hometown legends. When public address announcer Roy Steele introduced him before the game, the fans showered him with a rousing two-minute ovation. Billy waved his cap and blew kisses back. Another local kid was shining that evening. Twenty-one-year-old Rickey Henderson, the pride of Oakland

Technical High, was starting and playing in his first opening night ever. Bobbie, his mother, was cheering him on from the stands. Energized fans cheered, "Let's Go A's!" The Billy Martin era in Oakland had begun. Billy's inaugural A's lineup:

Rickey Henderson, LF

Dwayne Murphy, CF

Mike Heath, C

Jeff Newman, 1B

Jim Essian, DH

Tony Armas, RF

Mario Guerrero, SS

Mickey Klutts, 3B

Rob Picciolo, 2B

Rick Langford, P

The Twins roughed up A's starter Rick Langford early and held a 5–0 lead through six innings. The A's—highlighted by Henderson's three-run blast—came roaring back and exploded for seven runs in the bottom of the seventh. Henderson's shot electrified the Coliseum and gave the A's a 7–5 lead heading to the ninth. But the bullpen couldn't preserve the lead. Bob Lacey coughed up a game-tying, two-run single to Willie Norwood, sending the game to extra innings. Billy was forced to bring McCatty in relief in the 11th. An inning later, he allowed solo home runs to Roy Smalley and Rick Sofield and the A's went down 9–7. Despite the Opening Night loss in front of a decent crowd, A's players were encouraged by the way they fought back and rallied back from a five-run deficit. The A's played noticeably more confident and disciplined under Martin.

Smalley sensed a new energy surrounding the A's and acknowledged the lively crowd at the Coliseum after the game. Visiting teams were used to playing in front of tiny crowds in Oakland. "That was the best opening game I've ever played in," said Smalley. "I loved it. The Oakland fans are going to have fun this season. Billy Martin will see to it."

A few games later, Martin entertained the hometown fans in signature style. On April 14, the Mariners hammered McCatty for five runs in the second inning. Billy, on his way to yank his pitcher from the game, charged toward first-base umpire Larry McCoy to argue about a called ball four that cost the A's a double play and prolonged the inning. McCoy kicked him out of the game and Billy kicked dirt on McCoy's shoes before being restrained by home plate umpire Don Denkinger. Billy climbed into the stands during the ninth inning to finish watching the game before leaving the Coliseum without speaking to reporters. "He would fight you, the opposition, umpires and his toughness rubbed off on some of those players," said Ken Phelps, a former American League slugger. "He was the kind of guy you wanted to fight for and fight with. It was always fun to watch him argue with umpires. That's something we really miss today."

The young A's responded to Billy's ejection by reeling off seven consecutive wins. On April 20, the A's swept a doubleheader against the Angels to climb into first place in the American League West with an 8–3 record. The Angels, who boasted a $5 million pitching staff, occupied the cellar. Baseball experts thought they were in the twilight zone. The lowly A's, the franchise everyone hoped would go away, owned the second-best record in baseball, behind only the 10–1 Cincinnati Reds. Baseball was taking notice of Oakland's hot start. They won their first six games against the Angels and felt delight in beating them down.

The A's were becoming an eyebrow-raising story without any local radio broadcasts. Billy was especially proud of how his A's were playing but was frustrated that fans couldn't hear the action over the radio. "It's developing, but it hurts when we don't even have a radio station," Billy said at the time. "We go 4–3—we could be 5–2—and nobody knows about it. It hurts, especially when we suicide squeeze twice and nobody's heard about it."

The A's early surge helped secure an agreement with a local radio station. On April 21, 11 games into the season, the A's signed with Berkeley's KDIA 1310, a 5,000-watt AM rhythm and blues station. KDIA announced that

Red Rush and Dom Valentino, Martin's close friend and a former play-by-play announcer for the Yankees, would be the A's broadcast tandem. Finley added twenty-three-year-old Ted Robinson, the A's promotion director, to spell Rush and Valentino. The Notre Dame graduate told Finley he wanted a job in sports broadcasting, so Finley allowed him to call an inning of each home game in addition to his duties as promotions director. "Because the A's got off to a red-hot start, Carl Finley, Charlie's cousin and front office manager, got a deal with KDIA three weeks into the season," remembered Robinson, who went on to broadcast for the San Francisco 49ers. The A's first radio broadcast was on April 29 in Anaheim. Wayne Walker and Harmon Killebrew were the A's television commentators on KPIX-Channel 5.

The A's first road trip in late April, which included a stop in Minnesota, cooled them off and tested the limits of Billy's temper. Martin, who led the Twins to a division title as a rookie manager in 1969, was returning to the scene of his fight with a traveling marshmallow salesman in a suburban hotel lobby six months earlier. During the series opener at Metropolitan Stadium in front of 2,664 fans, Billy pulled Keough from the game in the first inning after the Twins jumped on him for four runs. As he walked back to the dugout, a fan in the stands showered him with marshmallows. Martin glared behind the A's dugout and challenged the culprit to come forward. He told coach George Mitterwald to monitor the stands behind the dugout. The fan showered Billy with more marshmallows in the ninth. The distraction stopped the game for several minutes and created a scene. A's players walked to the top step of the dugout and stared into the stands, while a furious Billy opened the gate leading to the stands preparing to go after the fan.

During the sixth inning of the next game, fans tossed more marshmallows at Billy. Police arrived and three fans were ejected. Billy thought they should have been arrested. In a scene that looked like something out of "Willy Wonka Meets Bull Durham," marshmallows covered left field. More significantly, the Twins swept the A's and knocked them out of first place. The A's were outscored 35–15 in the three-game series.

On April 30, when the A's were in Anaheim to play the Angels, the buzz wasn't about candy thrown from the stands. It was about spitballs thrown from the mound. After the A's lost to the Angels 2–1 in Anaheim on April 30, Angels manager Jim Fregosi, a Billy rival and A's nemesis, and catcher Tom Donohue accused starting pitcher Matt Keough of throwing spitballs during the game. "Keough got beat on a spitball, of which he threw many," Fregosi claimed. Word was spreading around the league that Fowler was teaching the A's young staff how to throw spitballs.

Billy seemed to be four innings ahead of opposing managers and his presence was felt all over the field. Billy repositioned his infielders during the flight of a pitch. "He'll move me two steps, and the batter will hit the ball right to me," second baseman Rob Picciolo once said. He could psychologically shake up and wear down opponents. Billy's steal-happy A's wreaked havoc on the basepaths, throwing off infielders and managers. The players' newfound confidence under Billy's direction was a winning formula. They pressured opponents into making mistakes. "That was a young team that just believed everything Billy told them," said Wayne Hagin, a former A's radio voice. "They followed every word he said. He always used that chip on the shoulder to beat the opposition, to beat the other manager and to dictate whatever happened in his conversation. It enabled him to be the success he was."

The A's were causing chaos for opponents. The national media began running stories and features on the A's miraculous start with virtually the same players from their embarrassing 108-loss season in 1979. Billy was the only difference. "For the first time since I signed with this organization in 1973, I'm really proud to be an Oakland A," Wayne Gross said at the time.

Intrigued fans, hearing about the A's exciting brand of baseball under Billy, began showing up to the Oakland Coliseum. Through the A's first twelve home games, they drew 81,405 fans, an increase of 35,393 from the first twelve home games in 1979. It marked the biggest percentage increase in the league and biggest numerical jump of any club at the time. "You had the excitement of the unknown," said Wayne Hagin. "He did things as a manager that very few others would even conceive of doing. He was capable of doing anything. You couldn't wait for an argument with the umpires because he would put on the theatrics. He was as good as [Baltimore Orioles manager] Earl Weaver on any given day when it came to giving it to umpires."

By May 1, the A's were on top of the American League West. "Billy Martin has brought excitement back to baseball in this city that has always played second banana to San Francisco across the Bay, that has endured the decline of the A's and Warriors, the utter failure of hockey, and the intentions of the Raiders to blow town for Los Angeles," wrote Norm Miller of the *New York Daily News* on June 14, 1980.

Jim Essian, who had played for the A's since 1978, noticed the climate around the ballpark changing after Billy's arrival. "It was inspiring to see Billy bring excitement back and see fans in the stands," Essian said. "We had a ball and loved it in Oakland. Billy fielded a pretty good team back then, if you consider the players we had. My son was a batboy and we had a great time."

On May 3, Martin got into the head of Jack Morris, the Tigers' starting pitcher, on a Saturday afternoon at the Oakland Coliseum. With the A's trailing 2-1 in the second with two out, Wayne Gross reached third-base on a Jeff Newman groundout. Third-base coach Clete Boyer asked Gross if he wanted to steal home to tie the game. Henderson had stolen home against the Angels on April 20 and Gross wanted to follow suit. Gross wanted to steal home on the first pitch and Martin nodded his approval to Boyer from the dugout. Gross slowly drifted off third and broke toward the plate as Morris started his windup. When the ball tipped off the glove of catcher Lance Parrish, Gross slid home headfirst safely to tie the game. Parrish had called for a slider. Morris threw a fastball and crossed him up.

The A's weren't finished torturing Morris. They loaded the bases with two outs the very next inning. With Newman at first, Mitchell Page at second and Dwayne Murphy at third this time, Billy called for a triple steal.

Roger Craig, pitching coach for the Tigers, warned Morris to pitch from the stretch to keep Murphy close to the third-base bag. But Morris pitched from his full windup, and Newman, Mitchell and Murphy took off. Morris's pitch again glanced off Parrish's glove and Murphy swiped home easily to give the A's a 3–2 lead. Page tried to score from second base on the play, but Parrish tagged him out. The A's successfully executed the triple steal. Murphy's steal of home was the A's third of the season. Morris and Parrish couldn't believe it. "I'd never seen so many guys stealing home," remembered Dave Newhouse. "You thought he couldn't get away with it again, but he did."

Tigers manager Sparky Anderson's had heard reports about the A's running, squeezing, and stealing coming into the series, but they weren't prepared for Martin's full arsenal of tricks. A disgusted Parrish smashed a water faucet with a bat when he returned to the dugout. Morris hurled his glove into the dugout in frustration and fired the ball into center field. Billy conquered the Tigers. "We played a different type of baseball," said Newman, one of three catchers on Oakland's roster in 1980. "There's no way in the world you could do it today. We stole runs through a lot of trickery. It worked for the time being until opponents caught on and it stopped working. That's why we were in first place early and then it just sort of stopped." The A's had stolen a total of four bases in the game.

The A's surprising start inspired local businesses. Cornell C. Maier, chairman of Oakland's Kaiser Aluminum, sponsored a "Salute the A's" night on May 6 at the Coliseum. The purpose of the night was to rally the community to celebrate the A's revival. Kaiser Aluminum donated $10,000 worth of free gifts for fans attending the game. The A's drew 24,309, their third-largest crowd since 1978. "We want to make it clear that this is a big league area in every respect—and we intend to keep it that way," Maier insisted.

He also hosted a special banquet with local dignitaries and civic leaders to honor A's players and wives. Maier, fifty-five, was a loyal Oakland enthusiast and community-minded leader. He was determined to form a group of investors to buy the A's and keep them in Oakland. He recognized that Billy had suddenly made the A's into a marketable product for potential local buyers. "I wish I had the wherewithal to do it myself," Maier told the *San Francisco Examiner* in 1980. "I'd love to buy the club. But, while I don't have any immediate prospects, I think there will be local ownership. I have a couple of ideas for putting together a group, but it would be premature to mention any names right now. There are one or two of 'em I haven't even talked to yet."

Maier didn't want to lose the pride and economic perks that professional sports brought to Oakland. He was often criticized in some circles for his involvements in Oakland's professional sports landscape. Although Maier could see the Raiders slipping from the hands of the city, he was more hopeful of keeping the A's. The A's still had seven years left on their lease with the Coliseum board and a twenty-year option. He was confident a local group would keep them, and in light of the miracle A's renaissance under Billy, he recognized the timing was right to solidify their long-term stay. "He was very much a cheerleader for the whole idea of keeping the A's in Oakland," remembered Roy Eisenhardt, former A's president. Eisenhardt worked with Maier to facilitate Finley's sale to Walter A. Haas Jr. in August.

By mid-May, *Sports Illustrated* and *People* ran stories on the A's resurrection that no one saw coming except for Billy. NBC and CBS produced and aired features on the A's surprising resurgence under Billy. The A's played on NBC's popular *Game of the Week* on May 17 in Toronto.

The A's notorious baserunning exploits continued. During a 6–3 victory over the Royals on May 28, they rattled starting pitcher Rich Gale and catcher John Wathan in the first inning. Murphy had stolen home on a double steal with Page. Page then scored on a passed ball. The A's prolonged the inning when Gross and Newman walked. They ended up on first and third with two out. With the score tied at 2, Billy called for a double steal play that the A's rehearsed religiously in spring training.

With Gale on the mound facing Klutts, Newman broke for second base and intentionally fell to the ground. A confused Gale, focused on nailing the vulnerable Newman between first and second, fired to Royals first baseman

Willie Aikens. Gross suddenly charged to the plate. Aikens—caught off guard—made an off-balance throw to Wathan as Gross scored the go-ahead run. Newman, meanwhile, bolted toward second and beat Wathan's throw. It was the A's second double steal of the inning as they stole seven bases in the game. "It was brilliantly reckless," said Bruce Jenkins, describing the A's style of play. "It was quite reckless because Martin had to try a lot of things with a tremendously flawed team. But there was wisdom behind all of it."

Kit Stier, former A's longtime beat writer for the *Oakland Tribune,* remembered how the excitement surrounding the A's gained momentum after their surprising start: "I don't recall the team generating any interest until they started winning some games. They were exciting. Beyond the three outfielders, Henderson, Armas, and Murphy, though, they really didn't have a very good team on the field. Billy made sure people talked about them. Billy himself would generate a lot of interest because he was so fiery. He spoke his mind even sometimes when he shouldn't have. He just made people interested and they started to win. As the summer went on, there was more and more interest in the A's."

The A's scrappy style of play under the fiery and larger-than-life personality of Billy played well in Oakland. Fans connected with the hustling group of unknowns who were taking baseball by storm and bringing respect back to the Oakland A's. Billy's presence alone created excitement for the once dispirited fan base. "It was very exciting times for the city and we were happy to see the stands filling up," recalled former A's infielder Mickey Klutts, who was conditioned to play in front of embarrassingly tiny crowds. "No one minded that they jumped on our train. We wanted it. If you put a good product on the field, people will come. Plus, you had an unpredictable manager and you never knew if he was going to fight or get thrown out of a game."

Mike Heath, the A's popular catcher, said Oakland's working class connected with the battling mentality of A's players. They were scrappers and hustlers and nothing came easy for them. Billy brought everything together.

"Our fans related to a bunch of hard-nosed guys going out and performing every day and that was the Oakland mentality. They want hard-nosed players. The appeal of it was that Billy was no nonsense. He came from the Bay Area. They were waiting for that team to rise again and Billy put that spark in the organization. The whole hype was really good for the area and brought life into the Oakland Coliseum, which was dead in 1979. We loved it and thrived on it."

No one could have forecast the A's sudden resurrection. Even knowing Billy might bring some excitement to the area, no one expected them to lead their division by two games in May. Stephanie Salter, who covered the A's for the *San Francisco Examiner*, recalled the fan enthusiasm building about the A's: "Being a part of that atmosphere that season was like nothing else I covered in sports. The crowds kept growing and growing. It was lightning in a bottle. It was the perfect intersection of Billy having something to prove, Charlie giving him the go-ahead, and the emergence of the young players."

The A's season wasn't without adversity, though. Many experts figured it was only a matter of time before the league caught on to Billy's managerial antics and the young A's faded. They experienced their first rough stretch of the season on a torturous 2–7 road trip through Toronto, Detroit, and Kansas City in late May. The team returned home in third place, two games behind the White Sox, with Billy fuming over mental mistakes. On May 23, for example, Billy was incensed when catcher Jim Essian and third-baseman Wayne Gross coordinated a pickoff play in the sixth against Texas at home without his approval and without tipping Rick Langford, the A's pitcher. The plan was for Essian to catch Texas center fielder Mickey Rivers leading off third-base after Langford's pitch, but Al Oliver laced a two-run single to right instead and the A's eventually lost 3-1. After the game, a reporter asked Billy about the botched pickoff play. "Play? What play are you talking about? A furious Billy asked. "I gave no play. There was no [bleeping] play on. Our pitcher should have won, 1-0. I didn't call a [bleeping] play."

The A's were 25–25 after 50 games, 4 1/2 games behind the first-place Royals. After the hot start, the A's offense was inconsistent, often unable to combine good hitting with good pitching. During that stretch, the A's boasted a home record of 17–9, but a poor 8–16 on the road. Billy's biggest concerns were his unreliable bullpen and defense at second base. He knew he had to set things straight quickly; the A's were on the verge of playing their next 17 games against the heavyweights of the East: Baltimore, Boston, and New York.

The A's went 3–3 against the Red Sox and Orioles. On June 13, the first-place Yankees brought their 34–20 record to Oakland for a four-game series. The series garnered national interest because Billy was facing his former club for the first time that season. Before the series, reporters asked Billy if beating the Yankees would give him any extra satisfaction. "I'm not concerned about the Yankees," Billy said. "I'm not wearing pinstripes now. The only team I'm concerned about is the Oakland A's."

Fans seemed to care about the Yankees, however. The A's drew a monstrous crowd of 47,768 for Friday's sold-out doubleheader. Through 34 home games, the team had already surpassed its total season attendance in 1979 of 306,763. It was the A's second-largest crowd to watch a regular season game at the Coliseum since June 6, 1970, when the A's and Tigers drew 48,758. A's fans exploded in the opener when Mickey Klutts clubbed a walk-off home run off Ron Guidry leading off the bottom of the ninth to muscle the A's to a 4–3 victory. "Billy told me that Guidry would try to bust me inside and that's exactly what he did," recalled Klutts. "I was able to get around on him. My mom flew in for the doubleheader."

The A's lost the next three games to the Yankees, putting their record two games below .500. But Oakland had other reasons to smile. The weekend crowd of 121,364 was a club record, and drove the A's season attendance to 410,075, an increase of 104,000 over the previous season in only 35 home games. "I'm very proud of our fans," Billy said after the series. "We're giving them exciting baseball and they're supporting it like I knew they would. This was one of the few times the A's fans outnumbered the Yankee fans here."

The media hype was building for Billy's highly anticipated return to Yankee Stadium for a three-game series starting on June 20. He admitted to being uptight before the series. Billy's return was the hottest ticket in New York and happened to fall on the weekend of the annual Old-Timers' Day. If all had gone according to George Steinbrenner's original plan, Billy would have been managing the Yankees in 1980.

Instead, Billy returned to New York as the manager of a scrappy, hustling team he'd fashioned in his own image. He was also scheduled to film a Pepto-Bismol™ commercial. Steinbrenner wanted Billy to wear pinstripes one last time for the pregame ceremonies on Old-Timers' Day on Saturday, despite Martin's vow after he was fired to never wear pinstripes again under Steinbrenner's ownership. Steinbrenner was also feeling pressure from Billy supporters to retire his old No. 1. Unable to reach Billy by phone in New York, the owner sent a telegram he later wired to the press: "Fact you are no longer my manager making it increasingly more difficult to reach you by phone. Tried you yesterday and today, but hotel said you were not taking any calls. So what's new? Really would like you in uniform Saturday if you can see your way clear. If you don't, I'm going to pour the Pepto-Bismol all over you Friday. Regards, George."

Later that day, Billy received a standing ovation at Yankee Stadium when he trotted to home plate to present the lineup card before the first game of the series. Some fans tossed marshmallows on the field. Old friends visited Billy in the visitors' clubhouse throughout the weekend. Martin proudly spoke to the New York media about the A's turnaround. He also voiced resentment over not getting enough credit for his turnaround skills. "I'm proud of the fact that we've proven Oakland can be a good franchise that can draw fans. I really want the franchise to stay there." Billy told reporters. "I've never gotten the credit for the fact that I do help baseball wherever

I've been. When I was in Texas, we managed to take the Cowboys off the front page for a while, too."

In the end, after conferring with his players, Martin agreed to wear his old No. 1 Yankee uniform on Old-Timers' Day. "It wasn't an easy decision," Billy said. "I remember when I left here, I said I'd never wear a Yankee uniform again as long as Steinbrenner owned the club. And if I wasn't here with the Oakland A's, I wouldn't have done it. I've been preaching the Oakland A's to my players."

When broadcaster Frank Messer announced Martin among other Yankee immortals such as Mickey Mantle, Joe DiMaggio, Roger Maris, Whitey Ford, and Yogi Berra during pregame ceremonies, Billy received the loudest and longest ovation from the sellout crowd of 51,598. An emotional Billy, choked up behind his dark shades, waved his cap to the fans. While Billy was building a cult-like following back in Oakland, Yankees fans showed him he was still a fan favorite in New York. It wasn't the electric reception he received during Old-Timers' Day two years earlier; it was a calculated show of appreciation and respect for his work improving the A's. On the field, though, the A's were mired in their longest skid of the season. The Yankees wound up taking two of the three games from the A's, dropping Oakland's record to 31–36.

From there, the A's road troubles continued. They struggled miserably with a 7–21 record in June and sank into fourth place, 12 games behind the Royals, who were separating themselves from the rest of the division. The A's weren't scoring runs and the bullpen was faltering badly. The starting rotation lacked run support. The A's were no longer capitalizing on the blunders of opponents, something they had done early and often to start the season. After a 5–2 loss to the Brewers in Milwaukee on July 1, the A's dipped to 32–43, a season-high (or low) 11 games under .500. Frustration mounted in the clubhouse and the team was at a crossroads. They had lost 15 of their last 18 games. Dave McKay and Mike Norris, both intense competitors, engaged in a shoving match in front of reporters in the clubhouse at County

Stadium. Langford and Henderson restrained McKay. Revering and Newman restrained Norris.

Dwayne Murphy, who was named team captain by Billy in late June, refused to accept losing again. Murphy was the A's first team captain since Sal Bando in the mid-'70s. "I think we are a better team than this," Murphy said after the game. "This is not reality. This is not the real Oakland A's." Only time would tell.

8

HAAS-MINDED

It is the responsibility of a business to give back to the community some of what it takes out. Levi Strauss is a classic example of this kind of thinking and the Oakland A's will be run with the same philosophy.
—Roy Eisenhardt, former A's president, August 23, 1980

August 1980: Mike Norris was sleeping comfortably in his Oakland apartment at sunrise when the phone rang. Charlie Finley was on the line, calling from Chicago. Norris rarely heard from Finley in those days. The last time Finley phoned Norris was when the pitcher's landlord complained to the A's about his loud music. Finley got wind of it and lectured Norris over the phone about keeping his music down.

Finley didn't have much to scold Norris about in 1980. After all, Norris, a Cy Young Award candidate, was 17–7 at the time and on pace to become the A's first 20-game winner since 1975, when Vida Blue went 22–11. Norris had mastered a tantalizing screwball that was unhittable for left-handed hitters.

After five rocky years in the organization, Norris was finally putting together a kind of season the A's had hoped for. Finley drafted him as the twenty-fourth overall pick in the 1973 January amateur draft from San Francisco's Balboa High. Norris—who received a $25,000 signing bonus—

had come a long way. It was on the diamonds of Balboa High where Juan Marichal, the Giants' All-Star pitcher, visited and taught Norris how to throw a screwball. The plan was for Norris to replace Catfish Hunter, the A's departing ace who signed as a free agent with the Yankees after the 1974 season. In fact, Norris was going to wear Hunter's old uniform No. 27 to begin his career, but A's manager Alvin Dark didn't want to add any more pressure on the slender 6-foot-2 rookie. Dark, a devout Christian, called Norris his "Jeremiah," after the biblical prophet of hope.

After tossing 16 consecutive innings without allowing an earned run to begin his rookie campaign in 1975, Norris was sidelined by elbow surgery for most of the season. Removing the calcium deposit in his elbow didn't translate into wins when he recovered. He wasn't the same pitcher. "I lost so much velocity and movement on my fastball from my elbow surgery, I had to learn how to pitch all over again," remembered Norris. "My fastball straightened out like a string. My career was on the line, so I needed to develop a screwball."

Norris was 6–17 over the next three seasons and Finley contemplated releasing him. Although Norris was in and out of Finley's doghouse through his ups and downs in the organization, he looked to the owner as a father figure. Like real sons and fathers, the two had their ups and downs. Finley demoted Norris from Triple-A Vancouver down to Double-A Jersey City in 1978. He fined Norris and suspended him without pay for one week for reporting a week late to Double-A Jersey City. Norris was one of the many disgruntled A's players who thought they deserved more money than Finley was paying them. But playing for Finley made them scrappy, tough, resourceful and aggressive. It made them think independently and grow up fast. Norris entered the 1980 season with a career record of 12–25.

On that early morning in late August, though, Norris was finally a healthy, happy, winning pitcher. Speaking with Finley for almost an hour, he noticed that Finley was not talking like an owner. The shrewd Finley— knowing Norris was only earning $35,000 and eligible for free agency after the 1981 season—proposed to be his agent. Finley tried to convince him of how much money he could land in the free agent rush. This was the same Finley who twice cut Norris's salary by 20 percent. The offer didn't sit well with Norris, so he declined. He knew there was more to Finley's proposal than met the eye. "I felt that I would have been straddling the fence," chuckled Norris. "It would have been a catch-twenty-two situation, and I wanted no part of it." Norris concluded that Finley was on the verge of selling the A's. He was right.

Cornell Maier, the leading voice of the Oakland business community, had already pitched the A's to the deep-pocketed Walter A. Haas Jr., chairman of Levi Strauss & Co., in July. Maier told Haas that Finley was ready to sell after several failed attempts to move the A's out of Oakland. Finley had re-signed Billy's entire coaching staff over the weekend. Billy maintained he was still in the dark about what was going on. "The last time I talked with Charlie, he asked me if I liked my coaches," Billy told a reporter. "I said 'Yes, every one of them.' I know that the contracts of the coaching staff were renewed through 1981 and some players were called. But I have no idea what's going on. If I did, I'd tell you." Renewing contracts in August was uncharacteristic of Finley; he usually bargained in the spring. Many saw it as another sign the A's would soon be in the hands of a new owner.

Under Martin, the A's had almost tripled attendance and the value of the franchise had increased by millions in only six months. Through 61 home dates in 1979, the A's drew 262,379. In 1980, they had already drawn 676,165 through the same number of home dates. "When Charlie sells the club, he should give 30 percent of the money to Billy Martin," White Sox president Bill Veeck said in 1980. Billy had made the A's attractive for local buyers who saw renewed fan interest in the team. Eddie Sapir, Billy's longtime friend, asked Finley how he planned on compensating Billy for enhancing the value of his franchise and sparking fan interest. "He said, 'I told the new owners to give him an attendance clause because he'll put a lot of butts in the seats,'" remembered Sapir.

The generous, warm-hearted Haas came from a pioneering, prominent, distinguished and wealthy San Francisco family with a strong sense of philanthropy and social responsibility. He taught his three children at an early age to donate a portion of their money to the poor. With deep roots in the Bay Area, the community-minded Haas family had long fought social inequity. "He was so benevolent," recalled Dave Newhouse. "The Haas foundation, to this day, gives away tons of charity. You'd visit him in his office and he was so self-effacing. He was just the kindest man."

The son of Walter A. Haas Sr., Haas was the grandnephew of Levi Strauss. Young Levi, a German immigrant, moved to San Francisco, building his empire by using fabric from tents and wagon covers to make durable trousers for Gold Rush forty-niners in 1853. He called them "waist-high overalls." The popular trousers became so synonymous with Strauss that customers started calling them Levi's.

In 1951, Haas Jr., a third generation San Franciscan, was named Outstanding Young Man of the Year for his business acumen and community work. The humble and unassuming sixty-four-year-old Haas was also a trustee of the Ford Foundation. "The Haases were some of the nicest people you'd ever meet in your life," remembered Steve McCatty, former A's pitcher. "You never knew what Mr. Haas did. You'd never know if he had $100 in the bank or $100 million. That's just the way he carried himself. They were wonderful. They finally promoted the team."

A graduate of UC Berkeley in 1937, Haas earned a varsity letter in tennis. The Haases were deeply rooted in the university. He earned a master's degree from Harvard Business School in 1939. After spending five years in the army, the twenty-three-year-old Haas started at the bottom of the totem pole at Levi. His brother, Peter, was president and CEO of the company.

Haas, an avid trout fisherman, lived in the Pacific Heights neighborhood of San Francisco next to Bob Lurie, owner of the San Francisco Giants. "He was always a gentleman and I considered him a very good friend," Lurie wrote in an email. One of the criticisms of Oakland was that there were not enough corporate headquarters in the city to support its professional sports teams. Maier's Kaiser Aluminum was the only major one. If the A's, Raiders, and Warriors wanted to sell corporate sponsorships and season tickets to businesses, the businesses first needed permission from their New York headquarters. Levi Strauss, boasting annual sales approaching $3 billion at the time, was headquartered on a 28th floor executive suite in the Levi Strauss building at the Embarcadero Center in San Francisco. All of Haas's interests were in San Francisco. Oakland, located in the East Bay, did not boast the sizzling business market San Francisco did.

Haas believed a professional sports team was a unifying force in a community. "It's important to a community to have a baseball club. It brings jobs, pride and so forth," Haas said in 1980. He said years later that when he returned home after meeting with Maier, he surprised his family. "I went home that night and told the family I had said 'no' and they said, 'What?!'" Haas chuckled.

Maier approached Haas at the perfect time. The Haases had been interested in investing in their first local sports team for a long time. Haas Jr.'s son, Walter J. Haas, whom everyone called "Wally," and son-in-law Roy Eisenhardt were ready to take on a new challenge. The Dartmouth-educated Eisenhardt was married to Betsy, Haas's only daughter. Wally, thirty, had been grants manager of the community affairs department for Levi Strauss and managed a rock band, "Sons of Champlin," on the side. Eisenhardt, forty-one, was an attorney and a visiting law professor at UC Berkeley. He also served as a real estate specialist and president of San Francisco's rent board. He coached the men's heavyweight rowing crew for UC Berkeley. Eisenhardt recalled his involvement in the A's sale. "He recruited me to help him acquire it. I didn't plan on staying in, frankly. I figured I would help him acquire it and set up an organization for him. Wally would stay there, of course. I was going to return to teaching at UC Berkeley and coaching men's freshmen rowing. The only reason I stayed longer there is because I couldn't find the right talent immediately to implement our ownership philosophy. I could find people who knew a lot about baseball, but I couldn't find somebody who could implement our mission of serving the community and doing good things."

Haas viewed the A's franchise as a neglected public landmark he wanted to restore and preserve in Oakland. Serving the community was his primary mission of ownership. Maier quickly delivered a letter of intent to Finley's Chicago home to purchase the A's. Finley and Haas began negotiating. "We discussed it among ourselves, had some financial and demographics analyses done," said Eisenhardt. "And we came back to Cornell and said, 'yes.'" Haas insisted the purchase be kept top secret until a formal announcement was made.

Eisenhardt and Wally flew to Chicago to meet with Finley and signed the agreement four days later. "Walter was contacted by several businessmen in the early summer of 1980," Eisenhardt wrote in an email. "We met with Finley's attorney in Chicago and settled on the terms."

On Thursday, August 21, the A's announced that a Saturday morning press conference would be held at the Kaiser Center in Oakland two days later at 10:00 a.m. The reason for the press conference was kept a mystery. "It was kept about as hush-hush as one can do in circumstances like that," recalled John Hickey, former A's beat writer. "Word leaked of the sale the day before, but no one knew who the buyer was."

Rumors and speculation swirled. Some fans remained skeptical because they had heard rumors of A's potential sales for years. With the presser being held at the Kaiser Center, many thought Finley was selling the A's to Maier, who had already invested a significant amount of Kaiser money in promoting the A's in the community. Maier had also recently publicly claimed the A's were staying in Oakland. Billy Martin Appreciation Day, sponsored by Maier, was scheduled at the Coliseum the next day. Billy's former Yankee teammates, Mickey Mantle, Joe DiMaggio, Hank Bauer, Roger Maris, and Whitey Ford were scheduled to be on hand to honor him. "The assumption was that Maier would put together a group of investors, including Mr.

Martin stands between former Oakland Oaks teammates Cookie Lavagetto (left) and George
Metkovich (right) in Oakland on Casey Stengel Day, August 1968. Billy played for the Oaks
from 1947 to 1949 before moving up to the Yankees in 1950.
(COURTESY OF RON RIESTERER)

Under Martin, the Detroit Tigers won 91 games in 1971 and the AL East in 1972. In
1973, the league suspended him for ordering spitballs and he was fired late in the season,
with a record of 71–63.
(COURTESY OF RON RIESTERER)

Billy Martin inherited an ailing A's franchise in 1980. The aggressive brand of baseball he brought to Oakland resulted in a tripling of the team's home attendance during his first season.

Martin waving his cap to Oakland fans on Billy Martin Day in August 1980. Former Yankees Joe DiMaggio, Roger Maris, Hank Bauer, Whitey Ford, and Mickey Mantle were on hand for the celebration.

As the A's wins piled up, the media wanted to hear from the architect of Billy Ball. Martin holding court with reporters in front of the visitor's dugout at Fenway Park in Boston, 1980.

Martin in vintage form, barking at the home plate umpire while another umpire, Ken Kaiser, tries to intervene in Oakland, 1980.

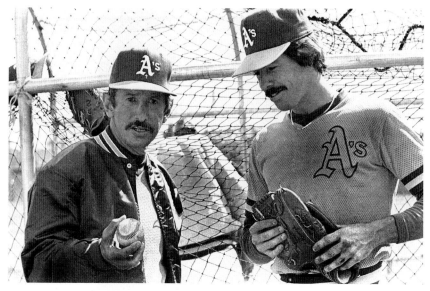

Billy with A's pitcher Matt Keough during spring training, February 1980. Keough, who was 2–17 in 1979, won the American League Comeback Player of the Year in his first year playing for Martin with a record of 16–13.

(COURTESY OF RON RIESTERER)

Billy and Rickey Henderson discuss the finer points of bunting during spring training in Arizona, February 1980. One of the most dynamic players in baseball history, Henderson flourished under Martin.

(COURTESY OF RON RIESTERER)

Billy addresses the young A's during spring training in Arizona, February 1981. Martin's mentor, Casey Stengel, once said of his protégé, "He may think he knows more about baseball than anybody else, but it wouldn't surprise me if he was right."

(COURTESY OF RON RIESTERER)

Martin during spring training in Arizona in 1981, the same season he led the A's to their first division title since 1975.

(COURTESY OF RON RIESTERER)

Billy and his mother, Joan Downey, in the A's dugout before the Opening Night game against the Twins on April 10, 1980. Joan threw out the ceremonial first pitch.
(COURTESY OF RON RIESTERER)

Walter A. Haas Jr. viewed his purchase of the A's in 1980 as preserving an Oakland landmark and believed a professional team was a unifying force in the community.
(COURTESY OF THE EVELYN AND WALTER HAAS, JR. FUND)

Behind the scenes, Andy Dolich, the A's vice president of business operations, partnered with advertising agency Ogilvy & Mather to create the brilliant, Clio award-winning "Billy Ball" campaign.
(COURTESY OF RON RIESTERER)

Martin on hand at an October 16, 1980 press conference introducing veteran Bay Area broadcasters Bill King and Lon Simmons as the A's new radio play-by-play radio voices for the 1981 season. From left to right: Walter J. Haas, Billy, Roy Eisenhardt, Jim Myers, Bill King, Lon Simmons.
(COURTESY OF RON RIESTERER)

A's players celebrate by mobbing closer Dave Beard in Oakland after sweeping the Kansas City Royals in the division miniseries to advance to the American League Championship Series, October 9, 1981.

(COURTESY OF RON RIESTERER)

Haas," recalled Eisenhardt. "But we thought buying the whole thing would be better, to make the tough early decisions, and then, if desirable, bring in additional investors. That never occurred."

Billy was told to be at the press conference at 9:15 a.m. Lee MacPhail, American League president, was even flying to Oakland for the big announcement. The A's front office leaked that Finley would be in attendance as well.

On August 23, 1980, the press conference was packed as cameras flickered inside the glass-enclosed twenty-eighth floor suite of the Kaiser Center. Built on seven acres in 1960, the slender, $45 million architectural marvel—the largest office building west of Chicago at the time—towered over Lake Merritt, a popular large tidal lagoon in the heart of Oakland. Eisenhardt and Wally had met with Martin for forty-five minutes in Maier's office prior to announcing the sale. Billy donned a suit and tie with large tinted glasses. "From the moment we met, I felt a friendship and warmth," recalled Eisenhardt. "He had good coaches. He knew how to get the most out of players and was caring for people off the field as well. He was very accepting and understanding. We were going to rely on people to give us honest opinions about issues when we'd have questions. He was very forthright and straightforward in his opinions. It was great. I really enjoyed my time with Billy."

The A's would now be run by wealthy philanthropists intrigued by Billy's baseball acumen. The Haases were aware that Billy had led the A's miraculous resurgence. He was the difference maker that attracted them. Plus, Martin was a hero to the working class. The Haases essentially purchased Billy Ball. "When the Haas family purchased the team, they assured us that we didn't have to sell Billy to them," said Sapir. "They believed he was the best manager in baseball. They told us to write our own ticket and we did. It was a beautiful ticket."

Eisenhardt, who grew up in New York, remembered Billy's infamous series-saving catch in Game 7 of the 1952 World Series against the Brooklyn Dodgers at Ebbets Field. He admired how Billy always hustled and maximized his talent. "I think that's why he was a good manager for young players," said Eisenhardt. "He knew how to utilize baseball skills to the fullest. He stood in contrast to the 'naturally' skilled players such as DiMaggio, Mantle, and [Phil] Rizzuto. Billy was always playing hard, no matter what the circumstance."

The Swingers, the A's colorful pep band, performed, "Back Home Again in Indiana" as Finley swaggered inside the suite. The last press conference Finley hosted was at the Drake Hotel in Chicago when he announced the masterstroke hiring of Billy on February 21. Oakland mayor Lionel Wilson and Coliseum president Jack Maltester were some of the local dignitaries on hand. Oakland A's pennants hung on the wall behind the podium. "There's no question in my mind that without Cornell Maier's incredible determination and dedication we wouldn't be here today with this wonderful family owning the A's," proclaimed Wilson.

Ted Robinson, A's director of promotions at the time, recalled how Maier's persistence brought Finley and Haas together. "Maier really took the lead from Kaiser to be the civic leader for Oakland and help the team get some traction to stay in Oakland," said Robinson. "By midseason, the Haas family was on the scene."

Representing Haas, Eisenhardt and Wally showed up to confirm the purchase. No one had any idea the Haas family would be involved in the announcement. Finley walked behind the podium and wiped a tear from his right eye when he announced that he was leaving baseball after two decades of ownership; he had purchased the franchise exactly twenty years before. The agreement stipulated that he would sell the A's to Haas for $12.7 million but would retain control until November 6. The transaction took only thirty days. "You mean that he can still fire me?" Billy asked tongue in cheek during the presser. Billy was Finley's last manager. "Billy Martin is the first manager I ever had who didn't need my help," Finley said. "He should be named manager of the century."

The agreement was contingent on the approval from American League owners. Finley—who purchased the A's for $4 million in Kansas City—moved them to Oakland in 1968 and would leave them there in 1980 when he departed from the game. While the mood inside the Kaiser suite was one of celebration and relief, Finley was still bitter about essentially being forced out of the game he helped innovate in many ways. Finley left baseball and Oakland with three world championships and five division titles in thirteen years. "The main reason I'm leaving baseball is because I can no longer compete financially," an emotional Finley told the crowd during his thirty-minute speech. "When the game was a battle of wits, no one could compete with us. But today it's no longer a battle of the wits. It's how much you've got on the hip. It's money."

Eisenhardt said that Finley recognized that his business model couldn't survive baseball's new economics. Eisenhardt noted that Finley was "fascinating," very smart and acutely understood baseball and how to network with other team officials to evaluate talent: "He could no longer keep his players because of the combination of arbitration and free agency spiraling the salaries up. His business model was to scout and sign good players and keep them for a long time. He saw the interaction between arbitration salaries and free agent salaries. Free agent salaries were driving awards up for arbitration-eligible players. He realized he was not able to sustain the economics of the payroll."

Finley—who blamed Commissioner Bowie Kuhn for the beginning of his exile from baseball—claimed that trying to move the A's out of Oakland was not his idea. The offer came from Coliseum chairman Robert Nahas, he contended. "About five years ago, Nahas offered me an opportunity to move the club if the American League would give Oakland $2 million," Finley insisted. "Then they raised the ante to $3 million and later they wanted the Giants to play half of their games in Oakland. It wasn't Charlie Finley who wanted to leave Oakland. I must say I didn't want to leave, but it was Nahas who came to me with the offer." The Coliseum board never allowed Finley to break his twenty-year ironclad lease to free the A's to another city.

The Haas family signaled a different approach going forward, one that would be more community-oriented. Eisenhardt would serve as president of the A's and Wally, the executive vice president. Wally, thick haired, bearded and scholarly looking with glasses, stressed that the motive for purchasing the A's was not only for profit, but also for creating a great experience for fans at the Coliseum. "Levi Strauss has never maximized profits at the expense of the community," he said. To the Haases, owning the A's was never a money commitment. It was an emotional commitment fueled by wedding the A's to the community and restoring fan trust. "The Haas family made the team into a great organization," said Mike Heath, former A's catcher. "They really treated us well. It was a breath of fresh air to have someone come in and inject some money into the team and make the right moves. I wanted to play the rest of my career in Oakland and never leave the Bay Area."

Eisenhardt, articulate, thin, handsome and tan with a sharp chiseled jawline and perfectly groomed, black-parted hair, stepped behind the podium. He announced plans for a new community-centered era of Oakland A's baseball. He said their ownership would be a partnership and romance with the city. Eisenhardt stole the show.

"It is the responsibility of a business to give back to the community some of what it takes out. Levi Strauss is a classic example of this kind of thinking and the Oakland A's will be run with the same philosophy.

"We have to create the mood of a team that's part of the community, rather than a private or personal activity of the owner. We'll be reaching out to senior citizens, youth groups, students—areas of the community that haven't participated in the A's before."

Asked about coexisting with the neighboring San Francisco Giants across the bay, Eisenhardt emphasized synergy between the two clubs. He maintained that if sports teams are successful in the Bay Area, they feed off each other. That contradicted the consensus among many, including Giants owner Lurie, that the Bay Area could not sustain two major-league teams. "Particularly when those two teams are successes, we intend to create a baseball fever in Northern California and the A's benefit from the enthusiasm when the Giants are a successful, competitive team," Eisenhardt said. "Our goal is to see the Giants compete for the National League pennant at the same time we are winning the American League pennant."

Brian Kingman, who pitched in the A's organization since 1975, recalled the brains, sophistication and intelligence the Haases brought to the archaic franchise and to baseball. "Going from Finley to the Haases was like going from the typewriter to Silicon Valley," said Kingman. "They were sophisticated guys wearing suits. I felt like hanging around them to get smarter. I was happy we stayed. I was hoping we wouldn't go to Denver. As a pitcher, you hear stories about the ball flying in Colorado. Why uproot everything and move there and we obviously didn't."

Glenn Schwarz, who covered the A's championship years of the early '70s for the *San Francisco Examiner*, figured the team would be in good hands with the Haases. "It was most welcomed from somebody who'd been through that era and saw all of the backroom stuff that went on. You had to figure that with the reputation of Walter A. Haas Jr., his family, and Levi Strauss, they would take on the team as a civic responsibility more than just being worried about making a dollar. They were very fortunate to have inherited Billy because he was already there. Finley picked him up when he was unemployed."

Eisenhardt knew he lacked the experience of a baseball executive and inherited a skeletal franchise, but he saw the making of a great organization. Some of their focused improvements were to increase access for the handicap, establish free days for children and senior citizens, improve clubhouse conditions, and create user-friendly ticket booths. Eisenhardt said their plan was to build the team through a strong farm system, investing their money in their scouting department, instructional leagues, and minor-league affiliates.

Lee MacPhail, who tried for three years to facilitate the A's move out of Oakland, couldn't help being impressed by the new owners. But he insisted he had no regrets about his previous attempts to relocate the team. "I know in the past I have said two teams in the Bay Area would never work out, but after meeting these new Oakland owners, I have a feeling they will prove me wrong," MacPhail said. "We've had some interesting owners in baseball over the years, but we've never had a college professor."

Robinson said that MacPhail wasn't only on hand to witness the purchase announcement. He was there to make sure Finley followed through with the sale. "MacPhail's real mission there was to make Charlie sign the papers and not change his mind," Robinson said. "Charlie needed to get out because he was getting divorced. Baseball had enough of Charlie and wanted him out."

The A's were scheduled to play a nationally televised game on NBC against the Orioles at the Coliseum that afternoon. Infielder Mickey Klutts recalled the optimism in the A's clubhouse when players first heard the announcement. "Obviously the youth of the owners and their commitment to upgrading the organization was promising," Klutts said. "I'm sure baseball was happy about the sale considering their battles with Charlie."

One of Eisenhardt's priorities was to repair a strained relationship with the Coliseum board and Oakland officials, a hostile one highlighted by litigations and distrust. He planned on forging a strong partnership with Jack Maltester by making significant and long overdue Coliseum improvements, including addressing fan and player comfort. The A's had seven years remaining on their Coliseum lease, and Eisenhardt confirmed they would honor the lease in addition to the twenty-year-year option that would keep them in Oakland until at least 2007. "We had known for years that Charlie was going to sell the club, but the surprise was that he sold it and it stayed in the area," said McCatty. "[Oakland] went from a place you didn't want to play to one of the best places to play."

9

THE MIRACLE WORKER

I never wanted my dad to leave Oakland because he had so much less stress there. He had a belly. He ate better and was healthier. He was under so much less stress. The media in Oakland wasn't anything like the media in New York. The show was "Billy Ball" and he was home.
—BILLY MARTIN JR., OCTOBER 2018

IT WAS BILLY MARTIN'S WORLD IN OAKLAND AND LOCAL CIVIC LEADers made sure they showered him with appreciation. Not that the A's were drawing sellout crowds every night, but Billy had started a revival in Oakland and silencing naysayers who had buried A's baseball in the city. The stadium was filling up and Billy brought respectability to the team. In contrast to the previous year, when the team averaged less than 4,000 fans for every home game, an average of 11,000 fans walked through the turnstiles per game. "He was like the gunslinger of the west," said Wayne Hagin, one of the A's radio voices. "When we came to town, fans weren't really looking for our players. They only looked for the manager. He was that big. He was a different guy. He had the cowboy hat and a presence. Even though he was a little guy, you knew that was Billy Martin."

The black cloud over the franchise was giving way to hope and excitement. Cornell Maier was chairman of Billy Martin Day set for August 24 at the Coliseum. Maier, who came up with the idea of honoring Billy, organized a group of local dignitaries and some of Billy's friends from around the baseball and entertainment world to pay homage to the Berkeley-born A's manager. Eisenhardt and Wally joined Finley in his private box to see the festivities and watch the A's play the Orioles afterwards.

A crowd of 18,160 was on hand on the Sunday afternoon to honor Billy, who was holding the 63–61 A's in second place. Billy's mother, stepfather, and sister, wearing A's Starter jackets, joined in the celebration. A highlight came when the master of ceremonies announced, "Some of Billy's friends wanted to drive out to see him." A car carrying Billy's former Yankee teammates Mickey Mantle, Joe DiMaggio, Roger Maris, Whitey Ford, and Hank Bauer suddenly emerged from the center field fence and cruised toward Martin, who was standing near home plate. As the car approached the infield, the driver dropped off Maris at third-base, Bauer at second, Mantle at first, Ford on the pitcher's mound, and DiMaggio at home plate. Billy's friends then walked behind him as he addressed the crowd. "After thirty years in baseball, to get a day is just a really great thing," Billy said. "It's very emotional."

Billy was showered with $30,000 worth of gifts, including a glistening new burgundy Cadillac Eldorado, courtesy of Finley. Ed Daly, World Airways president, presented him with 1,000 gallons worth of gasoline. He received a trip to Hawaii, a box of grapes, a portable TV radio, and a shotgun along with many other gifts. George Steinbrenner called him to congratulate him and Frank Sinatra sent a telegram. Billy and his former Yankee teammates partied with the Raiders later that evening.

Billy was enjoying rock star status in Oakland. And his autobiography, *Number 1*, co-authored with Peter Golenbock, had been released in May. Golenbock spent five weeks with Martin and the A's in 1980 and witnessed the excitement for himself. "Coming from Berkeley, Billy was the absolute perfect person to manage the A's. He was so popular with that team, he could have been the mayor of Oakland. It was so much fun traveling with them. It was very interesting to see the loyalty those players had for him."

It was a timely romance between Martin, the A's and a lonely fan base. "Billy was one of their own," said Bob Lacey. "He was from the Bay Area and played for the Oakland Oaks of the Pacific Coast League. They took ownership of him."

"Billy Ball was fun," said Kit Stier, who covered Martin for the *Oakland Tribune.* "It was a good sign there was some baseball interest in Oakland." As much as fans embraced the excitement Billy brought, he loved being near his mother, who loved the attention that came from her son's homecoming. Cigarette dangling from her mouth, she autographed scorecards, balls, and souvenirs for fans in the stands when she attended games. There were fewer distractions for Billy. He kept a low profile and the temptations were far less in the town of Danville, California, where he lived, than in the fast lanes of New York.

There was not a world-famous Sardi's Restaurant or Mickey's Bar in Danville like there were in Manhattan. Instead, Billy lounged at the laid-back Danville Saloon.

The pressure was not as intense managing in Oakland. The expectations of taking over baseball's cheapest club coming off 108 losses were less burdensome than managing a club expected to win with the highest payroll and biggest egos in the game. Finley left him alone, made him the highest-paid manager, and granted him free reign to manage the team as he saw fit. He always wanted that control. Life was smoother, slower and relaxing for Billy. He was home, happy, winning and finally found the peace and contentment he had been pursuing for years. "I'd guess it was one of the happiest times of his life," remembered Stephanie Salter. "He was home, surrounded by his cronies, and molding a bunch of eager players into winners."

Danville was an emerging East Bay suburban residential farming community. The new owners wanted Billy living comfortably. "I never met anyone fairer than Roy, Sandy [Alderson], and Wally," said Judge Eddie

Sapir, Billy's attorney. "They asked me what they had to do to make Billy happy. We got everything we wanted. It wasn't because I was some great negotiator, but they wanted a real happy manager. They knew they had the best manager in baseball." Billy lived in a $650,000 home purchased and owned by the A's. His contract with the new owners allowed him to use the house rent-free for ten years. Sapir and Eisenhardt were discussing a ten-year deal for Billy, according to Sapir. "They let Billy pick out a home and make some improvements," said Sapir. "The two biggest improvements were very expensive landscaping and a new swimming pool. The reason they didn't mind doing that was how we structured the deal. Oakland would own the home and Billy could live in it. If, for some reason, things didn't work out, Billy could still live in the home as long as he wanted. If Billy no longer had any use for the home, the owners could sell it and get back the amount they purchased it for. Any profit would go to Billy. They couldn't have been fairer. He got the home he wanted."

Steve McCatty, who pitched for Billy in Oakland, observed that Billy was more relaxed without the pressures and temptations that came from managing in New York.

> He was really relaxed out there. He lived in the Blackhawk community of Danville, an absolutely beautiful area. The drive home after games was really relaxing. There was a lot less temptation for him out there. There weren't a lot of places for him to get into trouble. He went straight home after games. He really looked good. There was a lot less pressure. The Yankees expected you to win and the expectations can almost be crippling if you don't.

Billy Martin Jr. never forgot the intense pressure and enormous media scrutiny his father was under in New York. The stress thinned him out, discolored him, and drove him to the bottle on many occasions. Billy Jr. knew that his father's heart would always be with the Yankees, but coming from a son who worried about his well-being, he was much more at peace with him being back home. Billy had gained twenty pounds since joining the A's. His face had filled out. Billy Jr. saw the difference:

If you compare photos, his skin was pale; he was gaunt-looking and looked withdrawn in New York. In Oakland, he had more color and had a belly. He ate better and was healthier. As someone who just cared about him, I wanted him in Oakland because I saw how much healthier he was there. He wasn't as stressed out and skinny. You could see his face. He was happy. It was like driving around with the pope. It felt so right for him to be there. It's where he belonged in a lot of ways. I loved it when he was there. I wish he had another length of time with the A's. I would have loved to see him take them to the postseason again.

Mickey Morabito, the A's traveling secretary and public relations director who Billy brought with him from the Yankees in 1980, said at the time that Martin was living a more quiet and carefree life. Nobody bothered him. "Martin is leading a more normal life with less things gnawing at him," Morabito told the *Los Angeles Times* in 1980. "The only pressure is self-imposed. He doesn't come to the park and face all the media pressure. He doesn't look out of his office and see all those personalities. He doesn't continually have to react to something that happened a week ago, month ago. He got a bunch of kids who were dying for help and leadership and he was able to give it to them without a Steinbrenner second-guessing him."

During the winter meetings in Dallas after the 1980 season, Billy acknowledged he was comfortable, happy, and settled in Oakland, especially since the Haas family made him the director of player development—which was essentially the general manager. "I feel this is my niche," Billy said to a group of writers. "The community is great, and I've got a chance to work with young kids who want to win. As general manager, I've got control I've never had. With the long-term contract and the other wonderful things they've given me, well, Oakland is right up my alley." Billy, a staunch Roman Catholic, believed in God and attended Sunday Mass. "No matter how much he drank or where he was after a day game on Saturday night, he was at church for Sunday morning Mass at 6:00 a.m.," recalled Mike Norris.

Billy pinned a gold cross under the A's logo on his baseball cap. While managing the Yankees, he fastened the cross in between the letter "Y" on the interlocking logo. Dave Heaverlo, a former A's reliever, asked Billy about the cross on his hat one day during a restroom visit standing in their stalls. "He told me that when it's all over with, he only had to answer to one person," said Heaverlo. "There was a religious side to Billy that a lot of people never saw. He may not have walked the walk all the time, but there were signs that he was a God-fearing man."

A reporter once asked Billy why his combative reputation and proneness for self-destruction followed him everywhere he managed. Billy blamed the media for painting that image of him and took the opportunity to disclose his Christian faith. "That's because of the press I've gotten," Billy said. "I don't think people really get a chance to know me. People don't know that I go to Mass every Sunday and that I love Jesus Christ. This is my own business. I don't care if they know it or not. He knows it. That's the most important thing."

Ray Negron, one of Billy's longtime confidants dating back to his managing days in New York, described his profound and private faith centered on a personal relationship with God. "That's the Italian side. In his heart, he felt a strong bond with God. Billy taught me that his relationship with God was his and his alone. He didn't have to tell the world that he believed in God and worshipped Him. He knew that God knew. That's all that mattered."

McCatty never heard Billy talk much about religion and couldn't confirm how regularly he attended Mass, but he did witness him help a lot of players. "He had a really big heart," said McCatty. "He helped some players with money and former players who were short on time with their pensions. He hired them so they could have enough service time. He never talked much about it, but he did it. I think he always felt pretty good about being able to help people and I'm sure he did that a lot more than we know."

Mickey Klutts, former A's infielder, said that although he never heard Billy share his faith, he observed his generosity. "It's not something he talked about," said Klutts. "It was a touchy subject for him. He possessed a lot of Christian values like generosity and his love of family. I'm sure a lot of people questioned his beliefs."

Former A's first base coach Jackie Moore contended that Billy's tussles off the field overshadowed his heart to help people in need. Once the game started, however, Billy had no mercy for opponents on the field. "Billy had a huge heart," said Moore. "You don't hear much about his big heart. He helped a lot of financially troubled former players. He would always reach in his pocket and help in any way he could. He had a lot bigger heart than most gave him credit for. But once he put on the uniform, the war was on."

While Ernie Camacho was a rookie pitching for Billy in 1980, he was hanging out with other A's players in the bar of the Edgewater Hyatt House in Oakland. Billy was also present. Camacho had never met Billy and never introduced himself. Camacho said Billy dropped money in his pocket when he passed him. "I remember him walking right by me and a hand coming over my shoulder," said Camacho. "He put a $100 bill in my pocket. He shoved it in my pocket and kept on going. As I reflect on it now, I wish he would have sat down and talked to me." Camacho figured that was how Billy showed his appreciation.

Wayne Hagin said that Billy used to meet with him and Bill King, the A's lead radio voice, after day games to give them private in-depth analysis of the game in his office. Billy wanted to teach them the game of baseball from his eyes. He told them to bring their scoresheet and pencil. "He'd go through all nine innings and tell me what he was thinking," said Hagin. "He'd look at me and say, 'Tell me what was going on in the sixth inning.' He'd tell me why he put on a hit and run. We'd go over all the different elements of the game in the confines of his office at the Coliseum. He did the same for Bill King, who had not done baseball since filling in late in 1962. He was amazing."

Hagin said Billy and King formed a connection because neither of them had a college education. Both were self-taught. King was an intellectual who never attended college. Hagin recalled a conversation between Billy and King on the team bus in Cleveland. "They were talking about the Civil War forever," recalled Hagin. "Billy thought he was an absolute expert on the Civil War, but Bill knew everything, too. Billy loved leadership and talking about the generals." King, who died in 2005, was a posthumous recipient of the Ford C. Frick Award in 2017 for broadcasting excellence.

Hagin said that Billy walked off the team bus one day in Anaheim after hearing Lon Simmons, another A's radio voice who joined the team after previously broadcasting the Giants, argue with coach Clete Boyer about which player was better: Mickey Mantle or Willie Mays. Mantle was Billy's friend. Stuck in traffic and a few blocks from the hotel, an annoyed Billy walked the rest of the way. Billy was always seated in the front right side of the bus. "He had enough of hearing Lon talk about Mays," said Hagin. "That was the first time I saw the temper. He had enough about Mays. Lon was just talking about the virtues of Mays. He [Billy] loved Mantle. In his eyes, anyone put up against Mickey was not nearly as good."

Rod Carew, the Hall of Fame batting master who owned a career average of .328 and collected 3,053 hits in 19 seasons in the majors, said that Billy worked with him for hours when he was a young prospect in the Twins organization. Billy pushed the shy Carew to come out of his shell. Carew said Billy was a battler, smart, aggressive, and knew how to handle players. He said that Billy promoted the theory of aggressive baserunning, forcing opponents into making mistakes. In 1975, Carew asked Billy to be the godfather of his second child, Stephanie Alyce. "Billy and I became good friends," said Carew. "He helped me on and off the field giving me meaningful fatherly advice when I really needed it. I was proud he agreed to be my daughter's godfather. He also encouraged me to open up. I was very shy, but I started chattering it up in the infield just to let the other players know I was there."

10

ACES AND THE OUTFIELD

It was an awakening and so much of a growth for us. Before Billy got there, we always felt that some of us got the opportunity on a false pretense because we were so bad. We started to realize we belonged there. He made us believe. He fought for us.
—STEVE MCCATTY, FORMER A'S PITCHER, JANUARY 2019

THE REVITALIZED A'S OF 1980, ON THE VERGE OF NEW OWNERSHIP, caught fire after sinking to a season-low 11 games under .500 on July 1. They won 30 of their next 43 games and climbed back into sole possession of second place. It was a distant second place because the first-place Royals held a convincing 13-game lead. The Royals were running away with the division and their hitting machine George Brett was flirting with a .400 batting average. Billy's bold spring training promise that the A's would finish ahead of the Angels was materializing. The Angels were in fifth place. Martin, recalling Bobby Grich's insult after the A's manager had earlier predicted that his team would finish ahead of the Angels, looked at the standings and returned fire. "Tell Grich that I'll let 'em know what I'm drinking and he can tell his teammates," Billy said. "Maybe he can rub it on his legs and increase his range. If the Angels had played Kansas City as tough as I thought they would, the division would have been up for grabs."

The Angels finished the season 5–8 against the Royals and 3–10 against the A's. The aggressiveness and unpredictability that Martin fostered were key factors in Oakland's turnaround. But so were his five rubber-armed starting pitchers—Langford, twenty-eight, Norris, twenty-five, Keough, twenty-four, McCatty, twenty-six, and Kingman, twenty-five—all right-handed and all acquired by Charlie Finley before Martin arrived. Finley drafted Norris and Keough, and signed Kingman and McCatty as undrafted amateur free agents in 1973. He acquired Langford in a blockbuster trade with the Pirates during spring training in 1977. Finley had conceived Billy's staff and assembled the A's 1980 roster. "Generally overlooked amid the A's success this year is that Finley's allegedly impoverished farm system produced Norris, Keough, Henderson, Gross, Murphy, McCatty and Kingman among others, and Finley shrewdly traded for Armas, Revering, Page and Langford among others," wrote Ross Newhan of the *Los Angeles Times* in 1980.

Finley may have acquired the A's starters, but Billy was the one getting the most out of his rotation, partly because his bullpen was shaky. His pitchers were completing games at an unprecedented rate. On September 12, Langford remarkably tossed his 22nd straight complete game and 25th overall in the season, shattering Vida Blue's single-season record for an A's pitcher established in 1971. Langford's complete-game streak began on May 23 and ended on September 17. During the run, he had a string of nine consecutive complete game wins. A workhorse, Langford was a durable control pitcher with an effortless windup who wanted hitters to make contact. Averse to walks, Billy was partial to control pitchers like Langford. And Martin and his pitching coach prized durability. "Billy and Art's philosophy was if you started it, you better be able to finish it," said Dave Heaverlo, one of Martin's relievers in Oakland. "He didn't have a dominant closer like Goose Gossage in his bullpen like he had with the Yankees."

Billy's reluctance to pull his starting pitchers started drawing criticism nationally. "I want to see how their arms are next year," broadcaster Tony Kubek said during an NBC *Game of the Week* telecast in August. On July

20, Langford pitched all 14 innings of an A's 6–5 marathon win over the Indians at the Coliseum. It was his 12th consecutive complete game. When Billy opened his office to the media after the game, Dave Newhouse, a columnist for the *Oakland Tribune*, asked Billy why he didn't use his well-rested bullpen to offer Langford some relief. "He got outraged and asked me, 'Who was I going to use?'" Newhouse recalled. "I was just thinking about the guy's arm." Billy was thinking about a win.

Other A's pitchers were stacking complete games. By September, Norris had pitched 19, including one that lasted 14 innings and another lasting 11. Keough was right behind Norris with 17 complete games. Kingman, (9), and McCatty, (7), followed suit. "He used to tell us don't even look at the bullpen; there won't be anyone down there," Matt Keough later told the *New York Times* in 1999. "Billy's whole philosophy was, why should I bring in someone from the bullpen, lefty or righty, when they're not as good as the guys I have on the mound now?"

On September 7, McCatty pitched the A's 78th complete game of the season in Baltimore, breaking the Giants' 1968 record for most in a 162-game schedule. McCatty threw 150 pitches to break the record against Steve Stone, the eventual Cy Young Award winner. "Billy was leaving them out there," said Ken Phelps, who broke into the majors with the Royals that year. "He wasn't going to the bullpen. When it was their day to start, they were going to leave it all on the field. They weren't overpowering type of guys, but they pitched in that ballpark. They knew they could have success in that ballpark because it was big. There were all able to command their pitches and each of them had a good off-speed pitch."

McCatty handed the record-breaking ball to A's pitching coach Art Fowler after the game. It was the staff's 19th complete game in their last 28 games. Far from feeling overworked, the A's starting staff walked into Billy's office and thanked him. In 1980, Langford finished 28 of the 33 games he started. Norris completed 24 of 33, Keough 20 of 32, McCatty 11 of 31, and Kingman 10 of 30. Lefty reliever Bob Lacey oddly pitched a 4–0 shutout over the Brewers for the A's final win and 94th complete game of the season. The A's staff completed 94 of 162 games, 58 percent. They had totaled 41 in 1979, 25 percent. They pitched a combined 1,261 1/3 innings, the most of any starting staff since the 1950s. Langford's 290 innings led the way, followed by Norris (284 1/3), Keough (250), McCatty (221 2/3), and Kingman (211 1/3). Langford, Norris, Keough and McCatty each tossed fourteen-inning complete games in 1980.

Mickey Klutts said the A's starters battled Billy to stay on the mound. "They would argue with Billy and not want to come out. I don't believe Billy ruined their arms. Those pitchers did what they wanted to do. I thought the best pitcher on our staff was Kingman, and he ended up losing twenty games. He had nasty stuff, but we couldn't seem to score runs for him. I felt so bad for him. He always faced the ace of the other staff. They [the starters] were extremely competitive amongst each other."

Rene Lachemann was one of Finley's minor-league managers in the 1970s and worked with Keough, Norris, Kingman, and McCatty when they climbed through the A's farm system. "They all had a tremendous amount of ability," said Lachemann. "Kingman set a record for most losses in a season [by an Oakland pitcher], but you have to be pretty good if they keep putting you out there to pitch that much. They all pitched very well for me in the minors." Former A's catcher Jim Essian described the pitching makeup of the A's staff. "They weren't hard-throwing guys," recalled Essian. "They weren't super big and strong. They were control pitchers."

McCatty maintained that behind their complete game accomplishments, the starters were driven by wins and ultimately keeping their spot on the staff. Billy used an assortment of motivational tactics to keep them hungry and focused. McCatty said the starters expected to go nine innings every start: "If you pitched a complete game, you had a chance to win. It was about the win and what you were supposed to do. That's how you were paid. The big thing was winning. You wanted to go nine innings. You competed not only against the other team, but the other four starters. You didn't want to be the slacker. He tried to motivate you by patting you on the back, pushing your buttons, pissing you off, chewing you out, or having another coach piss you off. He would do both to me."

Billy felt that leaving his starters in the game gave him the best chance to win. "He had no bullpen in 1980," recalled Kit Stier, former A's beat writer. "Bob Lacey led the team with six saves." Bob Lacey, Craig Minetto, Dave Hamilton, Jeff Jones, Dave Beard, Ernie Camacho, Mark Souza, Rick Lysander, Alan Wirth, and Rich Bordi all came out of the A's bullpen during the season. Lacey, Jones, and Hamilton ate most of the innings.

Through smoke and mirrors, Billy managed to hide the A's glaring weaknesses and milk all their strengths into victories. He knew how to win with limited talent on his club. Others around baseball began taking note of how Billy was turning the A's around by his starters completing games. The A's starters were suddenly receiving unprecedented attention and relished every moment. "To me, it was the greatest thing ever," said Bruce Jenkins. "Billy Martin would kill himself before he relied on a pitch count. He was watching the games and those guys were dealing right through the tenth, eleventh and twelfth inning. Without a doubt, it was a little extreme—but I loved it. It was the best time of their baseball lives."

Martin was criticized for the workload he imposed on the A's starters. And the criticism sometimes suggested that he didn't have a complete grasp of major-league pitching. "He was not a pitcher's manager," said Tommy John, who pitched for him in New York. "He didn't understand pitching. I remember Fowler visiting me on the mound and I asked him, 'What's wrong?' He told me, 'I don't know, but you're pissing Billy off.'"

Ernie Camacho recalled a similar visit from Fowler. On June 8, Camacho had drilled Red Sox catcher Carlton Fisk square in the back in the ninth inning to load the bases. "Fowler came streaming out of the dugout and yells at me, 'Ernie, Billy's going to kill me.' I was wondering why Billy was going to kill him when I was the one who hit the guy. It was all psychology."

Jeff Newman recalled Billy bringing a young right-handed reliever into a game to face a righty batter. The reliever promptly coughed up a double. Billy marched to the mound to yank him. The reliever tried to convince him to keep him in the game, but Billy shook his head and grabbed the ball. "Billy looked at him and said, 'Son, don't ever say another word to me when I come out here,'" said Newman. "'The guy I wanted you to get out is standing on second base.' He handed Billy the ball and he was gone. There were a few more expletives thrown in there. Being there to listen to Billy come to the mound to take somebody out or chew them out was a treat."

Kingman, who compiled a record of 8–20 with an ERA of 3.83 in 1980, stressed the difficulty of losing that many games on a winning team under Martin, a notoriously hard loser. "Losing twenty games is hard enough. But how about losing twenty for Billy Martin?" Kingman explained. "There's no one else living who has lost twenty games for a winning team except for me. Everyone else had been on losing teams. The hardest part was Billy and how he handled losing. It was really depressing. Everyone else was succeeding and I was failing. I felt alone. I felt like something was obviously wrong with me. And then Billy was telling me I was a piece of shit."

Echoing Mickey Klutts, many of Kingman's former teammates insisted that he was a hard-luck loser who received little run support that season. Kingman was smart and sharp. At times, though, he felt that Billy was not only his manager, but also his enemy. "It got to the point that my biggest opponent in a game was Billy. Not the other team."

Not all of Billy's staff felt that way, though. Norris recalled convincing Billy on several occasions to keep him in the game. Norris insisted he would do it all over again.

"When he walked to the mound again, I used to tell him 'Billy, get the hell out of here,'" recalled Norris. "Then he'd look me in the eyes, put his hands inside his back pockets, and march back to the dugout. We had that kind of relationship. It was great."

Norris said the A's starting staff wanted to seize the moment and break the record. They knew the fierce competition facing pitchers to stay in the majors and refused to let the moment pass them by. "It became a matter of pride and being able to accomplish what some of the greatest pitchers in the history of the game had done," explained Norris. "Back in our era, a relief pitcher couldn't go through the lineup three times. A pitcher didn't stay in the majors with an ERA over 4.50."

Keough epitomized the A's resurrection, and thought the alarm over possible burnout was nonsense. "Rick, Mike, and I don't throw that many pitches," Keough told the *Boston Globe* in 1980. "None of us is a true strikeout pitcher; none of us walks many people. Rick went five straight games without throwing as many as 100 pitches. Mike and I average between 110 and 120. Some of those staffs that have been blown out involved strikeout pitchers and happened because, like [Angels pitcher] Frank Tanana's fourteen straight complete games, a manager was trying to save his job."

While the A's starting pitchers were embarking on history, left fielder and leadoff hitter Rickey Henderson was flirting with the record books on the basepaths. The twenty-one-year-old Oakland product and All-Star emerged as the A's offensive catalyst in 1980. Like Billy, Henderson was a local star who was fueling the A's resurgence. Many locals heralded Henderson as Oakland's version of Willie Mays, the complete player. Henderson found a home in Oakland when he arrived at age seven.

Born in Chicago on Christmas Day 1958, Henderson's mother, Bobbie, a nurse, moved the family to Oakland when he was seven. It was in Oakland where Henderson sprouted into a physical specimen and dominated in sports on neighborhood fields. Henderson starred in football, baseball, and track for Oakland Technical High School.

Henderson gained 1,100 yards rushing in his senior season, while also playing linebacker. He was offered a football scholarship to Arizona State University. The highly recruited, all-city running back thought about pursuing football after high school, but Bobbie convinced him to stick to baseball. "Because my momma's never made a bad decision," Henderson later explained. Henderson batted .465 and stole 30 bases in his senior year at Oakland Tech. A's scout Jimmy Guinn drafted and signed him as an outfielder in the fourth round in 1976. By June 1979, he was wearing an A's uniform and facing John Henry Johnson of the Texas Rangers, doubling in his first at-bat.

Martin's aggressive managing style and Henderson's explosive speed created scoring opportunities and pressured defenses relentlessly. On October 4, Henderson swiped his 100th base of the season in Milwaukee, making him only the third player in baseball history to steal that many bases in a season. A groundskeeper interrupted the game, lifted the base, and handed it to A's coach Lee Walls to keep for Henderson. "What I like about this record is that there aren't any cheapies in here," Billy had said while Henderson was pursuing the record. "Every base he's stolen has been to help us win ballgames, not for any personal glory." Henderson not only broke the A's single-season franchise record for stolen bases—established by Eddie Collins seventy years earlier when he swiped 81 in Philadelphia—he shattered Ty Cobb's 1915 American League record of 96 on September 30 in Chicago.

Only Maury Wills and Lou Brock, both National Leaguers, had 100 thefts in a season since 1900. Wills swiped 104 in 1962; Brock amassed 118 in 1974, holding the all-time record. Henderson joined the club in 1980. "Billy Martin brought it out of me," Henderson later said. "He made me become the best stealer I could be." Henderson maintained that playing for the right manager on the right team gave him so many opportunities to steal.

Henderson never forgot Billy's influence early in his career, even when he played for teams other than the A's. In *Chumps to Champs,* author Bill Pennington observed, "Henderson had never truly been happy as a Yankee unless his long-time mentor Billy Martin had been the manager."

Henderson's presence in the lineup and on the bases disrupted opponents. He ran wild, rattled pitchers, and forced errors. In his first full season in the majors, Henderson batted .303, clubbed nine home runs, and drove in 53 runs. His 117 walks were the second most in all of baseball. He stole four bases in a game three times.

Henderson was also a part of what had become the best outfield in baseball. Right fielder Tony Armas, twenty-six, and center fielder Dwayne Murphy, twenty-five, patrolled the outfield with Henderson. All three were center fielders coming up in the minors. The Venezuelan-born Armas climbed through the Pirates organization. Henderson arrived in 1979 as a center fielder to fill in for an injured Murphy. Murphy's return forced Henderson back to left field. "They were something to watch," said Kit Stier of the outfield. "Billy made sure he talked about them."

Born in Merced, California, on March 18, 1955, Murphy was a son of an Air Force sergeant. He was a tremendously athletic running and defensive back for Antelope Valley High School in Lancaster, California, so talented that Arizona State recruited him to play football. Murphy's football and baseball teammates called him "captain" because of his obvious leadership qualities. He was also a standout high school shortstop. His preference was football, though. But at age eighteen, two months shy of graduation, Murphy started a family and needed to financially support his girlfriend, Brenda, and newborn, Dwayne Jr. Murphy never received a scholarship offer for baseball, but after considering his options, he chose to sign a professional baseball contract.

The A's drafted him as a shortstop in the 15th round of the 1973 June amateur draft. He received a $6,500 signing bonus. Murphy was struggling to throw accurately from shortstop in rookie ball, so the A's moved him to center field, where he found a home. Murphy, the team captain, was a sure-handed, graceful center fielder and a self-sacrificing second-place hitter behind Henderson in the lineup. "Murphy was a very good center fielder," said Ken Phelps. "He could come get the ball and go get it." He led the league with 22 sacrifice bunts in 1980. Murphy played a risky shallow center, only about 275 feet from home plate, and threw with precision. He specialized in robbing players of would-be singles up the middle and keeping runners from going from first to third on singles.

The outfield of Armas, Murphy, and Henderson snatched virtually every ball that came near them. They knew what A's pitchers were throwing and moved pitch by pitch, and helped maintain the starters' stingy 3.46 ERA. The unit posted 43 outfield assists in 1980. Armas had 15 of them. "We use outfield as a collective noun," A's president Roy Eisenhardt said in 1982.

The strong-armed Armas was having a breakthrough season playing every day for the first time. Born on July 2, 1953, in Puerto Piritu, a town in eastern Venezuela, Armas was the son of an electrician and one of fourteen children. As a boy, he had to hide to play baseball because his father thought it was a waste of time. His determination paid off. The Pittsburgh Pirates, one of the pioneers in drafting Latin ballplayers, signed seventeen-year-old Armas for $5,000 in 1971. Armas looked forward to playing alongside Roberto Clemente in the Pirates outfield. He briefly cracked the majors with the Pirates in 1976 but was traded to the A's the following spring in the blockbuster deal that netted Pittsburgh Phil Garner. The presence of superstar Dave Parker made Armas expendable to the Pirates. He'd already realized that he never had a chance to play every day for a team that was stocked with so many talented outfielders.

Armas, who spoke soft, careful English, played with fearless abandon in the outfield, often running into the outfield wall, which led to knee and shoulder injuries. Physically, he was a question mark in spring training, having played in only 80 games in 1979 due to injuries. He posted subpar offensive numbers: 11 home runs and 34 RBIs. In 1980, it was a different story. Armas clubbed 35 home runs and drove in 109 runs. His hitting was a pleasant surprise because he had never hit more than 21 homers in professional baseball. "Billy has brought out the best in me," said the right-handed slugger in 1980. Armas played in 158 games, the most he'd ever played in a season in professional ball. He was finally healthy and getting a chance to play every day. Billy started marketing Henderson, Murphy, and Armas as the best outfield in baseball. Glenn Schwarz apparently agreed. On May 1, 1981, in a piece for the *New York Daily News,* Schwarz wrote, "[I]f the A's starting pitchers are the heart of the club, their outfielders are its soul. Left to right, Henderson, Dwayne Murphy and Armas collectively have few defensive peers in the league (more than one manager has raved that they form the best outfield he has ever watched). Offensively, they are equally exciting."

Dave Newhouse described the significance Billy's outfield played in the A's resurgence. They complemented each other in the lineup, too. Henderson reached base, Murphy moved him over, and Armas drove him home. The A's offense revolved around the outfielders. "Billy built the team on pitching and that outfield," said Newhouse. "He had an incredible outfield. Not only were they good at the plate, they threw guys out on the bases. Armas had a great arm and Rickey could nail guys at third and second. And Dwayne Murphy was a great defensive outfielder. He was okay on offense, but defense was his strength. He was the coolest outfielder you'd ever see."

The A's finished the 1980 season strong, winning 17 of their last 26 games. They won 51 of their final 87. They escaped the nightmare of 1979 and surged into a remarkable second place with an 83–79 record, 29 more wins than the previous season. Oakland finished 17 games ahead of the sixth-place Angels, who posted a 65–95 record. Some of the A's were ranked among baseball's elite for the first time. Keough, who was 2–17 in 1979, was crowned American League Comeback Player of the Year. He was 16–13 with a 2.92 ERA. "I was the epitome of our ballclub the last two years," Keough said after learning he won the award. "I was the prime example of the club being bad last year and good this year." Keough lost his first 14 decisions in 1979.

Mike Norris finished the season with a dazzling 22–9 record and a 2.53 earned run average, the second lowest in the league. His tantalizing screwball badly fooled lefty batters. Norris was at the forefront of Cy Young Award conversation. But Orioles starter Steve Stone, who was 25–7 with a 3.23 ERA, edged him out to win the American League's Cy Young. Norris trailed Stone 100–91 in points. Each pitcher received thirteen first-place votes. Three voters left Norris off the ballot. Norris praised Billy for injecting the confidence in him to pitch so well. "He made me believe in myself," Norris said. "He convinced me that I was someone around here, that I was needed."

Armas and Norris weren't the only A's to up their games in 1980. Rick Langford, also considered a Cy Young candidate, was 19–12 with a 3.26 ERA. He led the American League with 28 complete games and 290 innings pitched. The A's pitching threesome of Langford, Norris, and Keough were the major-league leaders in complete games with 28, 24, and 20 respectively. They were also baseball's winningest trio. The A's finished with the lowest ERA in the league at 3.46. Henderson, the Oakland speedster, became only the third player in history to steal 100 bases in a season, while hitting .303. Norris and Murphy won their first Gold Glove awards.

Billy was named American League Manager of the Year for a third time. He'd won it in 1974, when he resurrected the Texas Rangers to a second-place finish, and in 1976, when he led the Yankees to a pennant. He always felt he should have won it in 1969 as well, after leading the Twins to a division title in his first season as a major-league manager. In 1980, Martin was the overwhelming choice by the Associated Press. He energized, willed, and pushed the moribund A's into exciting contenders with essentially the same roster from 1979. The personnel didn't change, only the attitude, Billy insisted.

Billy grabbed the attention of the alienated fan base and spiked attendance in the same venue from 1979. A's season home attendance swelled to 842,259 in 1980, an increase of 535,496 from 1979. It was the most they had drawn since 1975, the season they won their last division title and also the largest attendance increase in baseball. "Billy Ball came to Oakland and it seemed a match made in Abner Doubleday's fondest dreams," wrote Stephanie Salter of the *San Francisco Examiner* in 1980. "The masterful managerial tactician taught the insecure, young players the fundamentals of the game and molded their minds into winners."

On Sunday, September 28, in the A's final home game of the season, Murphy dropped down a game-winning bunt single in the bottom of the ninth to beat the Brewers 3–2. When the game ended, Billy and his players walked back inside the clubhouse to prepare for a season-ending five-game road trip through Chicago and Milwaukee. But the fans weren't finished. Most of the crowd of 10,662 rose, stayed and roared, "We want Billy! We want Billy!" A's publicity director Mickey Morabito phoned the clubhouse and told Billy the fans were demanding a curtain call. He obliged them by bringing the entire team back out on the field with him for several minutes to celebrate the A's renaissance season. Don Anderson, the organist, played "Happy Days are Here Again."

11

THE RESURRECTION

Billy Ball stickers adorn the windows of the shops and restaurants in Jack London Square, not to mention the majority of the car bumpers in downtown Oakland. The lines at the Oakland Coliseum ticket windows are long, and the waiting raises the temperature of the fans who concede that they are happy, finally, to have reason to buy tickets to see the A's.

—ROSS NEWHAN, *LOS ANGELES TIMES*, MAY 1981

THE TURNAROUND BILLY MARTIN HAD ENGINEERED IN OAKLAND paid immediate dividends. On November 20, 1980, the A's handed Martin the security and control he had always wanted. The Haases presented him with a new five-year contract and made him the A's director of player development in addition to his managerial duties, a position that was essentially the general manager. Whitey Herzog also served in both capacities for the St. Louis Cardinals. It was unprecedented power for a field manager since former A's owner and manager Connie Mack controlled everything from 1901 to 1950 in Philadelphia.

Billy, the biggest star of the franchise, reported directly to team president Roy Eisenhardt. Eisenhardt announced that there would be no general manager under the A's reorganization. Billy would run all A's baseball operations and Eisenhardt would focus on contracts and securing players long-term. Billy would make decisions on players from the moment he drafted them and be responsible for the team's performance on the field. "It demonstrated that the Haases were smart businessmen, and they weren't going to try to tell baseball people how to run a team," said Dave Heaverlo. "That was a smart move on their part. The players certainly knew the power Billy had."

Martin's hustling brand of baseball would be preached to every prospect at all levels of the A's minor-league system. He wanted the entire farm system—which only fielded one winning team in 1980—playing his way. Billy had spent much of the offseason reshaping the badly neglected scouting department and farm system. Dave Newhouse recalled how Billy's role expanded and power increased with the new appointment: "Billy got what he wanted: all the power in the world. The Haas family was so benevolent to him. He got control of all of the player moves and decided on who came up from the minors. He had more power I bet at that point than any manager in history except for Connie Mack, who owned the A's. He was in the catbird seat. But the cat was really wild."

Billy persuaded longtime friend Dick Wiencek to be his director of scouting and minor league personnel. Wiencek was a West Coast scout supervisor for the Tigers based in Claremont, California, and had been scouting for twenty-seven years. Wiencek had scouted and signed major leaguers Graig Nettles, Jim Kaat, Lance Parrish, Alan Trammell, Bert Blyleven, Frank Tanana, Jason Thompson, and Jerry Remy. (Later, he was instrumental in drafting and signing Mark McGwire as the 10th overall pick in the country in 1984.) While both worked for the Twins, Wiencek taught Billy the finer points of evaluating talent. He also told Billy he thought he would make a good manager.

Martin hired seventeen scouts, including former players Eddie Mathews, Camilo Pascual, and Del Wilber. The A's retained farm director Walt Jocketty. Billy, Jocketty, and Wiencek were laying the foundation for what would later become baseball's premier farm system. The next year, Pascual, who scouted in Florida for the A's, discovered seventeen-year-old third-baseman

Jose Canseco from Miami's Coral Park High. The A's drafted him in the 15th round of the 1982 June amateur draft. "It was smart to give [Martin] all that power," recalled Bruce Jenkins. "Those two years were so special and resonate to this day. It's very hard to say it was a misfire on the A's part. It was Billy's show."

Billy was the professor of "Billy Ball" university. "There is no style of baseball more exciting than that taught by Billy Martin, and he is entrusted with implementing that stress on fundamentals and hustle at every level of our system. There is no more talented person than Billy for that job," Eisenhardt said during the announcement of Billy's new position.

Notwithstanding the turnarounds he engineered elsewhere or the championship he won with the Yankees in 1977, many baseball experts believed that Billy's impact in Oakland was his most impressive accomplishment as a manager. Billy always attributed the A's success in 1980 to the freedom he had to run the show without meddling by the team owner. Billy did it his way. "He has managed teams to pennants and world championships, but Billy Martin's greatest managing job was last year when he took the rag-tag A's and brought them in an impressive second in the AL West. It happened, he said, because he was allowed to do things his way," wrote Phil Pepe of the *New York Daily News* in 1981.

Billy's frustration over not having enough control of his players had always fueled his notorious clashes with previous owners. Billy felt that if a manager was responsible for winning, he should have more control of the makeup of the team he fields. Billy's new bosses were enthralled by Billy Ball and wanted to keep him happy.

"All my baseball life all I ever wanted was a little security," Billy told reporters at the news conference. "But all I ever got was bounced from one ballclub to another. I'd improve a team and then someone would decide how easy it was and send me down the road. Now, I've got the kind of security I've always wanted.

"For the first time in my baseball life, I feel wanted. With the A's and their new ownership, I feel like part of the family. Now, I can make plans, long-range plans both for myself and the ballclub and not worry about someone cutting the rug out from under me."

That same day, the A's announced the hiring of their new vice president of business operations: Andy Dolich, former general manager of the dissolved Washington Diplomats of the North American Soccer League. Dolich was a sales and marketing specialist with a master's degree in sports management from Ohio University. The A's retained Carl Finley, cousin of Charlie, as vice president of baseball administration; Mickey Morabito as traveling secretary and director of media relations; and Lorraine Paulus as director of ticket sales. Dom Valentino, one of the A's radio play-by-play announcers in 1980, became the director of the new speakers bureau, which dispatched A's players around the community. The A's office swelled to almost forty employees.

Eisenhardt brought in Sandy Alderson, the A's general counsel (and later the Mets GM), to help negotiate contracts and arbitration hearings. Eisenhardt was Alderson's mentor. Like Eisenhardt, Alderson practiced law, attended Dartmouth and was a former Marine. A graduate of Harvard in 1976, Alderson was the son of an Air Force pilot. Nothing on his résumé suggested a talent for finding baseball talent. The new owners were transforming the A's into a first-class organization. A Christmas tree suddenly appeared in the A's office during the holidays for the first time since the club moved to Oakland. The A's and the Coliseum board poured $1 million worth of cosmetic improvements into the stadium. A new sound system was erected behind the centerfield fence. The radio booth and clubhouses were renovated. A lounge area for players was added to the clubhouse. Thousands of light bulbs were added to the light towers to meet major-league standards. New ticket booths were installed to accommodate the anticipated demand. The scrambled scoreboard was repaired. The dangerous outfield fences— made of hard plywood and steel posts—had been a major concern for player safety. Armas's numerous shoulder injuries were associated with him barging into those fences chasing balls. The Haases finally padded the fences. "We are going to be organized as a business," Eisenhardt emphasized. "We will be divided into a baseball operation and a business operation."

On February 7, Kool & the Gang's disco-infused "Celebration" soared to No. 1 on the *Billboard* Hot 100 chart. Heralded as the party song of 1981, "Celebration" was the theme song for Super Bowl XV in New Orleans between the Raiders and Philadelphia Eagles and provided the soundtrack when fifty-two American hostages were freed from Iran after 444 days of captivity on January 20, 1981. Eager to jump on the upbeat bandwagon, the A's introduced "Celebration" as their theme song for the 1981 season. The tune would be played through the Coliseum's upgraded sound system and center field speakers after every win. "When that song came on after we won a game, our fans literally stayed around and partied for twenty minutes," Mike Norris remembered. "Those fans would lose their minds in the stands. Instead of going straight to the clubhouse, we'd stay on the field to watch them party."

The A's made a bold statement on the radio airwaves. On October 16, 1980, the A's finally secured a stable radio flagship station, signing a four-year contract with KSFO, a popular and well-established AM station based in San Francisco. The station was the flagship of the Giants from 1958 to 1978 before the Giants moved to KNBR in 1979. Radio was the optimal delivery medium for fans not at the park. The A's and the station held a press conference at the Kaiser Center to make the announcement. A new and stable flagship was only part of the surprise. To complement the A's new radio home, Eisenhardt introduced veteran Bay Area broadcasters Bill King and Lon Simmons as the team's new radio play-by-play radio voices for the 1981 season. The respected King, fifty-three, and Simmons, fifty-seven, brought with them rabid followings from their decades of being at the forefront of Bay Area broadcasting. King was the longtime play-by-play radio voice for the Oakland Raiders and Golden State Warriors. The deep-voiced Simmons, a former minor-league pitcher, was a longtime voice of the Giants and Forty-Niners. Eisenhardt explained how they strengthened radio broadcasts to keep fans engaged: "We wanted a very strong radio presence and KSFO offered that. Not only did they have a strong signal, their daytime on-air talent was of high quality and popular. Additionally, KSFO could create networking alliances with other stations outside of their signal range, such as Sacramento. Finally, their general manager, Jim Myers, was a class act and very pleasurable to work with. Thus it was a decision that really didn't take a lot of analysis. And it worked out great, particularly with the strength of Lon and Bill as the on-air talent for the games."

King, a dogged researcher with an extensive vocabulary who meticulously painted the field action for listeners, would be juggling his play-by-play duties with the Raiders and Warriors. Both he and Simmons were premier announcers and brought intelligence, humor, and entertainment with their commentary. The radio voices had been paired across the bay twenty years before. They had teamed with Russ Hodges to call Giants games on the radio from 1958 to 1962. In the arrangement, King would work for the A's and Simmons would be paid and employed by KSFO, where he was the longtime sports director for the station. King became the A's director of broadcast operations. The move brought the A's instant credibility. The A's hired a third radio voice in January, twenty-five-year-old Wayne Hagin, to spell King when his obligations with the Raiders pulled him away. The young broadcasting prodigy grew up in San Jose, California, and idolized King and Simmons for their broadcasting prowess. A graduate of San Jose State University, Hagin went on to have a long career broadcasting major-league games. Hagin insisted that pairing King and Simmons, the two most celebrated broadcasters in the Bay Area, together in the broadcast booth was a brilliant move by the Haas ownership: "It was astonishing to watch. King had not done baseball since 1962 and Simmons was two years removed from the game. To blend Simmons, the focal point of any play-by-play broadcast on the San Francisco Peninsula, with King, so well-known in the East Bay with the Raiders and Warriors, was brilliant. It made the A's on par with the Giants broadcasts."

Dolich, meanwhile, was piecing together the most powerful marketing movement in Oakland A's history. The anticipation was growing for the A's second season of Billy Ball. Dolich's emphasis on customer service and building trust among fans was a perfect fit for the restructuring A's. He was a graduate of American University with a degree in government. Around the time he found out he couldn't enter law school, he heard about a one of a kind master's program in sports management that Ohio University was offering. He jumped at the chance and enrolled. He earned his master's degree in 1970 and began his career as an administrative assistant for the Philadelphia 76ers in 1972. His dream of working for an NBA team was fulfilled.

Dolich moved on to become business manager for the Maryland Arrows of the National Lacrosse League in 1974. After the NLL folded in 1976, Dolich joined the NHL's Washington Capitals as their marketing director. He then became general manager of the Washington Diplomats of the North American Soccer League in 1979 before the team folded in 1980. During his time with the Diplomats, Dolich marketed Dutch soccer legend Johan Cruyff and helped increase attendance dramatically. Dolich explained his marketing philosophy: "I was a big proponent of the Disney form of marketing. To serve your guests at Disneyland because the fan base is really the most important part. Yes, you want to have a great team and terrific players, with community involvement, but if you don't have a fan base that trusts you, you really don't have anything."

While working for the Diplomats, Dolich networked with Matt Levine, a savvy sports business futurist in the Bay Area. He ran Pacific Select Corporation. Dolich was moved by Levine's prophetic outlook on sports business. Levine knew the Haases from his time serving as a consultant for the city of Oakland and the County of Alameda during their litigation against Finley in 1979 for not promoting the A's. When the Haases purchased the club, they hired Levine as a consultant to help them strategize and position themselves in the market during their crucial early days of ownership. Levine found out the A's were hiring a vice president of business operations and remembered Dolich's innovative work in Washington.

Levine suggested Dolich to Eisenhardt. Dolich believed that Dick Vertlieb, a former executive for the Warriors, was the frontrunner to land the position. After flying from Maryland to San Francisco with his wife, Ellen, to interview with Eisenhardt and Wally, the new owners offered him the job. Dolich initially declined the A's offer because of the anxiety of uprooting his family on the East Coast, moving them cross the country, and planting them in California, foreign territory to them. But while he was relaxing at home with Ellen and son Cory one night in their suburban Maryland home, he changed his mind and took the job. His task was to build a fan base. "I always viewed it as an amazing opportunity because of everything Finley hadn't done," said Dolich. "I always say, 'Thank you, Charlie Finley.' He left the cupboard bare and we stocked the shelves in a fashion that worked. I never viewed it negatively. In a month or so, we put together a sales staff of thirty."

Dolich recalled his first day working for the A's on December 3, 1980. He only interviewed in San Francisco with Eisenhardt, so walking into the A's office in Oakland for the first time exposed him to the bare-bones state of the A's. "It was like a ghost town," he remembered. "In the reception area, I saw a desk leaning toward one side because one leg was lower than the other. There was nobody behind the receptionist desk. I saw a sign that read PLEASE DIAL 0 FOR ASSISTANCE on the leaning desk next to a phone. I finally got somebody on the phone and came in the office."

The A's commissioned over thirty sales reps to sell tickets throughout the Bay Area. David Rubinstein, former A's director of sales, once asked Lorraine Paulus, the ticket manager, to show him the season ticket holder accounts in 1981. "She brought out a shoebox with 3 1/2 index cards in it," said Rubinstein. "It was very much stone age kind of stuff, operationally. They had only 105 accounts in a size five shoebox. We ended up knocking on around 10,000 doors. We went from 300 season tickets to 3,000 in only a three-month period. We wanted to give people a good time. It pretty much didn't matter what the team was doing. We had a good foundation built. Our position was to always control the controllable. We assumed the team wasn't going to win a game, and sometimes they obliged us."

Shortly before Dolich arrived in 1980, the A's assigned Levine and his firm to conduct a market study throughout the Bay Area to better understand fans and gauge regional variances. The research—marketing research methodology—included facilitating focus groups and interviewing fans by telephone. The focus groups in particular offered fans a voice to express themselves. They interviewed current and former A's fans who abandoned the club. The research revealed that Billy Martin fascinated the fans. "In these focus groups, fans would tell us how much they would love to be inside the mind of an opposing pitcher with runners on base trying to guess Martin's next move," said Levine. "We started documenting these free-forum comments from fans about how exciting going to an A's game was, sitting on the edge of their seats, and not knowing what's going to happen next with Martin leading the show. It made for an exciting experience. We asked fans to tell us what 'Billy Ball' meant and they described it as being unpredictable and the ability to get inside of people's heads."

Fans were enamored with Billy. They wanted someone like him in their corner. "They translated that into a style of play that they had never seen before and a risk-taking willingness on the part of the A's under his leadership," said Levine. "It was anti-establishment. It had a rogue-like character to the way they played. It was yielding more success than they had before."

The A's were searching for an advertising agency and ultimately signed with Ogilvy & Mather, a major global advertising firm with offices in every major city. Dolich and Levine showed brand genius Hal Riney, an innovative advertising mogul who had opened up an agency for O&M in San Francisco in 1976, an overview of what kind of campaign they wanted back from them; one built on philanthropy, season tickets, excitement, and community involvement. Riney was a creative giant in the industry and a perfectionist in commercial advertising.

The A's required the agency to build the campaign on the marketing research insights they collected through focus groups and telephone interviewing. The presentation needed to convey the commitment and dedication of the Haases to reinvent the franchise through the community. "We were telling a story that people were willing to buy into," said Dolich. "The greatest opportunity was the only preexisting thoughts that fans had about Finley not caring, losing interest, and the perception that they were less than a minor- league team. But these new enthusiastic owners were painting the stadium, bringing in new scoreboards and attending community breakfasts. We developed momentum even before we went to spring training."

Levine said that inheriting the A's skeleton office made it less complicated to rebuild. "With the cupboard bare, it made it easier in a way because they didn't have to unravel anything," Levine said. "On one hand, they were in a deep hole. On the other hand, they were filling a vacuum. And the Haases, even before purchasing the A's, always had a strong community bent. They viewed the A's as an investment in community. It became a community asset in which people had pride."

O&M, the fourth-largest advertisement agency in the world at the time, boasted a portfolio of heavyweight accounts from Rolls-Royce and American Express to IBM and General Foods. They had just helped Marriott's Great America market the opening of their 100-acre amusement park in Santa Clara. The agency, one of three finalists to land the A's account, came back to the A's with a colorful, humorous and clever campaign built on Billy Martin that challenged fan involvement, "Billy Ball . . . It's a Different Brand of Baseball."

Billy was the defining larger-than-life personality behind the movement. Riney, heading the creative process with the help of copywriters Rich Silverstein, John Crawford, and Jeff Goodby, made "Billy Ball" a fan experience. "Billy Ball" was entertainment. It was a state of mind. Not just a person. The

A's were blown away by their presentation and gave them the account. "They knocked it out of the park," said Levine. "They took our marketing research and ran with it. They took it so that not just watching a game was an unpredictable experience; getting in line to buy a ticket was, too. We gave them the account, and we virtually implemented the commercials they had developed for that speculative presentation with some minor refinements."

Dolich remembered how the "Billy Ball" campaign brilliantly captured the essence and enthusiasm of what the A's were trying to convey. "They went into a completely different direction using Billy as the focal point in the different brand of baseball," Dolich said. "We weren't guaranteeing that people were going to see a winning game, but with 'Billy Ball,' we were guaranteeing that fans were going to have a good time."

Riney paired Goodby and Silverstein on the creative end of the A's campaign. Silverstein was the graphic designer and Goodby was the baseball lover. Riney later added veteran freelance writer Crawford to the project. Goodby remembered being cautioned not to build the campaign around the fiery Billy because of his stormy reputation. "It was communicated to me that Billy might not be the best idea to build the campaign around," Goodby recalled. "But if there were any reservations about using Billy, they melted away when we presented the campaign. Everyone was into it." Silverstein insisted that he was the perfect personality to build the campaign on. "There was no one like Billy Martin," said Silverstein. "You had to take the chance."

Goodby said Riney loved the "Billy Ball" idea when he mentioned the phrase nonchalantly to him in his office. Riney knew little about baseball, so Goodby educated him about the baserunning, dirt-kicking havoc Billy was famous for. Riney immediately told Goodby to start on the campaign. "The hidden ball tricks and double steals came from a fountain of craziness from the A's dugout named Billy," Goodby said. "The fans embraced it. It brought a kind of crackle to everything at the Coliseum. The appearance of Billy at the Coliseum was different because of the 'Billy Ball' campaign. It made the experience more fun. The A's planted flowers in left field that spelled out 'Billy Ball.'"

Silverstein, the graphic designer who created the "Billy Ball" logo, said the campaign was ahead of its time in sports marketing. No sports advertising at that level existed. It predated Nike's legendary Michael Jordan ad campaigns. The product was "Billy Ball." "Before there was reality television, he was reality baseball," said Silverstein. "We tried to make the marketing like the crazy and smart way he managed the A's. I started learning about stealing home and sandlot baseball. I was fascinated by the hidden ball trick. He was such a character and so ahead of his time. People wanted to be a part of Billy Ball. It showed a lot of people we can have fun in sport."

Goodby and Silverstein saw firsthand the significance of their work when they saw the "Billy Ball" logo appear on the big screen on Opening Night at the Coliseum. Billy was officially the face of the A's. Over the next three months, they produced "Billy Ball" promotional print ads for mass mailing, radio and television spots, and created hilarious television commercials starring Billy at the A's spring training facility in Phoenix. Billy was always the center of attention. "He loved it," said Billy Martin Jr. "He was home and they treated him like royalty. It was stress-free."

Goodby worked with Billy and A's players on commercial shoots and revealed that Billy was a seasoned, talented actor. Billy knew when to turn it on when the cameras were rolling. On Billy's busy days, Goodby cleverly dispatched a beautiful production assistant to keep his attention and direct him to each commercial shoot. Billy always followed. "It was easy to get Billy on board," said Goodby. "He had a good sense of humor about things. He had a naughty twinkle in his eye. He was ready to go at all times, and I mean that in every fashion. He was amazing, even though he was kind of a prickly character. When it was an acting situation, he turned it on. He knew what was funny." As Billy brought immediate success to the A's on the field, he was also shouldering their advertising campaign. He was the hope. "This whole dream was riding on the shoulders of this troubled, flawed guy with a track record," said Stephanie Salter.

Off camera, the genial face of the A's advertising campaign could turn in an instant. Goodby recalled being at Arizona State University's Packard Baseball Stadium with Billy filming a commercial on the field. The Arizona State coach politely told Billy that his team needed to take quick infield practice and they could have the field back after. "No fucking college coach is going to tell me what to do!" Billy yelled. Goodby said Billy turned around, got in his car, and drove off. Bill Rigney, a scout for the Angels, was able to convince Billy to come back and finish filming the commercial.

Some of the ads celebrated Billy's East Bay homecoming under local ownership with a team committed to staying in Oakland. The commercials made light of Billy's stormy temper. "Baseball is all about hope and belief in magic, and Billy embodied the hope of baseball and the magic," said Goodby. "He gave the place a bolt of energy. People suddenly wanted to see it. It jump-started from nothing. Instead of focusing on the A's deficiencies, fans focused on the positive fusion of Billy's energy."

In one commercial, a take-charge Billy grilled a fan at a ticket window before handing him over tickets to the game. "We wanted to get across that this isn't quantum physics," Dolich said. "Let's not take everything so seriously. This is baseball, and it's supposed to be fun." Billy dominated the A's promotional material. "I hate finishing second. So this year, we're going to run harder, throw harder, slide harder, and think harder. And you're going to come out to the park and yell harder, right?" Billy was quoted as saying in a promotional blurb on a 1981 A's pamphlet.

The "Billy Ball" campaign logo graced the cover of the A's 1981 media guide. "When I saw Ralph Wiley's *Oakland Tribune* column mentioning 'Billy Ball,' I thought the concept had enough flexibility that our fans could write whatever chapters they wanted," said Dolich. "The campaign was aided by the fact the team was playing better."

Three of O&M's "Billy Ball" commercials won prestigious Clio Awards, the Oscars of the advertising world. The A's captured marketing awards for their award-winning season ticket campaign and TV ads. The groundbreaking commercials changed how people perceived baseball. International advertising tycoon David Ogilvy, the agency's founder, even awarded the San Francisco firm for the campaign. "It was brilliant," recalled Bruce Jenkins. "It was a great campaign and it totally worked. Every time you went to the park you realized it was about Billy and his style of ball." Goodby believed the trailblazing commercials were the first to showcase athletes acting funny in dialogue. "That advertising campaign was revolutionary," said Dave Newhouse. "Baseball hadn't advertised itself before with such creativity, and the A's marketing genius, Andy Dolich, brought baseball into the modern age with his out-of-the-batters-box thinking with the considerable help of Ogilvy & Mather. I haven't seen any baseball advertisements any better or more imaginative in the ensuing nearly forty years."

Wayne Hagin, one of the A's radio voices in 1981, said the marketing prowess of Dolich was as much of a force behind the success of "Billy Ball" as Billy himself. He believed Dolich never received enough credit for making "Billy Ball" bigger than life. "If Mickey Mouse was important to Walt Disney, Billy Martin was Mickey Mouse and Andy Dolich was Walt Disney," said Hagin. "He was so good at marketing. He was doing things that the Oakland A's had never seen before. He was a genius. If Billy Martin put the A's back on the map, Dolich kept them there."

Commercials were one thing. Billy Martin's main objective heading into the 1981 season was to prove that 1980 hadn't been a fluke.

12

URBAN COWBOY

There was some optimism heading into the season. Things had gone pretty well in 1980. The starting pitchers were all back after ninety-four complete games and the outfield remained the same. Of course, by that time, it was all about Billy Martin and the Haas family.
—John Hickey, former A's beat writer, September 2018

December 9, 1980: Billy Martin, crowned with a feathered, wide-brimmed cowboy hat, swaggered into baseball's annual winter meetings in Dallas lusting for a right-handed designated hitter. Martin wasn't alone in his affection for the cowboy look. Many Americans were flirting with the country-western craze. After a significant spike in country music's popularity in the late 1970s, the 1980 cult classic film, *Urban Cowboy,* starring John Travolta, triggered a western movement across the country. The movie soundtrack was a huge commercial success and the country caught country fever.

At the Anatole Hotel, the headquarters of the winter meetings, there was more hype about Billy than George Brett, the American League's Most Valuable Player who had just missed becoming the first player since Ted Williams to bat .400, finishing at .390 in 1980. "Martin drew more excited attention than George Brett at the *Sporting News* Player of the Year conference, and nearly as much as the perfumed, fashionably dressed women heeling around the snazzy Anatole Hotel," wrote Glenn Schwarz of the *San Francisco Examiner* on December 10, 1980.

Billy created more noise when he and Eisenhardt made a trade with the Chicago Cubs to acquire thirty-three-year-old right-handed slugger Cliff Johnson for minor-league pitcher Mike King. The trade reunited Martin and Johnson, who had played for Billy in pinstripes in 1977 and 1978. Johnson destroyed southpaw pitching and would be Billy's right-handed designated hitter behind Armas. Johnson also brought with him pinch-hit power off the bench.

One of Martin's other offseason goals was to shore up the A's defense. Oakland converted only 115 double plays in 1980, the fewest in the majors. In early November, he acquired veteran infielder and double-play specialist Fred "Chicken" Stanley from the Yankees for A's former first-round draft pick Mike Morgan. The plan was for Stanley to platoon with Rob Picciolo at shortstop. Shortstop Mario Guerrero was sold to the Mariners.

Billy added Jackie Moore, who coached for Martin in Texas, as the fifth coach alongside Fowler, Boyer, Mitterwald, and Walls. Moore, forty-two, was the youngest coach on the staff. He would alternate as first-base coach with Walls.

All of these moves by Martin were designed to prove that the revitalized A's of 1980 were not a fluke. The new season, 1981, after all, would be one of great expectations. "There was some optimism heading into the season," said John Hickey, former A's beat writer for the *Daily Review*. "Things had gone pretty well in 1980, the starting pitchers were all back after ninety-four complete games in 1980 and the outfield remained the same. Of course, at that point, it was all about Billy Martin and the Haas family." Heading into the '81 season, the A's were anticipating the largest single season attendance total in team history.

Across the bay, the San Francisco Giants were making major moves of their own. Giants owner Bob Lurie hired forty-five-year-old Oakland product Frank Robinson, baseball's first African American manager in 1975 with the Cleveland Indians, to manage his club. Lurie had relieved manager Dave Bristol of his duties in December. Although the Giants had a more stable fan base than the A's, they wanted to create momentum of their own and improve on their fifth-place finish in 1980. Lurie wanted a manager who players would respect after back-to-back losing seasons and fired managers.

Robinson knew firsthand how quickly Billy could land back on his feet as a manager. While Robinson was managing the Indians in 1975, the Rangers had fired Billy in July that season. A few weeks later, Robinson was in Yankee Stadium on Old-Timers' Day delivering his lineup card to home plate before the Indians played the Yankees. When he looked up, he saw Billy handing him the Yankees' lineup card. George Steinbrenner had hired Martin as manager that morning, replacing Bill Virdon. "What's the secret?" Robinson asked him. Robinson, who was fired by the Indians in 1977, wasn't so lucky. He wasn't offered another managing job until the Giants hired him three years later.

In Oakland, the Haases had tripled the A's payroll from 1.3 million in 1980 to $3.8 million in 1981. They signed several key players to multi-year contracts. Pitcher Rick Langford signed a six-year deal with the club worth $600,000 annually, making him the A's highest paid player. Management also locked up left-handed designated hitter Mitchell Page for five years in a deal worth $1.9 million and secured catcher Jeff Newman with a $1 million, five-year contract.

The A's signed Matt Keough to a four-year contract and Rickey Henderson to a one-year deal worth $150,000 plus incentives. Wayne Gross also signed a one-year deal with Oakland. Norris and Newman were the only A's players who predated 1977. Pitcher Steve McCatty was happy seeing his teammates being financially rewarded and the A's owners preserving the chemistry of the club. "We had a special bunch of guys. We all got along well, but we also gelled at the right time. We were all friends. We used to say that the Angels had twenty-five cars headed in twenty-five different directions after games, but we had twenty-five guys having beers at the same bar. We all hung out together. We generally liked each other."

Salary arbitration played a big part in the A's efforts to prepare for 1981 as well. The A's won arbitration cases against arguably their best pitcher and outfielder of 1980. Mike Norris, who was seeking $450,000 in his arbitration case, lost to the A's offer of $325,000. Tony Armas was seeking $500,000, but an arbitrator ruled in favor of the A's offer of $210,000. Despite losing their cases, both received significant raises. The A's lost five arbitration hearings in 1980, costing them $167,500. The A's arbitration wins in 1981 under the Haases saved them $340,000.

With contract and salary disputes behind them, the A's and Billy prepared for the '81 season. Martin required A's pitchers and catchers to report to spring training on February 14, the earliest camp-opening date among the twenty-six major-league clubs. Billy's deadline for position players was March 1. "We're going to win it," Billy said to open spring training. "I'll be honest with you. That's how I feel." Billy was glowing in the A's success and his new latitude in the organization. He predicted more suicide squeezes than the previous year. The young starting pitchers drew a lot of media attention in spring training. Norris, Langford, Keough, McCatty, and Kingman were touted as the best starting staff in baseball and some started comparing them to the A's championship rotation of the early 1970s featuring Jim "Catfish" Hunter, Vida Blue, Blue Moon Odom, and Ken Holtzman. Reporters and photographers from major magazines descended on Scottsdale Stadium for feature stories on the rubber-armed staff. "They were like a rock band without instruments," Stephanie Salter said of the five starters.

But the threat of a season-ending work stoppage was looming behind the A's optimism. The players set a May 29 strike deadline if a settlement wasn't reached on free agent compensation, the crux of the dispute. Owners wanted premium compensation—roster players—for losing free agents but the players refused to give up their bargaining power. It would be the first strike in baseball history to interrupt the majors in midseason. The owners were determined to regain the leverage they lost after the repeal of the reserve clause, which had allowed teams to retain the rights to a player after the expiration of a contract. While both sides negotiated behind closed doors, the season was slated to start as scheduled.

Signaling a new direction for the team, Billy and Eisenhardt instituted a new dress code for A's players. They were required to wear green traveling blazers, featuring the A's logo on the breast pocket, with dress shirts and ties on all team flights. The new dress code was meant to emphasize unity instead of individualism. It also represented the professionalism the Haases intended to convey. On the field, the A's would no longer wear green jerseys. They would don white at home and gold on the road.

Courtesy of new ownership, thirty-three of the A's thirty-seven flights during the season would be on chartered planes. And they looked to be traveling more, since the team was becoming more popular. The A's were scheduled to play the Hall of Fame game against the Reds on August 3 at Doubleday Field in Cooperstown. The Haases upgraded all the A's equipment. A's players were enjoying a special romance with their new owners. Ownership hosted gatherings for A's staff poolside during spring training at the Safari Hotel.

With the season approaching, Martin continued to make moves. On March 27, Billy traded reliever Bob Lacey and minor-leaguer Ray Moretti to the Padres for infielder Kevin Bell and two minor-leaguers, infielder Tony Phillips and pitcher Eric Mustad. Lacey was 3–2 with a 2.94 ERA in 47 appearances for the A's in 1980. Lacey and Billy had a stormy relationship and clashed on several occasions, but they coexisted most of the time. It got so bad that Billy banned Lacey from the A's clubhouse in Scottsdale before trading him. Martin alleged that Lacey had bumped him as he passed by on the field after throwing a pregame bullpen session. "After getting beat up for awhile, you get tired of it, give in, and do what he says," Lacey admitted. "But I wasn't that bright and didn't make the adjustment." The Padres traded Lacey to the Indians five days later. He was back in the American League.

Since the A's had become a great story, who constructed the A's was a topic buzzing around camp. Jack McKeon, general manager of the Padres, told the *Arizona Republic* that he and Finley were responsible for building the A's current club. McKeon, comparing the makeup of the Padres to the young A's players of 1977–78, reminded everyone that he helped build the club everyone was buzzing about. "We have the same age kids here that we had in Oakland when Charlie [Finley] and I were putting together the team that is so good now," McKeon told the paper. In fact, some credited the A's resurgence to McKeon's days managing the A's in 1977, when he spearheaded a blockbuster trade with the Pirates that netted Page, Langford, and Armas.

Expos manager Dick Williams, the A's former manager who led them to three division titles, two pennants, and two world championships in three years, told UPI in April that Finley and McKeon deserved some credit for the A's sudden success. "Remember, he's the one who got Martin," Williams said of Finley. "Charlie made all the deals and most of the players with the club now were because of his doing. In that regard, Jack McKeon deserves some of the credit also. He helped Charlie make some of those deals when he was managing the A's."

Clearly, success had many fathers when it came to the 1981 A's. Still, heading into the season, there was still a great deal of uncertainty surrounding the A's bullpen. To replace Lacey, the A's acquired the well-traveled lefty Bob Owchinko from Pittsburgh late in spring for Ernie Camacho. They needed another left-handed reliever in the bullpen with Craig Minetto. A's rookie infielder Mack "Shooty" Babitt batted at a .529 clip in the spring and played solid defense at second base. The stocky, 5-foot-8 second baseman was a non-roster player and pleasant find for Billy. Babitt first caught Billy's attention during the Arizona Instructional League in the fall. Like Billy, Babitt played second base and attended Berkeley High. Babitt not only made the squad, he was the A's Opening Day starting second baseman.

With the roster more or less set, and after finishing with a Cactus League record of 17–10, the team flew to Minnesota to open the season on April

9 against the Twins. Billy announced that Norris would take the mound on Opening Day. Billy had complained that the club looked too lethargic at the conclusion of the spring. But when the season began, they turned it on. Behind the power of Armas—who batted a homerless .182 in the spring— and the starting staff, they exploded from the gate. In front of a packed house of 42,658 at Metropolitan Stadium, in what would be the Twins' final season before moving to the new Hubert H. Humphrey Metrodome, Norris tossed a six-hit, complete game, 5–1 victory. Twins batters flailed helplessly at his unhittable screwball. Armas fueled the offense by going 3-for-5 with a homer, three runs scored, and two runs batted in. "Get used to it, fellas," Norris told reporters after the game. "This is the way it's going to be all year."

The next three games appeared to prove Norris right. Langford followed suit the next day with a complete game, 6–3 win over the Twins as Armas blasted another home run. In Billy Ball fashion, A's second baseman Brian Doyle maneuvered the hidden ball trick to tag out a wandering Glenn Adams near second base in a crucial moment in the sixth. To complete the series, Keough and McCatty each hurled complete game shutouts. Through the first four games, Billy never used the bullpen. The A's 4–0 start, led by the A's rubber-armed aces, began raising eyebrows across the country and creating interest at home. Billy's scrappy A's were at it again.

The undefeated A's took their show to Anaheim to open a four-game series against the Angels. With Oakland trailing 2–1 in the eighth inning, Armas blasted a two-run homer to muscle the A's to a 3–2 comeback victory. Armas's late-inning heroics fueled the A's electrifying 5–0 start. Norris, Langford, and Keough strung together consecutive complete game wins to sweep the series, while Armas powered the offense. Two days after his heroics in the series opener, the Venezuelan slugger crushed an eighth-inning, three-run bomb to power the A's over the Angels, 5–3. He drove in eight runs in the four-game sweep. The A's had won 14 of their last 17 games against the Angels dating back to the previous season. While A's pitchers dominated the headlines, Armas was off to a torrid start. In his sizzling opening week, he batted .375 with four homers and 11 RBIs, including four game-winning hits. Armas was named the American League's first Player of the Week in 1981 by virtue of a batting average of .438.

After completing the sweep of the Angels, the streaking A's came home with a perfect 8–0 record and expecting a sellout for Friday's home opener with McCatty on the mound. The A's took control of first place in the West, leading Tony La Russa's second-place White Sox by three games.

The A's were eyeing the major-league mark for the best start in baseball history. In 1955, the world champion Brooklyn Dodgers opened the season with 10 straight wins. So did the 1962 Pirates and the Indians of 1966. The A's were three wins away from breaking the record. The A's 8–0 record represented the club's best start since moving to Oakland in 1968. The road sweeps inspired more fans to flock to the A's ticket windows. By Wednesday, Friday's home opener was completely sold out, the A's first sellout since the 1975 American League Championship Series.

The starting pitchers were the driving force behind the hot start. Norris, Langford, Keough, and McNatty completed seven of the first eight games and allowed only 12 earned runs in 72 innings. Even more incredibly, none of them had given up a home run.

The second season of Billy Ball was on and the A's were winning. In Oakland and elsewhere, the question was, would the success continue?

13

THE REVIVAL

You could have not written a better script. The stands filled up and the Coliseum jumped. Billy Ball excited fans and then the Haas family took over and brought in their first-class operation. It was quite a production.
—JACKIE MOORE, FORMER A'S COACH AND MANAGER, SEPTEMBER 2018

IN OAKLAND, FANS WERE LINING UP AT THE A'S TICKET OFFICE AND clogging up phone lines to watch the A's home opener on Friday, April 17. The A's had already sold 3,500 season tickets since the A's new sales force took over. Some diehards slept in tents overnight at the Coliseum for tickets to the home opener against Seattle. "Billy Ball" had become the hottest ticket in town.

In the early '80s, Mark Ibanez was a young weekend TV news anchor for local KTVU, and a baseball fanatic energized by the "Billy Ball" hype. On weekends, he covered the A's for the station; during the week, he partied in the stands as a fan. "We'd literally go to almost every day game and sit in the bleachers," said Ibanez. "I probably immersed myself in that Billy Ball season personally and professionally more than any other year. I felt quite fortunate because I got to know those guys personally and then I was in the bleachers with my buddies as a fan on other days. It was a really cool experience."

Ibanez had plenty of company. The upsurge in enthusiasm pushed the A's sales office to the limit. David Rubinstein, the A's director of sales at the time, said the A's antiquated phone system in the ticket office couldn't accommodate the response to the team's aggressive marketing push that started in the winter. "There were three rotary telephone lines and eleven of us," said Rubinstein. "We had to wait for someone to hang up to grab another line. If you misdialed, you lost your spot. They were renovating the offices and the PBX, the front lines of our phone system, blew up right before we opened our new offices."

On Friday, April 17, the atmosphere inside the Coliseum for the home opener was electric. Exactly two years removed from the day the club announced a "crowd" of 653 on a chilly Tuesday night, a franchise-record 50,255 fans crammed every level to watch the A's extend their streak to 9–0. "You could have not written a better script," said Jackie Moore. "The stands filled up and the Coliseum jumped. 'Billy Ball' excited fans and then the Haas family took over and brought in their first-class operation. It was quite a production."

"It was a party atmosphere," said "Krazy George" Henderson, a professional cheerleader hired by Kaiser chairman Cornell Maier in 1980 to help energize A's fans at the Coliseum. "The whole stadium was clapping and cheering. The whole crowd got involved." Glenn Schwarz, covering the game for the *San Francisco Examiner,* described the evening as a "baseball Woodstock." Baseball Woodstock, perhaps, but with better amenities. The repaired scoreboard shouted, WELCOME TO THE HOME OF WINNERS! The new stadium lights added during the winter brightened the A's white jerseys and sharpened the action. Inside the clubhouse, A's players returned to plush, new green carpeting, freshly painted walls, a new dining area, and director chairs in front of each locker, courtesy of their new owners.

Ron Fimrite, who covered the game for *Sports Illustrated,* described the A's magical home opener: "The single word CELEBRATION appeared on the Oakland Coliseum message board before the A's home opener last Friday, and celebration is what it was as a record crowd of 50,255 watched the all-conquering heroes demolish the Mariners. It wasn't just a large aggregation. It was a happy, optimistic, grateful one. The A's had come home in more than a physical sense. They had found a home. The "New Oakland A's" they are now called. Finleyless and carefree, they have charged into an early lead, largely on the strength of five supple arms."

Billy was welcomed back with a larger office with a large bathroom, dressing room, and walk-in closet. Next door, the Haases hosted an elegant "Opening Night Reception" in the Coliseum Arena and Exhibition Hall. Caviar and champagne were served to 3,000 invited guests, including Governor Jerry Brown, Cornell Maier, Golden State Warriors owner Franklin Mieuli, and Curt Flood. Krazy George fired up the crowd on top of the A's dugout. "People were excited about 'Billy Ball' in 1980," noted Wayne Hagin. "But it really came into existence in 1981."

On the field, the A's rocked the Coliseum and their new theme song "Celebration" inspired the crowd throughout the night. Sending ten men to the plate in the first inning, Oakland struck for five runs and routed the Mariners 16–1, extending their season-starting winning streak to nine. Henderson, Murphy, and Johnson each slammed homers, while Armas continued his offensive terror by smashing two more of his own. When Armas crushed his second long ball of the game, a three-run blast in the seventh, fans screamed "Tony, Tony, Tony" as he trotted back inside the dugout. They didn't stop standing and screaming until he answered two curtain calls. "People began calling my name, and I didn't know what to do," Armas told reporters after the game. "Nobody ever did that before." Overshadowed by the A's 18-hit offensive barrage, McCatty tossed another four-hit complete game.

The 9–0 A's were one win away from tying the major-league record for consecutive wins to open the season. They kept the streak alive. Led by Kingman's complete game 8–0 shutout over the Mariners the next game, the A's tied the record by going 10–0 in front of a crowd of 20,131. A's starters completed nine of Oakland's ten wins. The A's would have a chance to break the record in a Sunday afternoon doubleheader to wrap up the series. The potential record-breaking game would be in the hands of Norris, who already had two complete game wins under his belt.

In the first game, the A's wrestled their way to history. In the top of the second, Norris brushed back Seattle third-baseman Lenny Randle with an inside pitch. Randle, incensed, felt the pitch was too close and started going after Norris. But A's catcher Jeff Newman intercepted Randle and a bench-clearing brawl ensued. Norris was restrained on the ground by team-mates. Randle was ejected and Norris stayed in the game. When order was restored, Henderson fueled the A's attack with a two-run triple in the third, while Norris limited the Mariners to one run through six innings. Norris left the game with a stiff right shoulder and numbness in his right hand from the second-inning scuffle. The A's bullpen duo of Minetto and Jeff Jones blanked the Mariners the rest of the way to seal a 6–1 win.

When Julio Cruz strolled to the plate representing the final hope for the Mariners in the ninth, A's fans rose to their feet and cheered. Cruz flied out to left for the final out and the 11–0 A's broke the record established by the 1955 Dodgers, the 1962 Pirates, and the 1966 Indians for the fastest start in baseball history. The crowd of 29,834 erupted and hummed along with the party anthem "Celebration" after the final out. The roaring fans forced the team to come back on the field for an encore. The lyrics, "There's a party goin' on right here; a celebration to last throughout the year" represented the feeling of hope and pride for A's fans. "It was electric," remembered Wayne Hagin. "Excitement had returned. Had they opened the season 5–6 or 6–5, I don't think they would have quite captured the fancy. But starting 11–0 was amazing."

The A's celebration was short-lived. The streak was snapped at 11 when the Mariners took the second game by a score of 3–2. Still, by that time, the club extended their division lead over the White Sox to 4 1/2 games. Armas became the first player ever to capture American League Player of the Week honors in the first two weeks of the season. During the week, he batted .375 with four home runs, four doubles, and 14 runs batted in. He was the thunder behind the A's explosive start. The starting staff completed 11 of the A's first 13 games, including four shutouts. Lefty reliever Bob Owchinko didn't make an appearance until May 2. The rest of the league had a total of four complete games. The country's attention began to shift to the A's. "The first half of the '81 season was as exciting as anything I'd covered in seventeen years," said Glenn Schwarz, former A's beat writer. "It was amazing. They won their first eleven games and were 17–1. The whole national focus was on the A's."

As April gave way to May, A's players dominated most MLB performance categories. Armas led the league with seven homers and 23 runs batted in. As a team, the A's were leading in home runs. Norris, who landed a five-year deal with the A's worth $550,000 annually on April 24, was a perfect 5–0 with a 2.14 ERA. "I grew up in Los Angeles," Kingman told *Sports Illustrated* in 1981, "and I saw Nolan Ryan. And when I was a little kid I saw Sandy Koufax. They would just blow people away, but I wonder if anybody has made hitters look as bad as Michael has. He has guys missing the ball by two feet. He's our magic man."

Keough, leading the league in strikeouts with 24, was 4–0 with an ERA of 1.00. He was the American League Pitcher of the Month for April. Henderson led the league in runs scored, 22, and stolen bases, with 16. "Billy Ball" was the early story of 1981, but it wasn't the only one. Down south, Fernando-mania was catching fire. Fernando Valenzuela, a twenty-year-old left-handed screwball specialist for the Dodgers, started the season 8–0 with a 0.50 ERA with eight straight complete games. He was on his way to becoming the first player ever to win the Rookie of the Year and Cy Young awards in the same season.

The A's new owners were also interested in building the team's reputation nationally. The notion was that garnering national attention would not only help the A's draw better in other markets, but give them more credibility locally. So they created a position called director of media relations and hired Rick Moxley. "No one else in any other sport had the function," said Matt Levine, hired by the Haases as a consultant. "Rick started engaging national media." Mickey Morabito, the A's traveling secretary and director of press relations, handled local press and Moxley handled national platforms.

In late April, that focus on national media delivered the holy grail. Oakland's aces—Langford, Norris, Keough, McCatty, and Kingman— graced the front cover of the April 27, 1981 issue of *Sports Illustrated,* with a headline proclaiming, "The Amazing A's and their Five Aces." The cover showed the aces smiling and donning the A's yellow road jerseys in the visitors' clubhouse in Anaheim. The early dominance of the five starters silenced critics who forecasted arm burnout. "They all realized that Billy was real the story," said Bruce Jenkins. "Without Billy, you might have a manager who takes those guys out in the eighth inning, and they lose the game with that lousy bullpen."

The limelight was an adjustment for some players. People began recognizing them in supermarkets. McCatty remembered driving on the freeway one afternoon on his way to the Coliseum and hearing a passing car honking at him. The startled McCatty looked over and the driver pulled out the *Sports Illustrated* with him on the cover. McCatty, who had been with the A's for parts of four seasons, was never noticed like that in public. "We didn't know people knew who we were," said McCatty. "It was fun going to the ballpark. We were getting a lot of press generally because of Billy, but we were playing good and fans were showing up."

The story of the smoking-hot A's invaded popular culture. They were the cover story of *Time* magazine's May 11, 1981 issue, which featured an artist's rendering of an intense, weathered, and fiery Billy Martin. The cover headline "It's Incredible!" captured the remarkable story of the A's resurrection. "Oakland's record would be impressive if it belonged to the 1927 Yankees. The astonishing truth is that it is held by virtually the same team that, two seasons ago, was the worst in baseball. But there is one huge difference, a stormy, unpredictable figure with fire in his eyes and victory on his mind, Alfred Manuel ("Billy") Martin," wrote B. J. Phillips of *Time*.

That cover story skyrocketed the A's popularity across the country and made them a pop culture phenomenon. "That exploded the whole Billy Ball story," said Matt Levine. "That was really a very important aspect of the new organization." Others around baseball praised Billy's managerial prowess. "I'm just convinced he's the best manager I've ever seen," former Twins slugger Harmon Killebrew said at the time. "I saw that club two years ago—it was one of the worst clubs I've ever seen. He's turned that club around."

The A's owned the front page. Keough and Armas appeared on the cover of the *Sporting News* and a smiling Martin was on the cover of *Sport* magazine. The A's were featured on NBC evening news and CBS's *Sports Spectacular*. Billy made an appearance on ABC's *Good Morning America*. "The Bay Area media already knew the great story, but we were waiting for the rest of the country to catch up," recalled Stephanie Salter. "They were winning and it was a remarkable turnaround. There was a lot of visiting press. Instead of the press box being half-empty, everyone was coming. The New York writers were coming. It was a bandwagon you couldn't help but jump on."

The A's shot to 17–1 after 18 games and fans poured into the Coliseum. It took only eleven home dates for the A's to draw 319,099, surpassing the 306,763 fans they drew in the 1979 season. They attracted a total of 140,876 alone during a weekend series with the Yankees in early May. With 66 scheduled home dates left, the A's—averaging 30,641 a game—were on pace to obliterate their Oakland franchise record of 1,075,518 established in 1975. BART (Bay Area Rapid Transit) set a new record for average weekday ridership in April with 174,000 dropping off and picking up A's fans at the Coliseum station. BART revealed that 20 percent of A's fans were riding BART to the Coliseum for games. "The meteoric rise of the Oakland A's makes all other Cinderella stories seem like a rags-to-riches cliché. A team—indeed, a franchise—left for dead only two years ago has come joyously alive and already has surpassed its entire 1979 home attendance figure," wrote Paul Schnitt of the *Austin American-Statesman* in 1981.

Perhaps inevitably, the A's success and popularity brought negative attention as well. Longtime whispers of A's pitchers throwing spitballs escalated into public accusations. The Twins, Angels, and Mariners publicly accused A's pitchers of moistening the ball for extra movement. Batters regularly told home plate umpires to examine balls thrown by A's starters. Opposing players and coaches took their allegations to reporters. The critics had different theories on how the pitchers were applying the foreign substances like Vaseline, spit, or sweat on the ball. A's skeptics maintained that the sudden success of the A's five starters was directly tied to Billy and Fowler introducing them to the spitter when they arrived in 1980. The charges, according to at least one former A's player, weren't unfounded. "Playing for Billy, one of the pitches you had in your arsenal was a spitball," said Dave Heaverlo, a right-handed Oakland reliever in 1981. "You learned how to throw one."

Nonetheless, some of the charges against the A's bordered on the absurd. On May 8, Buck Rodgers, manager of the Milwaukee Brewers, played that night's game under protest because McCatty wore a long, white-sleeved sweater underneath his white home jersey. Rodgers contended that McCatty's arms covered in white made it difficult for opposing hitters to pick up the ball.

Long-sleeved or not, the A's were armed with a first-place 24–7 record when they began a ten-game, four-city Eastern swing through New York, Milwaukee, Baltimore, and Boston on May 12. In New York, after dropping by his downtown Manhattan western shop, Billy Martin's Western Wear ("Western duds for Eastern dudes"), Billy returned to Yankee Stadium in a stretch limousine. The Yankees proceeded to cool off the red-hot A's, winning two of three games, although Keough ran his record to 5–0 in the club's only win. The A's ended the trip through Milwaukee, Baltimore, and Boston with eight consecutive losses and returned to Oakland reeling from a 1–9 road trip, their lead having dropped from 7 1/2 to 2 1/2 games in twelve days. The A's big bats struggled on the trip, with the team averaging just 2.7 runs per game. Armas failed to drive in a run in his 8-for-39 effort and Johnson, Gross, and Heath were a combined 9-for-78. The A's pitching was uncharacteristically shaky, posting an ERA of 4.56 on the road trip.

Before the road trip was over, Oakland decided to make a move. On May 20, the A's and Yankees agreed on a five-player deal. The A's acquired veteran first baseman Jim Spencer and southpaw pitcher Tom Underwood from the Yankees for first baseman Dave Revering, outfielder Mike Patterson, and minor-league hurler Chuck Dougherty. While Revering had a career batting average of .282, he was hitting only .230 and not playing much. He needed a change of scenery. Spencer was a sure-handed first baseman with some left-handed pop. He was batting only .143 with two homers for the Yankees. He had a clause in his contract with the Yankees that could have blocked a trade to the A's, but he agreed to rejoin Martin. Underwood was used primarily as a starter for the Yankees and struggled with a record of 1–4 and 4.41 ERA. Billy planned on using Underwood as a spot starter against predominantly left-handed hitting lineups. Spencer and Underwood joined Stanley, Johnson, Klutts, Heath, and Doyle as former Yankees who joined the A's. Loyalty was important to Billy. It shaped how he assembled his roster and coaching staffs. He added familiar Yankees to the roster. The infiltration of pinstripes in the organization was obvious.

After the disastrous road trip, the A's reeled off five straight wins and maintained their hold on first place. But the May 29 strike deadline was casting a pall over the young season. A strike would kill the momentum of a dream baseball season for the A's organization on all fronts. Most players felt a strike was inevitable. The owners were crying that free agency was wiping them out, and the players demanded to see financial records to support the claim. Persuaded by the players, the National Labor Relations Board stepped in and filed an injunction against the owners. The NLRB accused the owners of refusing to bargain in good faith. They sought to rescind the compensation plan the owners unilaterally implemented on February 19, which required clubs that signed "ranking" free agents to part not only with a draft pick, but a roster player in return. With little hope of quickly settling the issue, players and owners appeared before a federal judge and agreed to postpone the May 29 strike deadline pending the administrative law ruling on the NLRB's injunction. Everyone waited.

The season lived on and the A's traveled to Toronto to open a six-game road trip. Billy started the road trip with headline-generating fireworks. During the A's series-opening loss to the Blue Jays at Exhibition Stadium on May 29, he bumped home plate umpire Terry Cooney in the bottom of the fourth. Billy was barking at Cooney all game about his tight strike zone for Keough. Cooney finally removed his mask and barked back at Billy. That was enough for Billy to explode from the dugout to confront him. Martin kicked and hand-shoved dirt on Cooney's gray slacks during what would be his first ejection of the season. Lee MacPhail suspended Martin indefinitely the next morning until the film of the incident was reviewed. A day later, MacPhail hit Martin with a seven-day suspension and $1,000 fine. It was the most severe suspension handed down by MacPhail in his eight-year tenure as AL president. Billy appealed the suspension and returned to manage the A's in Chicago for a three-game series against the second-place White Sox.

On June 4, before the series finale, Billy arrived at Comiskey Park and his adventurous road trip continued. A male had called the stadium anonymously the night before and said he was going kill Martin at 10:00 p.m. the following night. He then hung up. Measures were taken to protect Billy. The Chicago police and stadium security greeted Billy with a bulletproof vest. Billy fastened the vest underneath his gold jersey and green jacket before the game. Billy was assigned two security guards in the dugout, while additional guards surrounded the A's clubhouse. Billy kept his players in the dark about the threat and promised to stay in the dugout the entire game. But the unpredictable Billy barged out of the dugout on three separate occasions in the course of the game, including once slightly before 10:00 p.m. and once slightly after.

Dave Heaverlo was in the bullpen and watched the bizarre scene unfold. "Rick Langford threw about two or three pitches and there was suddenly a time-out," remembered Heaverlo. "Billy randomly walked to the mound and Langford looked at him like, 'What did I do wrong?' Billy didn't even make eye contact with Langford. He circled around the mound, looked into the stands and walked back to the dugout. Everyone was confused. We all wondered what Langford did wrong. Our bullpen coach, George Mitterwald, called the dugout to see what the hell was going on. Clete Boyer told him that someone had threatened to shoot Billy the minute he stepped on the field. But that was Billy. Billy was in charge."

The White Sox beat the A's 4–2, salvaging one of the three games. Billy received another death threat in Oakland when the club returned home. This time, on June 6, someone called the A's switchboard and threatened to shoot him. Security was beefed up around the A's dugout and Billy was left untouched in the A's 6–2 win over the Red Sox. After then taking two of three games from the Orioles, the first-place A's were 37–23 and a game ahead of the Texas Rangers. That was when the bottom fell out of everyone's season, at least temporarily.

On June 10, a federal judge, Henry F. Werker of US District Court in Manhattan, dismissed the NLRB's petition that would have tabled for a year the sticky issue of free agent compensation and kept the season alive. So the players walked out on June 12, baseball's first ever midseason work stoppage. The Player Relations Committee canceled the season "until further notice." Spencer's game-ending groundout in the A's 3-1 loss to the Orioles on June 10 would be their final swing of the season until August 10. "As directed by the executive board's unanimous decision, no games will be played on Friday, June 12, or thereafter until a settlement is reached and approved by a vote of the players," wrote Marvin Miller, executive director of the players' association, in the memorandum he sent to players. Many predicted the strike would last long because of the tension between both sides surrounding the leverage-swaying issue of free agent compensation. Jeff Newman, the A's players representative, remembered the work stoppage: "I'll never forget when they locked the doors. We had to work out on our own. We really didn't know where it was going from there. Thankfully, it only lasted fifty days. And if you're not doing anything, it was enough time to get out of shape. We worked out on high school fields and brought our own equipment because the teams couldn't supply anything."

For three weeks in June and all of July, major-league ballparks across the country were empty. Norris said the strike had changed his whole outlook on the season and that trying to get back into playing shape after a seven-week hiatus on short notice proved to be detrimental. "The strike screwed us all up," said Norris. "We all thought the season was over. We got totally out of shape. We came back pitching complete games, but our arms were out of shape. That's what led to our arm injuries." According to comedian Bob Hope, the A's manager had his own unique regimen for remaining sharp during the strike. "Billy Martin stayed in shape by kicking dirt on his dog," Hope quipped.

With owners collecting their final $100,000 per-game payments from their $50 million strike insurance that was expiring on August 5, and players already missing two paychecks, both sides were motivated to reach a settlement by August. There was pressure to reach an agreement around August 1, the final point to salvage a respectable 100-game season with a short window of time for players to reenergize themselves. "The owners knew they could hold us out because we weren't getting paid," said Mike Heath "We had no money to pay bills. People don't realize that."

The owners had a strategy and stuck to it as long as they could. The longest strike in sports history that erased baseball on the Fourth of July for the first time in the century finally ended. On Friday, July 31, 1981, at 5:30 a.m. EDT, chief negotiator Ray Grebey, representing the owners, announced that a tentative agreement was in place and baseball would be returning starting with the All-Star Game—originally scheduled on July 14—in Cleveland as planned on August 9. Representing the owners, Grebey and MacPhail had negotiated with players' counsel Donald Fehr and Marvin Miller for twelve hours on Thursday afternoon before finally reaching an agreement early Friday morning at 1:00 a.m. The agreement still needed to be ratified by the players.

The strike forced the cancellation of 713 of 2,106 scheduled games and cost the A's 22 home dates. The A's drew 819,892 in only 29 pre-strike home dates, averaging 28,272 per game. The A's only had 22 home dates left because of the strike-shortened season. "It's a victory for nobody and a loss for nobody," said Grebey. "It's a good collective bargaining agreement. There's something in it for both sides. The fans of America are the winners in this and the clubs will do everything they can to try to restore the confidence of the fans."

Miller, meanwhile, called the settlement a "victory for the spirit of the players."

To accommodate the postseason, the owners decided that the first half of the season would end with the games on June 11. No missed games were made up. The teams in first place in each division at the end of the first half automatically qualified for the first round of playoffs. The second half of the season would consist of games played from August 10 through October 4, the same scheduled end date of the regular season. The division leaders of each half would meet in the first round of postseason. That meant the A's had already clinched a postseason berth. But if they won the 49-game second half, too, they would play the team in their division with the second best record of the second half in an intra-division miniseries beginning on October 6. Every club was on even footing to open the second half. The Royals, for example, who trailed the A's by 12 games when the strike happened, were equal with the A's to start the second half. The 1981 A's lived on.

The A's, Yankees, Dodgers, and the Philadelphia Phillies, the four pre-strike division leaders, clinched playoff berths under the owner's split-season system. A's players gathered back in the Bay Area where team workouts were held at UC Berkeley's Evans Diamond to dust off the cobwebs. They played exhibition games against the Padres and Giants before opening the second season in Minnesota on August 10. The return of baseball was ushered in with the drawing power of Major League Baseball's 52nd All-Star Game in Cleveland on Sunday, August 9, the eve of the second half regular season schedule. AL Manager Jim Frey tapped Norris and Armas to represent the A's on the All-Star squad.

Armas struck out in his only plate appearance in the eighth and Norris allowed a homer to Dave Parker in the sixth. A massive crowd of 72,086 stuffed Cleveland Stadium to celebrate the return of America's Pastime. The final score, with the National League edging the American League 5–4, was almost an afterthought. Baseball was back. "It was the return of baseball," said Bruce Jenkins. "The place was totally packed and unbelievably exciting. That whole night, with the whole nation watching, the All-Star Game brought baseball back in a big way."

The A's had not played a game in sixty-one days before losing 6–2 to the Twins to open the second half. Given that Oakland had already clinched a postseason slot, there was little incentive to win other than trying to peak during the playoffs. That frustrated Billy, who felt the winner of both halves should be granted a bye before the American League Championship series. Even though the A's played only .500 since May, turnstile numbers suggested that fans were still enthralled with Billy Ball.

The A's surpassed the one million mark in attendance for the first time since 1975 when they drew 35,325 fans on a Sunday afternoon game against the Orioles on August 23, exactly one year removed from the date Finley announced the A's sale to Walter A. Haas Jr. That brought the season total to 1,014,803 through 38 home dates, only the third time the A's reached the million mark since moving to Oakland in 1968.

Playing hard in the second half seemed to be a matter of pride for the A's. Dwayne Murphy emerged as a second-half offensive catalyst and was having a breakout season. Climbing the center field wall like Spider-Man, the smooth and fearless Murphy robbed hitters of homers above the wall. As the hitter trotted around the bases, Murphy casually flipped the ball back to the infield, surprising everyone in the park. He got it done offensively as well, smashing 15 homers and driving in 60 runs in the A's 109-game season. Murphy also led the major leagues with 15 game-winning runs batted in.

The A's encountered some rough stretches in the second half and Billy, at one point, was concerned the club wasn't winning consistently enough and had acquired bad habits. Heaverlo remembered a frank discussion Billy had with his club after a tough loss in Baltimore: "We're in the clubhouse and Billy comes in and slams the door. Nobody dared get up to get a sandwich or a beer. Then Billy suddenly calls this meeting. He said, 'Gentlemen, as you know, I am the general manager and field manager; I negotiate your contract and fill out the lineup card. If we don't start playing better baseball and earn the money I'm paying you, I'm going to do one of three things: First, I will send you to the minors; or second, I will release you; or third, I will send you to Seattle.'"

It wasn't an idle threat. The Seattle Mariners were on their way to finishing the season with a 44–65 record. In their previous four years of existence, the Mariners lost more than 100 games twice and 95 and 98 games in the other two seasons, respectively. Getting shipped to Seattle was the baseball equivalent of a trip to Siberia.

In addition to putting fear in the hearts of his players, Martin took action. In late August, Billy called up third-baseman Mickey Klutts, highly touted first baseman Kelvin Moore, and outfielder Mike Davis. Klutts had been in the minors on a rehab assignment and needed to get back into shape. Playing for Triple-A Tacoma, Moore hit .327, clubbed 31 homers, and drove in 109 runs. Billy had benched Babitt and moved Dave McKay to second base. McKay, thirty-one, batted .323 in September/October with three homers. "Dave McKay turned out to be one of their better hitters down the stretch in 1981," said Glenn Schwarz. "He was hitting for power." Davis was a talented outfield prospect who was having difficulty cracking baseball's best outfield. The Yankees, leading the American League East, began sending five scouts to monitor the A's down the stretch.

On September 30, the A's final regular season home game, the team drew a crowd of 11,144, running its season attendance to a record 1,304,052 in just 51 home dates. In 1981, the A's averaged 25,569 per game and never drew fewer than 10,000. In 1979, four-figure attendance numbers had been the norm. The strike ultimately robbed the A's of drawing 2.3 million, close to two million more than they drew in 1979. The A's barely cleared a million during their championship years in the early 1970s. As much as winning was luring fans to the Coliseum, the effort by the Haas family to stimulate community interest was another factor that increased attendance and fan enthusiasm. "I don't think it was the winning," infielder Wayne Gross told reporters in 1981 on the A's attendance explosion. "I think it was the new ownership and the way the new owners approached baseball, making the community feel like it was their club, that it was part of Oakland."

Interest was certainly high as the end of the regular season approached. The A's trailed the first-place Royals by a game and a half as they headed to Kansas City for the final series of the second half. The outcome of the three-game series would determine home-field advantage for the American League West playoffs. If the A's swept the Royals, they would be champions of the second half and only need to play the first game of the best-of-five intra-division series in Kansas City. If the Royals won two of three, they would host only the first two games in Kansas City. Should the A's win two of three, leaving them only a half-game behind the Royals, they would force the Royals to make up a rained-out doubleheader in Cleveland to decide the division on October 5, the Monday after the season ended. "If it hadn't been for the strike, we'd have won by ten games," Billy said before the series. "We have the best pitching and had just shaken off our only slump. Kansas City is getting in on a [split season] fluke. You can't put them in the same category with New York and Milwaukee."

Despite Martin's slight, or perhaps because of it, Royals ace Dennis Leonard hurled a seven-hit, 3–0 shutout over the A's in the series opener. But the A's stormed back to win the next two games, forcing the Royals to fly to Cleveland for the makeup doubleheader the next day. Instead of starting the offseason, the sixth-place Indians were forced to play one more day. The A's, meanwhile, rested in Kansas City until the Division Series started the next day. The Royals ran over the checked-out Indians 9–0 on an 18-hit attack in the first game to clinch the second half. The second game was cancelled because even a Royals loss would have left them division winners over the A's in the second half by percentage points. With the Royals winning the second half, the A's would play the first two games in Kansas City and the remaining three in Oakland, if necessary, in the playoff miniseries. It was fitting that the A's would face the Royals in their first postseason appearance in five years. After all, in 1976, Kansas City was the team that had brought an end to Oakland's spectacular playoff run in the first half of the decade, including three consecutive championships. Now the two clubs would be battling for American League West supremacy in the 1981 postseason.

14

POSTSEASON DREAMS

The A's, to their credit, maintained the magic they established before to get themselves into that miniseries. They went in there and dominated the Royals, who were in the World Series the season before. That was the height of the A's under Billy Martin.

—Bruce Jenkins, *San Francisco Chronicle*, August 2018

The Royals, carrying a losing 50–53 overall record into the postseason, hosted the 64–45 A's on October 6 in the opener of their playoff miniseries. If the first-half division races remained alive after the fifty-day strike ended, the Royals would have ended the season trailing the A's by 11 games. Making the postseason even stranger was that the Cincinnati Reds, baseball's winningest team in 1981 with a record of 66–42, didn't make the playoffs because they finished in second place both halves. Since this was the A's first postseason appearance since 1975, Oakland's roster consisted mostly of playoff novices. Still, the A's were confident they could finish off the Royals fast in the miniseries and move on to the League Championship Series. The A's and Royals were 3–3 against each other during the season. The confident A's smelled blood. "We're going to whip their ass bad," Norris told a group of reporters before the miniseries. "They are afraid of us."

Dennis Leonard, the Royals' top starter who tossed two shutouts against the A's in the season's final month, faced Norris in the Tuesday afternoon series opener in Kansas City. Norris was 12–9 with a 3.75 ERA overall in 1981, but struggled after the strike with a 4–6 record and a 4.32 earned run average. Billy set the rotation for Norris, McCatty, and Langford to open the first three games. The A's pitching, power, and defense were on display in the series opener in front of 40,592 fans at Royals Stadium. Wayne Gross started the scoring with a three-run homer to right off Leonard in the fourth, and Dwayne Murphy took him deep with a solo shot in the eighth. Norris, meanwhile, shackled the Royals in a 4–0 shutout to snatch the first game. In the fifth, Gross had contributed with his glove as well. Playing third-base, he snared a fierce line drive off the bat of Frank White with the bases loaded that he turned into an inning-ending double play to bail Norris out.

In Game 2, Armas, despite a pulled groin muscle, went 4-for-4, including two doubles. McCatty tossed a complete game six-hitter to edge the Royals 2-1. McCatty continued his strong post-strike push on the mound and the A's were making quick work of the fading Royals. The series moved to Oakland for Game 3, the A's first postseason game in Oakland since October 7, 1975. A mob of 40,002 filled the Coliseum on October 9 to welcome playoff baseball back to Oakland and see the A's clinch their sixth division title since moving to Oakland.

Larry Gura, who killed the A's playoff hopes in 1976 by shutting them out 4–0 on September 29 that season, started Game 3 for the Royals. After being hitless in nine at-bats in the first two games of the series, Rickey Henderson ignited the A's, and the crowd. He banged two singles, stole a base, walked twice, and scored three runs in the A's 4–1 win to complete the division-clinching sweep. Dave Beard, Billy's newly minted hard-throwing, right-handed closer, struck out John Wathan to close the game out in the ninth and usher in the celebration. "The A's win the West!" exclaimed Al Michaels, ABC's play-by-play man, after the final out. Michaels could have been forgiven if he sounded surprised.

The A's, 54–108 in 1979, outscored the Royals 10–2 in the three-game sweep and advanced to their first American League Championship series since 1975. After striking out Wathan, Beard dashed to home plate, jumped into Heath's arms, and thrust his right arm in the sky in exhilaration. The A's rushed from the dugout to join Beard and Heath.

"The A's, to their credit, maintained the magic they established before to get themselves into that miniseries," noted Bruce Jenkins. "They went in there and dominated the Royals, who were in the World Series the season before. That was the height of the A's under Billy Martin."

With the supercharged sound system playing "Celebration" in the background, hundreds of fence-hopping fans flooded the field from the bleachers to celebrate with the A's. They also helped themselves to some swag, relieving more than a few A's of caps and gloves. Oakland players who had weathered the dry years under Finley in the second half of the 1970s were now spraying top-shelf champagne on each other in the clubhouse. "It was a happy night in Oakland," said Jackie Moore. "Every night at the ballpark was exciting."

After celebrating the AL West championship, the A's had to wait for the conclusion of the American League East miniseries between the Brewers and Yankees to determine where they were flying for the championship series, which would start on October 13. Because the A's closed the Royals out so quickly, they had three days off before the series regardless of the opponent. They welcomed the rest. The break gave Armas more time to heal his pulled groin muscle and rested the right arms of the starters. "I'm very proud of my team," Billy told reporters. "They are young and hungry and they know how to win. What more could a manager ask? The way we are playing now, I think we can beat anyone. Our pitching is solid, our defense is sound and we play aggressively when we get runners on base. This is Oakland A's baseball."

Like the best-of-five miniseries, the A's would open the first two games on the road and host the remaining three back in Oakland, if necessary. After a morning workout at the Coliseum on the Sunday before the series, the A's camped out at Vince's Restaurant, a mile from Oakland International Airport. "The plane was either flying to New York or Milwaukee," recalled John Hickey, who covered the series for the *Daily Review*. "At one point, Billy was suggesting we just get in the air and get going with the idea that once the winner was determined, we could finalize the course. Two things about that: Billy was drinking and you can't take off without a flight plan."

With bags already loaded on the chartered plane with no destination, A's players, coaches and wives watched the Yankees defeat the Brewers 7–3 in the decisive Game 5 at Yankee Stadium to advance to meet the A's. With the flight plan now finalized, the A's jetted to New York three wins away from the World Series. "The team stayed put until the Yankees won, so we got to New York pretty late," Hickey recalled. Most of the A's preferred playing the Yankees and figured the road to the World Series would pass through New York. Billy was pleased that the Yankees had used up pitchers Ron Guidry and Dave Righetti in the win-or-go-home Game 5 win. The matchup, replete with storylines about Billy and Steinbrenner's reunion, was a bonanza for the media, which would have no shortage of intriguing angles. Martin, the magazine star, baseball savant, and conquering hero, was returning to New York with the goal of taking vengeance on the team that had fired him just two years before. And his team was playing for the pennant.

Ray Negron, a former Yankee clubhouse attendant, remembered Billy's return to New York for the championship series: "Billy was my hero and I couldn't help wanting to see him do well. At the same time, I was naturally rooting for my Bombers to win. I couldn't help to wish that Billy could come back to New York with the Yankees, where he belonged. I knew that he was the missing link to us beating the Dodgers in the World Series that year. Bob Lemon was a good manager, but he was no Billy Martin when it came to the big-time games."

One upstate New York paper, the *Binghampton Press & Sun-Bulletin*, maintained the A's were "loaded with Yankee rejects." Reggie Jackson would be in his final days in pinstripes as a player. "A's–Yankees is a media maker's dream," A's president Roy Eisenhardt said in 1981. "You have West Coast against East Coast, George and Billy, the Oakland no-names against the Yankee names. It definitely would be exciting." Many New Yorkers billed the series as the "Billy and George" showdown in the Bronx, the real World Series. Everyone who knew Billy knew how badly he wanted to beat Steinbrenner. "He wanted to beat them so bad," said A's coach Jackie Moore. "Anytime we played the Yankees, it was on a different level. He couldn't stand to lose, but he really couldn't stand to lose to the Yankees." Martin made clear, in blunt terms, just how badly he wanted to take down Steinbrenner and the Yankees during the A's workout a day before the series started. "I'm not a Yankee fan . . . right now," Billy told reporters. "I'm a Yankee killer."

Back in Oakland, economists forecasted that hosting the championship series would generate $2.5 million in economic activity per game for the business community through hotels, transportation, dining, and concession and parking revenues. Hotels were booked throughout Oakland. After the Raiders brought a Super Bowl championship to Oakland in January, Billy's A's could bring the city more economic juice and attention with a World Series title that was seven wins away. On NBC's telecast before Game 1, baseball analyst Tony Kubek told viewers that "Billy Ball is the greatest piece of managerial gamesmanship in the history of the game."

Based on salaries, however, it shaped up to be a case of David taking on Goliath. The experienced and filthy rich Yankees boasted an estimated player payroll of $8,793,000, the highest in the majors. According to an August 20 piece on player salaries in the *New York Times* by Gerald Eskenazi, "Reggie Jackson, the outfielder and designated hitter, averages $525,000 a season under a five-year contract that expires in October. . . . [pitcher] Tommy John, another starting pitcher, averages more than $575,000 a season in total compensation."

The salary disparity aside, it was more a case of Goliath versus Goliath. The series featured two of baseball's most prolific home-run teams of 1981. In the strike-shortened season, the A's led baseball with 104 homers and the

Yankees were right behind them with 100. Armas led the American League with 22 home runs and 49 extra base hits, and Rickey Henderson was the league leader in stolen bases with 56. As for pitching, the Yanks' Righetti led the league in strikeouts per nine innings pitched with 7.60, while Guidry finished third with 7.37. The A's Mike Norris and Rick Langford were both 12-game winners, just two games behind the 1981 leaders including McCatty. Langford, McCatty, Norris, and Keough were all top-10 finishers in complete games, with Langford holding the lead at 18. McCatty led in ERA at 2.32.

Pitching was clearly on Steinbrenner's mind when he met with AL president Lee MacPhail on October 12 to persuade him to support umpires in upholding spitball violations in the championship series. "This is a championship that has to be decided within the rules," Steinbrenner said, according to Murray Chass of the *New York Times*. "The guys are going to have to be under strict and scrutinous surveillance. If that's going to be a factor, let's have it be enforced." When the A's played the Yankees at Yankee Stadium back on May 14, umpires examined balls Norris had been throwing throughout the game. The Yankees were one of the clubs who had accused the A's staff of doctoring balls during the series. It distracted Norris such that he couldn't escape the sixth inning. Billy accused Steinbrenner of bullying the umpires into harassing A's pitchers with mound visits and ball exams. This time, Martin vowed that history wouldn't repeat itself. "They made a farce of it. They bothered Mike so bad he lost the game. . . . I guarantee all the money in the world it won't happen. . . . My pitchers will walk to home plate, hand them the ball and lift their arms and let them check for spitballs or guns or whatever else they want."

With his line drawn firmly in the sand, Billy announced that Norris would open the series on the mound for the green and gold with McCatty, Langford, and Keough to follow. The Yankees rolled out Tommy John, Rudy May, and Righetti in that order, all lefties.

The headline in the October 13 *Daily News* shouted "George's Gall vs. Billy Ball" on the day of the series opener in the Bronx. "The thing that

George and Billy had in common was their desire to win," said Judge Eddie Sapir, Billy's friend and attorney. "That was the common denominator."

The deep Yankees quickly proved to be too much for the young A's. Yankees starter Tommy John tamed the A's lineup over six innings in Game 1 and Graig Nettles punched a first-inning, three-run triple, providing all the runs New York needed en route to a 3–1 win. The Yankees brought in hard-throwing relievers Ron Davis and Goose Gossage, the "Gold Dust Twins," to shut the A's down in the eighth and ninth in front of 55,740 fans at Yankee Stadium to seal the opener. Tommy John later revealed his Game 1 strategy: "I knew that Billy wanted to make me look bad," recalled John. "I was not the best at fielding bunts going over because I wasn't very quick. My plan was to keep them off second and third-base, so I wouldn't have to worry about any of Billy's stunts. I ended up beating them."

The A's hoped to steal Game 2 with Cy Young candidate Steve McCatty taking the mound against Rudy May the next afternoon. But the Yankees massacred five A's pitchers, McCatty, Beard, Jones, Kingman, and Owchinko, in a 13–3 daytime shelling to take a 2–0 lead. Piniella and Nettles each smashed three-run homers to lead the Yankees' offensive charge, while Dave Winfield made a spectacular leaping catch to rob Armas of a second-inning solo shot to left. "I'm going home ashamed, embarrassed," Billy told reporters after the game. "Two guys who I thought we would beat [pitchers John and May] both got off the hook."

Back in the Bay Area, a large segment of the A's faithful kept hope alive. After the losses in New York, hundreds of fans greeted the A's at the Oakland Airport when their late-night flight touched down. The A's were 35–21 playing at home, and hoped to accomplish what no other 0–2 team had in the thirteen years of the best-of-five series: win three straight. Billy tapped Keough to start Game 3 at home instead of Langford, who was recovering from a bruised ankle. Facing the twenty-two-year-old lefty fireballer Righetti in the twilight at 5:10 p.m. PDT was no easy task for the A's. Righetti, a local product who grew up in nearby San Jose, was starting Game 3 for the Yankees. He went 8–4 with a 2.05 ERA in the regular season and had already notched two postseason wins.

For ticket scalpers hovering on the street leading to the Coliseum before the game, business was booming. In front of a crammed house of 47,302 on a Thursday evening, the A's received ominous signs early. Murphy, 8-for-19 in the postseason, injured a ribcage muscle on a swing and left the game in the first inning. A's utility outfielder Rick Bosetti, acquired from the Blue Jays on June 9, replaced him in center field. In more deflating news, Henderson sprained his wrist during a fifth-inning at-bat and left the game, replaced by Mike Heath. The A's were battling for their playoff lives in a scoreless tie with the Yankees in the sixth inning with only one-third of the best outfield in baseball on the field. Murphy's departure would come back to haunt the A's. The Yankees took a 1–0 lead when Willie Randolph ripped a solo homer off Keough with two outs in the sixth. The game, season, and series ended for the A's in the ninth. With the bases loaded and two out, Nettles drove a ball off Underwood to right center that Bosetti badly misjudged. He appeared to camp under the drive, but it sailed over his outstretched glove and bounced on the warning track.

Nettles's base-clearing double scored three runs and put the Yankees ahead 4–0 with Gossage looming in the bullpen. He finished them off at 8:47 p.m. With two out and Armas on first in the bottom of the ninth, Gross lofted a swirling popup that Randolph snared in shallow center for the third out. The Yankees captured their thirty-third pennant. The A's remarkable season was over. The deflated A's watched the Yankees celebrate from the dugout. The Yankees outscored the A's 20–4 in the series. "In a short series, we didn't match up man-to-man well against the Yankees," conceded Jeff Newman. The Yankees were moving on to the World Series and the A's received a dose of reality. "When the money was on the table, the A's didn't play like the cocky young guys taking on the world. They looked more like a bunch of underage kids sneaking into the pool hall, hoping nobody would check their ID," wrote Scott Ostler of the *Los Angeles Times* after the series.

Jackie Moore acknowledged that the Yankees were the more experienced and deeper club despite the excitement surrounding the A's. The A's didn't have a Davis or Gossage in the bullpen. "On paper and in between the lines on the field, they were a better club than we were," said Moore. "They won the first game and took the series away from us. We were having so much fun and success, we didn't want the season to end." Mickey Klutts said the A's were outplayed by the hungrier team. "Sometimes I felt like we were just happy to be there," said Klutts. "The Yankees were going for it." Even if the A's rebounded to win Game 3, the injuries to Henderson and Murphy would have probably sidelined them for the remainder of the series. "When it was over, the A's were disappointed, but not crushed," Hickey said. "They thought they were on the first steps to some really big things. So while they were down, it wasn't the end of the world, just the end of an unexpectedly special season."

The *San Francisco Examiner*'s Stephanie Salter said that losing to the Yankees was Billy's biggest nightmare. "What can be worse than being swept in the playoffs by the Yankees of all teams," Salter explained. "This dream that had all this energy and momentum, but reality killed it." After the game, the A's Dave McKay looked back on Oakland's championship dynasty and figured they were right where they needed to be. "But I think history is going to be on our side," McKay told reporters after the game. "The old Oakland A's were swept by the Orioles ten years ago, then came back to win three straight world championships [1972 to 1974]. This is our lesson and we are following that tradition, because I am looking forward to winning the world championship for the next three years."

In the A's somber clubhouse, a teary-eyed Billy handed his game-used cap to A's owner Walter A. Haas Jr. In November, Martin was named UPI's and the AP's 1981 American League Manager of the Year for a second consecutive season and fourth time overall, which tied a league record held by Billy's mentor Casey Stengel. Billy was previously the league manager of the year with Texas in 1974 and New York in 1976. The *Sporting News* named Tony Armas American League Player of the Year. Henderson finished second in balloting. Henderson, Murphy, and Armas were selected on TSN's All-Star team.

The A's were leaders in other categories in 1981 as well. Murphy's15 fifteen dingers, along with Armas's 22 and Johnson's 17, helped power the A's to a league-leading 104 home runs. On the mound, McCatty pitched his way into Cy Young Award conversations and was the A's top starter in 1981. He was 14–7 with a stingy 2.32 ERA. He completed 16 of his 22 starts and tossed four shutouts. McCatty eventually finished second in Cy Young voting that season to Milwaukee Brewers' closer Rollie Fingers, who led baseball with 28 saves and boasted an ERA of 1.04.

Henderson's offensive production in 1981 made him a strong contender for the American League MVP. Besides his batting average of .319, Henderson led the league in hits, with 135, and runs, with 89. He also stole 56 bases. (Tim Raines, rookie left fielder for the Montreal Expos, led the majors in thefts in the shortened season with 71.) Henderson also dazzled with his defense in left as one-third of baseball's best outfield. Some peers anointed Henderson the best player in the game. A banner reading HENDERSON HEIGHTS hung over the second deck in left field at the Coliseum. Henderson purchased the section of fifty seats every game for Oakland's unprivileged kids. "Not enough players have that dash that makes people see them. In Oakland, the city baseball once left to die, Henderson is one of them. He is great and knows it. He's spectacular and he's got the magic flair," wrote Peter Gammons of the *Boston Globe* in 1981.

For Billy Martin and the A's, the magical, bizarre, unprecedented 1981 season had come to an end. In Oakland, for the second time in two years, fans, players, team management, and the manager all had good reasons to be optimistic about what lay ahead. "Wait 'til next year" was no longer an empty slogan.

15

RAINY DAYS

More successfully than any other manager, Martin has been able to make an entire collection of athletic bodies into an expression of his own will. Like everything else Martin does, this is the short-term strategy.
—BILL JAMES, AUTHOR, *THE BILL JAMES BASEBALL ABSTRACT 1982*

AFTER THE 1981 SEASON ENDED, A's PRESIDENT ROY EISENHARDT'S main priority was to lock up the A's core stars to long-term contracts with fair-market salaries. Many of the young A's had finally landed the money, lifestyle and security they dreamed of. Tony Armas inked a four-year deal worth $2.6 million in late January. Armas, living out of a hotel room during the season while his wife and children stayed in Venezuela, started looking for a home in Oakland to settle with his family. "I like the ballclub," Armas said after signing. "I think we have the best manager in baseball, I think we've got the best owner and I think we've got the best fans. They're giving me good money to keep playing here." The A's also inked Steve McCatty to a four-year pact worth $1.5 million that same day.

The A's payroll nearly tripled since the Haases purchased the club. In January, Eisenhardt had forecast the A's payroll for the 1982 season to hover around $3.5 to $3.8 million, not including signing bonuses. "Now, the players' parking lot at the Oakland Coliseum resembles a German car dealership. New management treats the players like kings. No longer do the A's take commercial flights. They travel only by charter. There is no more waiting in airport terminals. Those 5 a.m. wakeup calls are things of the past," wrote Kit Stier of Gannett News Service in 1982.

Mickey Klutts said that some A's players benefited financially from playing for Billy. "A lot of our guys were rewarded financially for '81," said Klutts. "Reading about how good we were, it was easy for complacency to creep into our psyche. Then you stop working as hard. A lot of us should have been very grateful to him. He got us some nice contracts, although it didn't last very long."

On February 6, 1982, an arbitrator awarded Rickey Henderson a $535,000 annual salary instead of $350,000 the A's had proposed. Henderson, who earned around $185,000 in 1981, became the highest-paid third-year player in baseball history. "We intend to pay them fairly, consistent with the overall payroll structure in baseball," Roy Eisenhardt said in 1981.

The A's headed into the winter pursuing a starting second baseman and depth. The A's success in 1981 rode mostly on the shoulders of only seven players: the outfield trio and the A's four aces. Being swept by the Yankees in the ALCS exposed holes—their lack of depth and experience. They were last in double plays for the second straight season with 74. Six players were used at second base in 1981: Babitt, McKay, Jeff Cox, Drumright, Doyle, and Stanley. Platooning Stanley and Picciolo at shortstop worked defensively. In 1981, the shortstop tandem made only eight errors, the fewest at shortstop in the league. Stanley had three; and Picciolo, five. Billy wanted stability at second base. As spring training drew closer, the A's acquired a second baseman: thirty-five-year-old Davey Lopes, a mainstay in the Dodgers infield since 1972. Lopes, coming off a record-breaking six-error performance in the 1981 World Series against the Yankees, had limited range at that point in his career.

The "Billy Ball" campaign lifted the 1981 A's into the national spotlight. Oakland players made public appearances coordinated by the A's new speakers bureau the new ownership had formed. "It made you proud to be Oakland A's fans," said Jackie Moore. "The fans felt a part of it and they were. When we'd go out to eat, fans would tell us how proud they were of us. That's what baseball's all about."

Other perks came the A's way as well. In February 1982, the A's participated in ABC's made-for-television special *Superteams* in Hawaii, having backed into the competition when the pennant-winning Yankees declined to participate. (After dispatching the A's in the ALCS, the Yankees had lost the 1981 World Series in six games to the LA Dodgers.) The show featured America's top teams competing against each other in beach-themed competitions. Henderson, Murphy, Gross, McKay, Norris, Keough, Stanley, and Newman represented the A's on the show. When the A's out-tugged the Cincinnati Bengals in the tug-of-war finale, despite being outweighed by the Bengals by 72 pounds, they won the *Superteams* crown. Each A's player received a purse of $14,100 for winning what was essentially a four-day, all-expenses-paid Waikiki vacation.

For Martin, the offseason was quiet. It was also marked by personal awards. During the annual banquet for the New York chapter of baseball writers on February 1, George Steinbrenner presented him with American League Manager of the Year honors from the Associated Press and United Press International. Billy had also been named Major League Manager of the Year by the *Sporting News*. Steinbrenner told the crowd that Martin "truly has to go down in history as one of the great managers in the game of baseball." Steinbrenner and Billy hugged and smiled in front of the flickering cameras. The bonhomie between the two carried over into Billy's remarks. He joked that he punched the marshmallow salesman in Minneapolis in 1979 because he was "knocking George Steinbrenner and the Yankees."

While Martin was winning awards, making jokes, and enjoying the adoration of A's fans, some critics were waiting for him to self-destruct. "I guess I've surprised everybody by making it through two years in a row now without any trouble," Martin said after winning his second consecutive Manager of the Year Award. "I'm very relaxed about the whole situation. Nobody tells me how to run my show. Nobody asks, 'Where was Billy thirty minutes ago?'"

Emerging baseball statistician Bill James, in his book, *The Bill James Baseball Abstract 1982,* released in April, was skeptical about Martin's shelf life in Oakland. "Martin creates an emotionally charged atmosphere," wrote James. "When you go into a clubhouse which is flat, stale and lethargic and charge that clubhouse with emotion, that's great. But to live in an emotionally charged atmosphere over a period of years is quite another matter. I don't see that it's going to be any easier here than it was anywhere else." James also wrote that "it is probably fair to say that Billy Martin can do more to help a team immediately than any other man in the world today, players included."

Fans would have to wait to see whether or not James's prediction would come true. Meantime, the A's made a number of changes ahead of the new season. They introduced new uniforms, connected their computer ticket system to local BASS and Ticketron outlets, and added an additional 1,500 bleacher seats at the Coliseum—which meant shortening the power alleys from 375 feet to 372 feet and moving dead center in from 400 to 397. Also, Andy Dolich continued his aggressive business-to-business season ticket sales campaign. In addition, the A's upgraded the antiquated telephone and ticket operations systems left over from the Finley era. This became a priority after the switchboard was unable to accommodate demand for tickets to the 1981 ALCS; only 17 percent of calls got through.

Spring training also had a different look for the A's in 1982. Not only did they move their spring headquarters from Scottsdale to Phoenix, it was crammed with players, instructors, and soaked with historic rainfall. It was a crowded organization-wide Billy Martin academy. The A's had bolstered their farm system and muscled up their scouting department thanks to a sizable budget from the Haases. They now employed twenty-six scouts, including twelve who worked full time under Dick Wiencek, director of A's scouting and minor league personnel. The A's had recently added their fifth and sixth minor-league affiliates—rookie-level clubs in Madison, Wisconsin, and Idaho Falls, Idaho.

Billy, who also served as the A's director of player development, decided he would evaluate his entire farm system that spring. The A's opened spring training with thirty-one pitchers and twenty-one catchers in the maxi-camp. The numbers swelled to 102 by February 19. Martin brought in nineteen coaches and instructors. With so many players, coaches, and instructors in camp, spring training resembled an NFL team in preseason. When players weren't waiting in long lines to take batting practice—with lines sometimes stretching back to the dugout—they were standing around doing nothing. Scott Foster, a non-roster catcher, was assigned No. 100. With that many players in camp, Martin could take a holistic look at the talent in the A's organization. But some thought the arrangement had backfired.

Wayne Hagin, one of the A's radio voices, said the chaos robbed the A's everyday players of work: "Because you put Billy Martin in that position, nobody got enough work in. He was out there trying to have everyone play in front of him, so he could evaluate them. We're talking lower-level players playing in spring-training games they had no business being in. Spring training was supposed to be for players like Norris and McCatty, and the everyday players, to get ready for Opening Day. Everyone lagged behind. It turned out to be a disaster for Billy Martin personally and the Oakland A's in 1982. They were not ready to start the season. No one had enough work because there was so much going on in spring training. There was too much evaluating instead of allowing players to get ready for the season."

Glenn Schwarz, who covered the A's in 1982, recalled the challenges of accommodating all the players in camp. "The pitchers didn't have enough mounds," recalled Schwarz. "The complexes were not as big as they are now. All they had was the main diamond at Phoenix Municipal Stadium and a small one behind it. It was ridiculous. None of the players could get in enough work."

Mike Norris remembered leaving spring training that year after having only pitched 14 exhibition innings. "He wanted all the minor-league guys to learn the system, so there were all these pitchers and players there. None of us got twenty innings in that spring. We didn't get our work in. We didn't realize that our arms were starting to break down in '81. It became inevitable in '82."

A's coach Jackie Moore defends the approach. Moore said that inviting so many players to camp that spring was a chance to give younger players in the system an opportunity to experience big league camp under the manager's supervision. The entire system could be indoctrinated at once to Billy's brand of baseball. Moore remembered arriving at 7:30 a.m. every morning that spring: "It was a jump-start for the organization. It was a matter of seeing a little bit of each player. We wanted the younger players in the system to feel important enough to be in big league camp. It was a great message to the organization. We wanted them to realize someone was watching them. There were groups of players leaving and coming in all day. The pitchers loved it because they could get their work in and go play golf or be with family. Don't ask me how, but we made it work."

Barry Weinberg—brought in by Billy in January as assistant trainer to help replace the retired A's trainer Joe Romo—recalled the challenges of accommodating so many players. "We had all those guys in a little tiny clubhouse," remembered Weinberg. "It took some imagination to put that many guys in that small of space."

Mother Nature added to the A's challenges that spring. Long stretches of fierce, stormy Arizona weather prevented them from working out consistently and wiped away several exhibition games. "We just didn't get the work in because of so many rainouts," said Mickey Klutts. Harsh rains in the Phoenix area puddled diamonds and rained out four of the A's first seven games of Cactus League play. Rain was so prevalent in Arizona that A's players helped spread tarps to keep Phoenix Municipal Stadium field playable. They became part-time groundskeepers. The rainouts were robbing the A's of games and workouts, causing concern. Players were never able to work out consistently. "We were rained out in spring training quite a bit and had zero indoor facilities for our pitchers," noted Mike Heath. "We couldn't work. Our pitchers couldn't work. The fields were terribly muddy. There were not enough mounds for guys to throw on and get their work in. Our pitchers came out of spring training with a limited number of innings. So our pitchers tried to pitch themselves into shape during the season. They weren't in shape."

McCatty surmised that because of the lack of consistent throwing and conditioning from that soggy spring, A's pitchers were unprepared to start the season. "None of us came out of spring training feeling good," said McCatty. "We had no inside mounds to do anything and we suddenly go into the season expected to pitch complete games. That spring was a precursor of what was going to happen: a slow slide downhill."

Another addition to the A's new tryout-atmosphere spring-training look was Martin's three-bedroom trailer behind the left-centerfield fence at Phoenix Municipal Stadium. Billy thought of having a private trailer to meet with his coaches because so many bodies were in camp. He made the trailer a private spot he could meet with his coaches and the media. Eddie Mathews and Art Fowler regularly cracked open beers inside the trailer, while Martin peeled and gobbled hardboiled eggs and held court every morning. A screen protected the trailer from balls flying over the fence. "Billy claimed he could see everything from there, but he really couldn't," said Schwarz. "He just sat in the trailer with his coaches and scouts. Billy was sort of isolated. He was pretty detached that spring."

The weather back home wasn't cooperating, either. Heavy Bay Area rains washed away the inaugural Bay Bridge Classic scheduled for April 3 and 4. It would have been the Giants' first ever appearance at the Coliseum. The teams made up the games by playing them in Arizona. "I'm concerned that we're not getting enough innings in," Martin said during the spring.

"But you can't fight the elements." The A's finished the soaked Cactus League with a record of 8–15, their worst since Martin took over the club in 1980. Most oddsmakers still listed A's as favorites to win the division for the second consecutive year. They figured the A's were the same club that won the division last season, but with additional depth. Despite the poor spring, it was hard to bet against Billy's bag of tricks. The expectation was for the A's to win again on the shoulders of a stellar starting rotation, though many insiders felt the Royals' acquisition of Vida Blue would take them over the top. Blue, who had a 2.45 ERA in 18 starts in 1981, had moved over to Kansas City in a six-player deal with the Giants.

As for the A's pitching in 1982, Martin opened the season with a four-man rotation of Langford, Norris, Keough, and McCatty, having optioned Brian Kingman to Triple-A Tacoma. Billy had dropped Kingman from the rotation after the strike ended in '81, and the pitcher had struggled badly in the spring. He was 0–3 with a 7.65 ERA.

Injuries also concerned the A's. Heath, Newman, Henderson, Rudi, Armas, Murphy, Picciolo, and Stanley all entered the season with an assortment of ailments. Hurt or not, A's players needed to pull it together for opening day.

The A's started the season at home against the Angels in front of 51,513 fans on April 6. It was the largest crowd ever for an Oakland A's season opener. One reason may have been the threat Martin had delivered to California earlier in the year. In the early 1980s, the A's and Angels had a history of bad blood—it was a rivalry marked by personal insults, charges of running up the score, and on-field brawls—and each team took special pleasure in beating the other. In February, Martin set the tone early on with this message to the Angels and his players. "We're not going to start a fight, but I'm putting the Angels on notice that we won't tolerate their petty intimidation," Billy declared. "If they start something, I'll tell my players to go and punch everybody's lights out. No rasslin' anymore. We're going to kick some ass."

Not surprisingly, it didn't take long for things to get testy. The Angels wanted revenge on the team they once bullied but that had owned them during the past two seasons. In 1980, the A's were 10–3 against the Angels; in 1981, Oakland won the season series 8–2. After the A's edged the Angels 3-2 in 11 innings on Opening Night, Angels' first baseman Rod Carew made a statement the next night to Norris and the A's. Carew, 3-for-24 against Norris in his career, banged two doubles and a single off him in less than five innings. After Carew's third hit, he told Norris "Nineteen eighty-one was over." Billy pulled Norris in the fifth and the Angels silenced the A's 7–0. Norris was the A's second consecutive starter not to go the distance. Uncharacteristically, Martin was grabbing the ball from his starting pitchers. The A's heralded starting staff, which had completed 154 games since 1980, finished off only one of the first ten games in 1982. In 1981, A's starters had completed nine of the first ten games of the season.

The A's bullpen was busy in April, playing in extra innings five times in the month, including three games lasting 16 innings and more than five hours. Billy used a lot of pitchers. The starters weren't finding the plate and Billy couldn't abide his pitchers allowing walks. Norris allowed 21 free passes in the month of April, Keough, 19, and McCatty, 18.

The A's 1981 record for the best start in baseball history with 11 consecutive wins lasted exactly one season. The Atlanta Braves exploded for 13 consecutive wins to start their 1982 campaign. Rickey Henderson, meanwhile, was setting the stage for greatness and another record-breaking season despite his club's uninspiring play. He compiled torrid offensive numbers as the catalyst of the A's lineup. The twenty-three-year-old A's star was living on the basepaths and stealing bases at an unprecedented rate. Henderson was reaching base almost 50 percent of the time through May, boasting a .444 on-base percentage. He collected 58 walks during that span.

A career .300 hitter, Henderson had stolen 100 bases in 1980, his first major-league season, thereby breaking Ty Cobb's 65-year-old American League record of 96. Early on in the 1982 season, Henderson was way ahead of that pace, having swiped 73 bases through June—a total he didn't reach in 1980 until September 8. Henderson was charging hard toward Lou Brock's 1974 all-time single-season stolen base record of 118, and was also on pace to break Babe Ruth's 1923 single-season record of 170 walks. As Henderson dashed from base to base and positioned himself in striking distance of the stolen base record, the chase created another narrative in the season. Henderson was on the heels of history.

The A's, 12–11, found themselves in fourth place and four games behind the division-leading Angels on May 1. The A's came off their most successful road trip through the East under Billy when they returned home 7–4 on May 6. But no series captured the collapse of the A's starters better than the one from May 6 to 9, when the Indians outscored Oakland 39–17 in a four-game series at the Coliseum. During the series, Langford couldn't survive the fourth, Norris was replaced in the third, and Keough was yanked after only 4 1/3 innings, as Oakland's starters combined for a total of only 16 innings in the four games.

Billy was running out of relievers and inserted Jeff Jones in the fifth inning of the Sunday afternoon Mother's Day series finale. In the Indians' 14–2 rout of the A's, Jones allowed eight runs in the ninth and was left to finish the game with no relief. Billy used up his entire eight-man staff in the series. Heath, a catcher, was warming up in the bullpen to pitch only if Jones' right arm fell off. The A's offense started games in a deep hole because the starters were knocked around early. "Hitting does not matter when you're down seven or eight runs all the time. Every time I go to the bullpen it's like putting kerosene in the fire," Billy said. The A's staff was in chaos and the defense committed 19 errors in the 11-game homestand. They committed an error in 17 games straight, a total of 28 during that stretch. A's pitchers led the majors in walks through May with 235.

The losses piled up and Billy's frustrations grew. He shook up the A's roster the next day. On May 10, the A's designated Rob Picciolo for assignment, demoted Jeff Jones to Triple-A Tacoma, and placed Mickey Klutts and

Jim Spencer on the disabled list. In corresponding moves, the A's brought up relievers Bo McLaughlin and Dennis Kinney along with designated hitter Danny Goodwin and shortstop Tony Phillips. With Picciolo's departure, Billy anointed Phillips as the club's future everyday shortstop. Phillips, a switch-hitter standing 5-foot-10 and weighing 160 pounds, was batting .350 for Tacoma. Phillips, acquired in the Bob Lacey deal with the Padres the previous season, had caught Billy's attention in spring training. Phillips reminded Billy of a shortstop he played with on the Oakland Oaks, Artie Wilson. Picciolo, a popular teammate, was traded to the Brewers for minor leaguers Johnny Evans and Mike Warren.

One glaring sign of the team's struggles: from May 4th to the 14th, the A's starters had a streak of ten consecutive outings without a single complete game. "This has been an unbelievable stretch for our pitchers," McCatty told reporters. "We can't believe it is happening to us, but it is." Many naysayers around baseball insisted Billy was paying the price for allowing his staff to complete so many games in the previous two seasons. Some A's pitchers partly blamed bringing in the fences at the Coliseum for their inflated earned run averages. McCatty was pitching with so much pain in his right shoulder that he only threw off-speed pitches in a home game start against the Tigers in late May. The pain wouldn't let him unleash a fastball. Norris, who'd lost the zip on his fastball, developed tendinitis in the rotator cuff of his right shoulder. Billy was so desperate for arms that he used relievers Beard and Jones to start two games each. He brought Langford in relief on July 11.

Some felt Martin's four-man bullpen was being overworked and everyone wondered what was wrong with Oakland's Four Aces. A's pitchers had allowed 354 walks in 88 games by the All-Star break. "They got off to a decent start and they were certainly looking like a contending team the first month or two of the '82 season," said Glenn Schwarz. "But then, piece by piece, the pitchers fell apart."

The A's, the most exciting team since 1980, were collapsing. When fans booed Billy in Oakland for yanking Norris out of a game in April, Phil Pepe, a columnist for the *New York Daily News,* sensed Martin's reign with the A's was coming to an end. Pepe noted the ungratefulness of the booing Oakland fans. He reminded readers of Billy's impact in rescuing the franchise from baseball hell. "This is the only man who pulled the A's—hell, the whole city of Oakland—up by the scruff of their necks, who brought them back from the dead, who turned around a moribund franchise," wrote Pepe on May 4, 1982.

But Martin was running out of ideas. "When they started going down the tubes in '82 while Billy was running the team, they really didn't have a lot of moves they could have made," noted Bruce Jenkins. "They had to keep the great outfield and the pitchers. They were kind of running out of ways to improve the team. As a general manager, Billy was kind of strapped."

Fans were still filling the Coliseum to see Billy's show. Through thirty home dates, 753,081 fans passed through the A's turnstiles, down 88,540 from the 1981 season. The A's passed the one-million mark in attendance for the second consecutive season on July 7 against the Yankees, totaling 1,013, 679 in 43 home dates.

On the field, the A's offense was sputtering so much that on June 23, Billy told Murphy, the team captain, to pick out the lineup from a coach's cap. Nevertheless, Martin reached the 1,000-win milestone as manager on July 8 at home against the Yankees, making him only one of four active managers at the time to achieve that milestone.

With both starting pitching and the offense underperforming, Rickey Henderson was the A's highlight of 1982. He had 84 stolen bases in 88 games at the All-Star break, 35 games ahead of Lou Brock's 1974 record pace. Henderson's popularity as a bona fide star grew nationally. Fans voted him to start the 53rd All-Star Game on July 13 in Montreal, the first Midsummer classic outside the US. Henderson was the A's only All-Star representative. Billy, the AL manager, tapped Fowler and Moore to join him in Montreal as coaches. Henderson, leading off for the American League, collected three hits, stole a base, and scored a run, but the National League defeated the American League 4–1.

By July 28, the A's, 41–60, were in fifth place, 16 games behind the first-place Angels and 19 games under .500. The club had lost 12 of 13 at the Coliseum during one stretch. Billy began publicly threatening to fine any players arriving late to games and missing signs. After some discarded bubble gum in the A's dugout stuck to his spikes, Billy ordered Frank Ciensczyk to remove gum from the clubhouse. He was taking the losses personally. He helped make some of his players millionaires and felt they had lost the hunger. The A's disappointing season quenched the enthusiasm of some fans. The crowd of autograph seekers who once mobbed the player's parking lot after games had dwindled.

Norris, who said that Billy had made him a millionaire, explained how the season got away from the A's. They could never gain any traction in the standings. "Billy wasn't as hands-on that season," said Norris. "He wasn't at the park as early as he used to be. He pretty much left things up to the coaches. Then our arms were shot. It was just a bad year. All the karma had left the building."

When Billy benched Murphy, his team captain and two-time Gold Glove center fielder on August 11 in Seattle for failing to flag down a Richie Zisk two-run double in the seventh the night before, it bothered many A's players, including Henderson. Murphy was further incensed that he got wind of the benching from coach Charlie Metro instead of the manager. "[Martin] was wearing on people after one loss after another," said Bruce Jenkins. "It got to the point that players were telling us off the record that it was getting out of hand. We all wrote stories at one point quoting anonymous sources. Nothing bugged Billy more than anonymous sources ripping him."

Despite the clubhouse turmoil, Henderson's chase of the stolen base record became the A's only drawing muscle in Oakland. Henderson said publicly he wanted to break the record at home, where he grew up, and A's fans wanted to be there to witness history.

On August 19, thanks to a crowd of 15,461 on a Thursday afternoon, the A's shattered their all-time franchise record for attendance by drawing 1,402,266 with 17 home dates left. The Kansas City A's held the previous record by drawing 1,393,054 in 1955.

But on the same day the A's set the record for its most attended season ever, Billy was walking an emotional tightrope. Billy and some of his coaches battered his plush Coliseum office after a 10–6 loss to the Milwaukee Brewers. The A's allowed five unearned runs in the game and some financial matters were weighing heavily on Billy. He was reportedly upset that he didn't have an attendance clause in his contract like other A's players had, and felt he deserved a bonus for bringing in so many fans. Billy also reportedly had a tax lien of $100,000 being garnished from his check and asked the A's owners for a loan to satisfy the lien against his sixth-year salary. The problem was, he'd signed only a five-year contract. Martin reportedly took out his frustration on his office. As Thomas Boswell put it in the *Washington Post,* "On Thursday here, after his A's had allowed six [actually five] unearned runs in a loss, Martin closed his door and went 10 rounds with his office. Martin had his fists. The office had pictures, furniture and walls. The office won." Martin had broken and bruised several knuckles.

Wayne Hagin, who hosted a postgame show on KSFO, the A's flagship station, was interviewing a Brewers player after the game in a supply room next to Billy's office. He heard chaos next door: "I heard yelling and stuff breaking. I walked inside the clubhouse when I was finished with my interview and saw Billy and some of his coaches taking down Billy's photos with the Yankees off the walls in his office. He was taking a bat and breaking things. He broke the television and toilet. He destroyed everything in sight. I was thinking to myself, My gosh, he takes losing hard. But I later found out it had nothing to do with the game at all. It had to do with him asking the A's for a $100,000 loan so he could pay his back taxes. But Eisenhardt and Sandy Alderson wouldn't do it, and I think Billy knew at that point he would not be coming back to the Oakland A's."

Peter Golenbock, the author of several books on Billy, said that what led to Billy's departure in Oakland was a phone call from Steinbrenner. "Unfortunately, the problem for Oakland was the day George called him and said, 'Billy, if you can get yourself fired from Oakland, I'd like you to come back to the Yankees.' Right after that conversation, he tore up his office. He got himself fired and returned to the Yankees."

Eisenhardt had Billy's office repainted the next day. "That's the price I have to pay. I like Billy a lot," he said.

Mike Heath recalled the day that marked Billy's departure in Oakland. "Clete [Boyer] came to McCatty, Murphy, and I, telling us that Billy wanted us to hang around after the game," recalled Heath. "When the clubhouse emptied and we were still sitting there, Clete told us Billy was not ready to see us yet. By the time he talked to us, it was late. We all sat down in his office. Billy was upset and his office was a little torn up. He was pissed. I don't blame him. That's who he was. The only photo not taken down was one of he and Mickey Mantle. He talked to each of us about how he thought we would be as players. He told us how he felt about us.

"When we left his office, the three of us decided to give him a departure he would never forget. So when he was showering in his on office, we went in there and beat the hell out of him. We were pushing him down, throwing ice water on him, and talking shit to him. We loved him. It was a gesture of love."

McCatty also witnessed Billy and his coaches destroy his office. "We were sitting there while he was doing it," said McCatty. "He punched the mirror in his bathroom and cut his hand wide open. That broke some of his fingers and it was bleeding like crazy. Billy was never good at holding his emotions."

Billy arrived at the Coliseum the next day with a splint on his left ring finger and a bandage on two fingers of his right hand. "I'm getting smarter as I get older," Billy said the next day. "I finally punched something that couldn't sue me." To lighten the mood, Dave McKay came on the field with all ten of his fingers taped up in splints. "Hey, skip, wanna go bowling tonight?" McKay asked Martin. The incident led many to believe that Billy would not be returning as A's manager for the 1983 season. "Billy was having a lot of off-field issues," said Glenn Schwarz. "He had tax issues and financial things were weighing on his mind. The last month of the '82 season was pretty ugly."

Henderson, meanwhile, was closing in on stolen base immortality fast. After stealing No. 100 against the Mariners on August 2, he became the first player in history to steal 100 bases in a season twice. Henderson was being pulled everywhere. He made appearances on NBC's the *Today Show* and ABC's *Good Morning America* as he approached the mark. On August 26, in Milwaukee, he stole base No. 118, tying Lou Brock's eight-year-old record. The next night, on August 27, with Wally Haas on hand at County Stadium sitting next to Henderson's mom, Bobbie, and fiancée, Pamela Palmer, he obliterated the record. In the third inning with two out, Brewers' pitcher George "Doc" Medich walked Henderson on four pitches.

While Henderson took his lead from first, Medich threw four times to first to keep him close. Henderson took off to second on Medich's first pitch—a pitchout—to Gross and slid ahead of catcher Ted Simmons's throw for No. 119, shattering Brock's record only 129 games into the season. Henderson, the new king of steals, pulled up the second-base bag and lifted it over his head. He met Murphy near the mound to celebrate and kissed his forehead. Play was halted for five minutes as fans applauded him and Brock and MacPhail congratulated him on the field. He stole three more bases in the A's 5-4 loss, increasing his total to 122. He was named American League Player of the Week. A sore shoulder made Henderson a part-time player the remainder of the season after he broke the record. He finished the season with 130 stolen bases. Billy was pleased the stolen base record now belonged to an American Leaguer.

After Henderson broke the record, the spotlight completely left the A's. By September, some Bay Area newspapers stopped sending reporters on the road to cover the team. Kit Stier of the *Oakland Tribune* was the only A's beat writer covering the club on the road. For a September 7 home game against Toronto, the A's drew their lowest crowd since 1980, when only 8,403 fans showed up.

Billy's frustrations continued. On September 15, he left in the fifth inning of the second game of a doubleheader in Toronto with the A's down 11–2. Before leaving the clubhouse, he flipped over the postgame spread prepared for the players. He told visiting clubhouse staff to hold the spread after the players were on the field playing for eight hours. The A's dramatically tied the game in the ninth, but lost 12–11. Billy was not there to see the comeback. Two weeks later in Texas, on September 29, with four games left in the miserable season, Billy was late. In Billy's absence, the players were horse playing on the field during batting practice. Kit Stier recalled the scene:

> Billy hadn't shown up to the ballpark and the team was on the field. Jackie Moore ran batting practice and Clete Boyer usually waited for Billy in his office to get the lineup card. The players were screwing around and weren't taking it seriously. They were goofing off in the outfield and not following the prescribed routine. Jackie was getting madder and madder—even yelling at them a couple times. He finally pulled the team off the field.

The season couldn't end soon enough for the 1982 A's. Billy later said he arrived late because he was with Mantle watching his son, Billy Jr., play baseball.

After the A's final home game of 1982, a 5–4 victory over the Royals on September 26, players rushed straight to the clubhouse to start packing for the final road trip of the season. Some players were embarrassed of how they played in front of their home fans and felt they let them down after two consecutive magical seasons. The A's were 36–45 at the Coliseum in 1982. It suddenly became a very emotional scene. Fans rose to their feet and kept clapping. While A's players were in the clubhouse, the grateful and energetic crowd was chanting, "We want the A's!" They demanded an encore, so players marched back on the field and saluted the fans. The A's finished with a season attendance of 1,735,493. In seventy-eight dates, they averaged 22,250. The fifth-place A's finished the 1982 season with a record of 68–94, the lowest finish in the standings ever for a Billy Martin team in a full season. They trailed the first-place Angels by 25 games.

The A's sour season didn't stop the revitalized farm system from producing. The A's six minor-league affiliates played at a .635 clip in 1982. Each of them—Idaho Falls (42–28), Medford (53–17), Madison (87–52), Modesto (94–46), West Haven (86–54), and Tacoma (84–59)—remarkably all finished first in their perspective leagues. Tacoma finished in second place in the second half of the Pacific Coast League season. The A's farm system was becoming a force.

16

THE STEINBRENNER SIREN

"I really think Billy wanted to stay here. I don't think he self-destructs, as some people are saying. He liked it here and wanted to finish his career with the A's . . . but sometimes things develop."
—MICKEY MORABITO, A'S TRAVELING SECRETARY AND
BILLY'S FRIEND, OCTOBER 1982

IN LATE SEPTEMBER, REPORTS SURFACED THAT THE YANKEES AND Indians received permission from the A's to interview Billy about a managerial position. Billy had three years remaining on his five-year contract, but Roy Eisenhardt insisted he wouldn't block Billy from a more attractive opportunity. "We won't stand in the way of Billy if he wants to leave," Eisenhardt said at the time. Billy made it clear he wasn't looking for another job. There were rumors that he would be relieved of his general manager duties after the season. "He wanted the title and acclaim, but the problem was that his focus and real genius was on the game," said John Hickey.

In mid-October, the *Chicago Sun-Times* broke a story that Martin would be leaving the A's to become the next manager of the Indians. He would work under Gabe Paul, one of his former bosses in New York. Former Indians manager Dave Garcia was forced to resign after the season. The Indians always toyed with bringing Billy in. The move never materialized.

Billy returning to the Yankees and reuniting with Steinbrenner was far more likely.

The Yankees, 79–83, finished the 1982 season in fifth place with Clyde King replacing Gene Michael as manager in early August. Steinbrenner needed a sparkplug manager to ignite his club back to the World Series. He knew firsthand about Billy's turnaround abilities. Steinbrenner fired him after the marshmallow salesman incident in 1979. Charlie Finley gave Billy another shot when he hired him on February 21, 1980. Returning to the Yankees at Steinbrenner's urging would be leverage Billy thrived on. "To come back to New York for a third term as a manager would be great vindication for him, especially when it appears that George Steinbrenner has come crawling on hands and knees, begging him to return. How could Billy resist?" wrote Phil Pepe in the *Daily News*.

Ray Negron, a former Yankees clubhouse attendant and friend of Steinbrenner and Martin, described their relationship. "The boss [Steinbrenner] loved Billy very much," said Negron. "He would not have hired him five times if he didn't. The boss always checked on Billy to make sure he was okay. They couldn't live with each other and couldn't live without one another. Billy could get very mad at the boss and call him every name in the book, but if he ever heard someone talk bad about the boss, he might slap you. No one loved the boss more than Billy in the game of baseball."

Martin's next managerial stop was the buzz of the 1982 World Series between St. Louis and Milwaukee and everyone wondered where the combustible, franchise resurrecting, gunslinger would end up. Amid the flying rumors, Billy said convincingly he wanted to stay put and had unfinished business in Oakland. "I have no deals with anybody at this time," Billy told the Associated Press in October 1982. "As far as I'm concerned, I'm staying with Oakland. I have a five-year contract with three more years to go and I intend to honor it. I got my hands full right now." Many figured, though, Martin was itching to manage the Yankees again. "The honeymoon was over," said Jackie Moore. "In the back of his mind, I really think he realized he had an opportunity to go back to New York."

The A's freed Billy to manage the Yankees when they fired him on October 20, the day of Game 7 of the World Series. Ted Robinson, working for KCBS radio in San Francisco, broke the firing on the air. "It wasn't a day that you're supposed break news like that," recalled Robinson, a prolific sportscaster today. "It was a national story. The timing wasn't great because it was on the seventh game of the World Series, but for some reason, the organization chose the timing."

Judge Eddie Sapir, Billy's longtime attorney and friend, flew to Oakland to meet with Roy Eisenhardt to discuss Billy's future prior to the firing being announced. Billy had gone hunting. Sapir revealed how Billy's departure unfolded: "Roy was certainly looking out for Billy. I never considered it a firing or dismissal. It had nothing to do with where the team finished or Billy's professionalism as a manager. It had nothing to do with his drinking. Roy told me, 'We think we need to make change for the sake of change. We don't think we're going to get a better manager and we hope we can bring Billy back in some capacity down the road.' Roy always gave me permission to talk with anyone we wanted. We had a choice between the Indians and the Yankees. It was a no-brainer for Billy. He was going to the Yankees."

Billy himself knew Billy Ball had run its course and the Haases were committed to building the A's through their farm system. "We stunk that season," said Mickey Klutts. "The attendance started to drop, and the billboards started coming down. It's really hard to keep a high level of play. Plus, we had some distractions. I think Billy wanted to go back to New York."

Eisenhardt and Sapir made Billy's exit as amicable as possible. Billy's record was 215–218 in his three years managing the A's, including the abbreviated 1981 season. Eisenhardt recalled the thought behind the firing: "With the team underperforming in 1982, I made it clear that we were entering a rebuilding mode, and Billy and I both understood implicitly that was not his preference at that point in his career. It was clear we needed to rebuild gradually through our minor-league system and not the free agency market. Billy understood that and our parting was cordial, as he returned to the Yankees. The Yankees intrigued him and my feeling was that was where Billy wanted to go in preference to a lengthy rebuilding period in Oakland. After we terminated his employment in late 1982, he signed with the Yankees."

In a statement released by Sapir after the firing, he indicated Billy had no hard feelings toward the A's and thanked ownership. "Most of all," said Sapir, "he would like to thank all of the great Oakland fans for their tremendous support. They saved baseball in the Oakland area. He hopes they will continue to support the A's. Seeing them come back to the ballpark was Billy's biggest thrill in baseball."

The man responsible for bringing Billy Martin to Oakland in the first place had a different take. Shortly after Martin's firing was announced, Charlie Finley told the *San Francisco Examiner* that he was the one who assembled the cast Billy used to turn the A's around. "He didn't turn the franchise around," Finley said of Billy. "I had already turned it around myself, with the players I had there. And I wouldn't have made half the deals they made after I left."

Martin received the siren call to return to New York. On January 11, 1983, Steinbrenner brought Billy back for a third time as manager. When asked why he would want to manage for the man who'd fired him twice already, Martin reflected on his relationship with the tempestuous Yankees owner. "There are a lot of good points about him, and there are a lot of bad points about him. There's one good point that I especially like about him. He wants the Yankees to win. He wants them to be the best, and he'd give his whole heart and soul for that. In that way, we're alike. That's why I came back, and that's why I think it's going to be different this time."

Billy managed the Yankees to a third-place finish in 1983 and was fired by Steinbrenner for the third time after the season. Back in Oakland, the progressive-thinking Eisenhardt, meanwhile, brought in forty-six-year-old

Steve Boros, the Montreal Expos' third-base coach, as the new A's manager. Eisenhardt was impressed with the intellect of Boros, who had graduated from the University of Michigan with a degree in literature. Boros promoted his use of the Apple II computer to help his managing strategy. The computer offered Boros instant access to endless amounts of data and statistics about the A's, opponents, and prospects. He reviewed printouts before and after each game. The data shaped his decisions and eliminated managing on a hunch. The A's were one of the first baseball teams to embrace the computer. But players were very skeptical about how influential the computer printouts had become in the organization. They scoffed at the idea of a computer dictating the lineup. "Billy Ball" gave way to "Computer Ball." With the departure of Billy, Sandy Alderson, rising fast in the organization, was named the A's new general manager.

EPILOGUE

ORGANIZATION OF THE YEAR

The Oakland A's were named *Baseball America*'s Organization of the Year in 1982, Billy's final season managing the A's. The prestigious award considered the total organizational body. The A's six farm clubs each finished in first place in 1982.

During the winter, the A's traded Tony Armas and Jeff Newman to the Boston Red Sox for third-baseman Carney Lansford, Gary Hancock, a first baseman, and a minor leaguer. The move finally opened the door for young outfielder Mike Davis to crack the A's outfield in right. They released Mickey Klutts and traded Cliff Johnson to Toronto. In the winter of 1984, the A's traded superstar Rickey Henderson to the New York Yankees for Jay Howell, Jose Rijo, Eric Plunk, Stan Javier, and Tim Birtsas.

The A's next reached the postseason in 1988 under the leadership of manager Tony La Russa. The stacked A's dominated baseball, making three consecutive World Series appearances from 1988 to 1990. They brought a World Series title back to Oakland in 1989 when they swept the San Francisco Giants in the earthquake-interrupted series. Down in the farm, the A's produced back-to-back back-to-back Rookie of the Year Award winners Jose Canseco, Mark McGwire, and Walt Weiss from 1986 to 1988 in that order.

After two more managerial stints with the Yankees—in 1985 and 1988—and almost two months after the A's captured their fourth world championship since moving to Oakland, Billy Martin, sixty-one, was killed in a one-vehicle car crash on a icy country road near his Binghamton, New York, home on Christmas Day, 1989. Joan E. Downey, Billy's eighty-eight-year-old mother, had died back home in Berkeley on December 10 and he had recently returned home for her funeral.

Billy, a special advisor to George Steinbrenner at the time, was one of the most popular figures in New York and one of the brilliant game managers of his time. Billy won division titles with Minnesota in 1969, Detroit in 1972, and Oakland in 1981. He led the Yankees to a World Series title in 1977 and American League pennant in 1976. There were reports that Billy would be returning to manage the Yankees a sixth time.

The A's released a statement after Billy's tragic death: "The A's organization is deeply saddened by the death of Billy Martin. Baseball has lost one of its unique and colorful personalities, and Oakland has lost a friend."

ACKNOWLEDGMENTS

First, heartfelt thanks to my Heavenly Father for your grace on this journey.

I've always considered "Billy Ball" an exciting era of Oakland A's history. But only when I placed a microscope on those years did I fully understand the significance. Thanks to Lyons Press, this amazing story has turned into a book. To Niels Aaboe, my editor at Lyons who gave my book proposal a publishing home, thank you for your razor-sharp guidance. To Stephanie Scott, another Lyons editor, thank you for sending along the proposal to the right person. To Ken Samelson, thank you for copy-editing the manuscript and your attention to detail.

To my brothers, Robert Tafoya and Richard Rodriguez, thank you for your love and support. To my nieces, Ava and Jeanette, and nephews, Ricky, Jeremy, and Robbie, keep making your uncle proud.

To Josephine Tafoya-Peraza, my aunt, and the rock of Tafoya town, thank you for your support, encouragement and always holding it down.

To the wonderful scribes who covered "Billy Ball" and shared their time with me to capture the story: Dave Newhouse, Bruce Jenkins, Kit Stier, John Hickey, Randy Galloway, Glenn Schwarz, Stephanie Salter, and Alan Fallick.

To Catherine Aker, the A's fantastic vice president of communications and community, many thanks for the organization's efforts in engaging the community. They will come.

Photographer Ron Riesterer is a Bay Area treasure and has delivered some wonderful photos in this book. Billy Martin Jr. and Judge Eddie Sapir were class acts and always generous with their time.

The late Michael Hamilburg, my first literary agent, landed my first book deal in 2007and gave me a platform. Hamilburg was a well-connected Hollywood agent and producer, but he took on first-time authors. I was one of them. To any aspiring writers, it only takes one "Yes!"

My sincere appreciation to the library staffs of *Sports Illustrated, Time,* the *Sporting News, Sport, Life,* the *Oakland Tribune,* the *San Francisco Chronicle,* the *San Francisco Examiner,* the *New York Daily News,* the *New York Times,* the *Dallas Morning News,* the *Detroit Free Press,* the Associated Press, Gannett News Service, the *Santa Rosa Press Democrat,* the *Chicago Tribune,* the *Chicago Daily News,* the *Boston Globe,* the *Daily Review,* the *Los Angeles Times,* the Oakland Public Library, *Beachwoodreporter.com, ESPN.com,* and *MLB.com.*

Special thanks to these individuals: Ken Korach, Carl Steward, Bud Geracie, Roy Eisenhardt, Wayne Hagin, Paul Gutierrez, Jorge Leon, David Beach, John Horne, Pam Kessler, John Underhill, Andy Dolich, Pete Gonzlaez, Seth Honeycutt, Hector Gomez, and Zdravomir Staykov.

Writing a book is like opening a business. Besides writing, researching and interviewing, you're emailing countless interview requests. Much appreciation to those who helped me secure them: Scott MacDonald, Matt Chisholm, Cheryl Zeldin, Kevin O'Brien, Josh Rawitch, Cory Parsons, Frank Pace, Jameson Lange, Bud Kennedy, and Janet Shields-Scott.

Beginning when Walter A. Haas Jr. purchased the A's in 1980, the Haas family propelled "Billy Ball" to the next galaxy. Working with the Haas family, specifically Denis Chicola, to set up an interview with Roy Eisenhardt for the book was wonderful. Roy was very cooperative and helpful. Everyone I interviewed in the book revered the Haas family and described how they transformed the A's into the best organization in baseball.

NOTES ON RESEARCH AND SOURCES

I NEVER KNEW THE SIGNIFICANCE OF THE BILLY BALL ERA OF Oakland A's baseball until I started researching a game at the Oakland-Alameda County Coliseum played on April 17, 1979. The A's drew a tiny crowd of 653 that night. The embarrassing crowd was a symptom of the A's decline in Oakland. But only ten months later, Billy Martin arrived and shook the franchise and city with his exciting brand of baseball.

While writing my first book, *Bash Brothers,* in 2004, I conducted hundreds of interviews. Many of the former players and team officials I interviewed stressed that 1980 was a crucial year in A's history. Charlie Finley had hired Billy right before the season. One player told me the A's transformation as a franchise in the 1980s started when Billy arrived in 1980. The late Dick Wiencek spoke with me for hours about the infant stages of the A's transformation into baseball's best organization. It persuaded me to delve deeper inside the baseball fever Billy brought to Oakland. Some of the research for this book started as early as 2004.

Even though the A's never won a World Series championship under Billy, how Billy Ball brought fans back was miraculous. Billy's ability to revive a sagging fan base is captured in the book. Even as a ten-year-old growing up in San Leandro, California, a city neighboring Oakland, I felt the excitement of Billy Ball. It hypnotized me. Billy Martin's face was everywhere. He brought electricity and hope. Billy Ball compelled Walter A. Haas Jr. to buy the A's from Charlie Finley and keep them in the city.

I was thrilled to encounter the same enthusiasm when I interviewed people for this book. Stephanie Salter, Bruce Jenkins, Dave Newhouse, Glenn Schwarz, Kit Stier, and John Hickey, talented scribes who covered the magical Billy Ball era, were very accommodating and generous with their time. It was fascinating to hear how the Bay Area story exploded nationally, drawing reporters from all parts of the country. Billy Ball was a Billy Martin reality show. They were there when he notoriously held court with the media. They saw the crowds grow.

Many principals interviewed emphasized that Billy Ball was a romance with the city. The scrappy, hard-nosed A's connected with the blue-collar community. The young A's were having the time of their lives. Many of them were anxious to share their Billy Martin encounters with me almost forty years later. They were with Billy, behind the scenes, at home, in the dugout, in the clubhouse, in bars, and on airplanes in every city.

I spoke with former players, executives, coaches, broadcasters, clubhouse insiders, scouts, advertising executives, owners, beat writers, and trainers. Complementing the interviews, digitized newspaper archives helped me confirm dates and times. I was excited to speak with Billy Martin Jr. about his father's time in Oakland.

Judge Eddie Sapir, Billy's longtime friend and advisor, offered me a rich glimpse into Billy.

The following is a list of people interviewed once or multiple times for the book:

Billy Martin Jr., Judge Eddie Sapir, Roy Eisenhardt, Andy Dolich, Rod Carew, Mike Norris, Jackie Moore, Mike Heath, Mickey Klutts, Brian Kingman, Bob Lacey, Dave Heaverlo, Jeff Newman, Jim Essian, Steve McCatty, Rene Lachemann, Tommy John, Bob Lurie, Stephanie Salter, Dave Newhouse, Bruce Jenkins, Randy Galloway, Barry Weinberg, Hal Ramey, Kit Stier, Rodney Scott, Glenn Schwarz, John Hickey, Ray Negron, Matt Levine, Sam Spear, Ted Robinson, David Rubinstein, Nancy Finley, Peter Golenbock, Ken Phelps, George "Doc" Medich, Steve Dunning, Stan

Bahnsen, Ernie Camacho, Alan Fallick, Ray Ratto, John Underhill, Mark Ibanez, Krazy George Henderson, Wayne Hagin, Rich Silverstein, Jeff Goodby, and Mike Morgan.

BIBLIOGRAPHY

Allen, Maury. *Damn Yankee: The Billy Martin Story*. New York: Times Books, 1980

Appel, Marty. *Casey Stengel: Baseball's Greatest Character*. New York: Doubleday, 2017

Creamer, W. Robert. *Stengel: His Life and Times*. Lincoln, Nebraska: University of Nebraska Press, 1996

Dickey, Glenn. *Champions: The Story of the First Two Oakland A's Dynasties and the Building of the Third*. Chicago, Triumph Books, 2002

Falkner, David. *The Last Yankee*. New York: Simon & Schuster, 1992

Finley, Nancy. *Finley Ball: How Two Baseball Outsiders Turned the Oakland A's into a Dynasty and Changed the Game Forever*. New York: Regnery, 2016

Fischer, David. *The New York Yankees of the 1950s: Mantle, Stengel, Berra and a Decade of Dominance*. Guilford, Connecticut: Lyons Press, 2019

Golenbock, Peter. *Dynasty: The New York Yankees, 1949–1964*. Chicago, Contemporary Books, 2000

———*Wild, High and Tight: The Life and Death of Billy Martin*. New York: Antenna Books, 1994

Green, G. Michael, and Roger D. Launius. *Charlie Finley: The Outrageous Story of Baseball's Super Showman.* New York: Walker Books, 2010

Hunter, Jim, and Armen Keteyian. *Catfish: My Life in Baseball.* New York: McGraw-Hill, 1988

Jackson, Reggie, and Kevin Baker. *Becoming Mr. October.* New York: Doubleday, 2013

James, Bill. *The Bill James Baseball Abstract, 1982.* New York: Ballantine Books, 1982

John, Tommy, and Dan Valenti. *T. J.: My 26 Years in Baseball.* New York: Bantam Books, 1991

Jordan, David M. *The A's: A Baseball History.* Jefferson, North Carolina: McFarland & Company, 2014

Kahn, Roger. *October Men: Reggie Jackson, George Steinbrenner, Billy Martin and the Yankees' Miraculous Finish in 1978.* New York: Harcourt, 2003

————*The Era, 1947-1957: When the Yankees, the Giants, and the Dodgers Ruled the World.* Lincoln, Nebraska: Bison Books, 2002

Katz, Jeff. *Split Season: 1981: Fernandomania, the Bronx Zoo and the Strike that Saved Baseball.* New York: Thomas Dunne Books, 2015

Kerr, Jon. *Calvin: Baseball's Last Dinosaur: An Authorized Biography.* New York: William. C. Brown, 1990

Libby, Bill. *Charlie O. and the Angry A's.* New York: Doubleday, 1975

Martin, Billy, and Peter Golenbock. *Number 1.* New York: Delacorte Press, 1980

Martin, Billy, and Phil Pepe. *BillyBall.* New York: Doubleday, 1987

Masters, Todd. *The 1972 Detroit Tigers.* Jefferson, North Carolina: McFarland & Company, 2010

Negron, Ray, and Sally Cook. *Yankee Miracles: Life with the Boss and the Bronx Bombers,* New York, Liveright, 2012

Pennington, Bill. *Billy Martin: Baseball's Flawed Genius.* New York: Mariner Books, 2016

————*Chumps to Champs: How the Worst Team in Yankees History Led to the '90s Dynasty.* New York: Houghton Mifflin Harcourt, 2019

Pepe, Phil. *The Ballad of Billy and George: The Tempestuous Baseball Marriage of Billy Martin and George Steinbrenner.* Guilford, Connecticut: Lyons Press, 2008

Piniella, Lou, and Bill Madden. *Lou: Fifty Years of Kicking Dirt, Playing Hard, and Winning Big in the Sweet Spot of Baseball.* New York, Harper, 2018

Shropshire, Mike. *Seasons in Hell: With Billy Martin, Whitey Herzog and "The Worst Baseball Team in History"—The 1973-75 Texas Rangers.* Lincoln, Nebraska: Bison Books, 2005

Silverman, Matthew. *Swinging '73: Baseball's Wildest Season,* Guilford, Connecticut: Lyons Press, 2013

Slusser, Susan. *100 Things A's Fans Should Know & Do Before They Die.* Chicago: Triumph Books, 2015

Tafoya, Dale. *Bash Brothers: A Legacy Subpoenaed.* Dulles, Virginia: Potomac Books, 2008

Turbow, Jason. *Dynastic, Bombastic, Fantastic: Rollie, Catfish, and Charlie Finley's Swingin' A's.* New York: Houghton Mifflin Harcourt, 2017

Newspaper/Wire Services

Associated Press
Berkeley Gazette
Boston Globe
Chicago Daily News
Daily Review
Detroit Free Press
Gannett News Service
Los Angeles Times
Newsday
New York Daily News
New York Post
New York Times
Oakland Tribune
San Francisco Chronicle
San Francisco Examiner
Santa Cruz Sentinel
Seattle Times
Washington Post

Magazines

Baseball America
Inc.
Life
People
Sport
Sports Illustrated
Sporting News
Time

Videos/Broadcasts

ABC, American League Division Series, 1981
PBS Index File, *Billy Martin and the Twins,* 2019

Mickey Mantle, *Mickey Mantle: The American Dream Comes to Life,* 1990
MLB Network, *Billy,* 2017
MLB Vault, 1952 World Series, 1952
NBC, American League Championship Series, 1981
Oakland A's, Billy Ball commercials, 1981–82
WFAA, Martin on being fired by Rangers, 1975
WPIX, Billy Martin Memorial, 1990
YES Network, *Yankeeography: Billy Martin,* 2018

WEBSITES

Baseball Almanac (baseball-almanac.com)
Baseball-Reference.com (baseball-reference.com/)
Destination America (pbs.org/destinationamerica)
National Baseball Hall of Fame (baseballhall.org)
Society for American Baseball Research (sabr.org)

INDEX

ABC, 171, 184, 195, 208

Adams, Red, 50–51

Air Force, 137, 146

Alameda County Athletic League, 47

Alameda County Land Development Committee, 29

Alderson, Sandy, 123, 146, 207, 215

All-Star Games, 87, 177–78, 204

Alyce, Stephanie, 128

Amburg, Van, 37

American Association, 27, 48

American Express, 152

American League, 15, 18, 26, 33, 35, 75, 90, 140, 161, 188, 205
    Championship Series, 57, 73, 164, 178, 185
    clubs, 6–7, 69
    Comeback Player of the Year, 59, 139
    Cy Young Award, 13, 139
    East, 180, 185
    leadership, 6, 17, 27, 29, 31, 34, 57, 71–72, 115, 117
    Manager of the Year, 59, 140, 191, 195
    MVP, 59, 62, 157, 192
    pennants, 119, 218
    Pitcher of the Month, 169
    Player of the Week, 164, 168, 208
    Player of the Year, 191
    records, 136, 201
    Rookie of the Year, 53, 59, 169, 217
    West, 19, 55, 86, 96, 99, 180–81

American University, 149

Anderson, Don, 141

Anderson, Sparky, 62, 100

Angels, California, 15, 23, 60, 71, 86, 93, 96, 98–99, 129–30, 135, 139, 155, 159, 163–64, 172, 200–02, 205, 210

Antelope Valley High School, 137

Apple II, 215

Arizona, 8, 27, 65, 79, 91, 198–99

Arizona Instructional League, 162

Arizona State University, 18–19, 135, 137, 155

Arizona-Texas League, 49

Armas, Tony, 21, 83, 87, 95, 137, 160, 191, 193, 217

Armstrong, Victor, 56

Arrows, Maryland, 149

A's, Kansas City, 15, 19, 26, 29, 52, 54, 73, 117, 129

A's, Oakland
   "Billy Ball." See "Billy Ball"
   and Billy Martin, 3, 6, 8, 24, 69, 71–79, 81–90, 93–107, 111, 114–17, 125, 129–36, 143–45, 157–75, 177, 179, 183, 185, 192–210, 217
   championships, 12, 16–17, 26, 48, 50, 71, 117, 119, 145, 160, 162, 164, 180–81, 183, 185, 187, 191, 217–18
   and Charlie Finley, 5–8, 12–19, 21–23, 25–26, 35, 54, 56, 69, 71–76, 78–79, 84–85, 92–94, 97, 109–11, 114–20, 122–23, 130, 149–50, 152, 162, 178, 185, 196, 212, 214
   early history, 5–9, 11–30
   fans, 27, 77, 79, 95, 102, 165, 204, 214
   Five Aces, 194
   Four Aces, 203
   negotiations, 31–35
   resurrection, 101, 103, 135, 143–56, 170
   vs. the Yankees, 104, 171–73, 187–91, 194–95, 204

A's, Philadelphia, 20

Atlanta Braves. See Braves, Atlanta

Babitt, Mack "Shooty," 162, 179, 194

Baer, Larry, 17

Bahnsen, Stan, 14–15, 23, 222–23

Balboa High, 109–10

Baltimore, Maryland, 131, 172, 179

Baltimore Orioles. See Orioles, Baltimore

Bando, Sal, 15, 107

Bank of America building, 33

Barnum & Bailey (of baseball world), 12, 77

BART (Bay Area Rapid Transit), 171

BASS ticket outlet, 196

Bauer, Hank, 52, 114, 122

Bay Area, San Francisco
   baseball fans, 82, 150–51, 189
   baseball teams, 6, 15, 18, 30–31, 75–76, 85, 103, 118–20, 123, 178
   "Billy Ball," 40
   broadcasting, 17, 147–48
   the Depression, 43
   immigrants, 41
   media, 20, 77, 91, 171, 209
   politicians, 32
   prominent families in, 112
   sports business, 149
   weather, 199

Bay Bridge Classic, 199

Baylor, Don, 15

Beard, Dave, 133, 184–85, 189, 203

Bears, Denver, 27, 54, 75

Bell, Kevin, 161

Bench, Johnny, 62

Bengals, Cincinnati, 195

Bergman, Ron, 30, 73

Berkeley High, 45, 47–48, 162

Berkeley Hills, 45

Berkeley Historical Society, 44

Berkeley Pier, 42

Berndt, Lois Elaine, 51

Big Red Machine, 62

The Bill James Baseball Abstract 1982, 193, 196

"Billy Ball," 1, 9, 40, 86, 89, 115, 121, 123, 140, 143, 145, 149, 151–56, 163–67, 169, 171, 178, 187–88, 195, 213, 215

Billy Martin Appreciation Day, 114, 121

Billy Martin's Western Wear, 172

Birtsas, Tim, 217

Blackhawk, 124

Blair, Paul, 63

Bloomington, Minnesota, 66, 73

Blue, Vida, 15–16, 109, 130, 160, 200

Blue Jays, Toronto, 30, 174, 190, 209, 217

Blues, Kansas City, 48

Blyleven, Bert, 144

Bonds, Bobby, 61

Bordi, Rich, 133

Boros, Steve, 215

Bosetti, Rick, 190

Boston, Massachusetts, 172

Boston Braves. See Braves, Boston

Boston Red Sox. See Red Sox, Boston

Boswell, Dave, 56

Boswell, Thomas, 206

Boyer, Clete, 77, 84, 88, 99, 128, 158, 175, 207, 209

Boyes Hot Springs, California, 48, 49

Braves, Atlanta, 84, 201

Braves, Boston, 48

Brett, George, 129, 157

Brewers, Milwaukee, 15, 22, 87, 106, 132, 141, 172, 180, 185–86, 192, 203, 206, 208, 212

Bristol, Dave, 159

Brock, Lou, 136

Broncos, Denver, 27

Bronx, the, 187–88

Bronx Bombers, 51

Brooklyn Dodgers. See Dodgers, Brooklyn

Brown, Jerry, 167

Burbank Airport, 23

Burbank Junior High, 43

Burke, Glenn, 78

Burrell Jr., Stanley, 17

Burroughs, Jeff, 59

Cactus League, 90, 162, 198, 200

Cadillac Eldorado, 122

Caen, Herb, 20

California Angels. See Angels,
    California

California
    Depression-era, 38
    immigrants, 41, 42
    Northern, 119
    Southern, 33
    University of, 39
    University of, Berkeley, 45, 46

Camacho, Ernie, 127, 133, 162,
    223

Campaneris, Bert, 15

Canseco, Jose, 145, 217

Capitals, Washington, 149

Cardinals, St. Louis, 143, 212

Carew, Rod, 53, 87, 128, 201, 222

"Celebration," 147, 166–68, 185

Chalk, Dave, 21

Chambliss, Chris, 61, 62

Chass, Murray, 64, 188

Cherry Hills Village, 25

Chicago police, 174

Chicago White Sox. See White
    Sox, Chicago

Ciensczyk, Frank, 11, 12, 205

Cincinnati Bengals. See Bengals,
    Cincinnati

Cincinnati Reds. See Reds,
    Cincinnati

Claremont, California, 144

Clemente, Roberto, 138

Cleveland Indians. See Indians,
    Cleveland

Cleveland Stadium, 178

Clio Awards, 156

Cobb, Ty, 136, 201

Coliseum board. See Oakland
    Coliseum board

Comiskey Park, 174

"Computer Ball," 215

Contra Costa Hills, California, 45

Cooney, Terry, 174

Cooper, Joseph, 66

Cooperstown, 2, 161

Copacabana nightclub, 52, 61

Coral Park High, 145

Corbett, Brad, 58–60

County of Alameda, 149

County Stadium (Milwaukee), 22,
    208

Cox, Jeff, 194

Crawford, John, 152–53

Cronin, Joe, 57, 71

Crown Center Hotel, 64

Cruyff, Johan, 149

Cruz, Julio, 168

Cunningham, William, 31, 35

Cy Young Award, 13, 109, 131,
    139–40, 169, 189, 192

Dallas-Fort Worth, 58–59

Daly, Ed, 122

Danville, California, 123
Danville Saloon, 123
Dark, Alvin, 18, 54, 71, 110
Dartmouth College, 113, 146
Davis Oil Company, 25
Davis, Marvin, 6, 25, 26
Davis, Mike, 21, 85, 179, 217
Davis, Ron, 189
Denkinger, Don, 96
Denver, Colorado, 6–7, 25–27, 29–30, 32–35, 55, 59, 71, 75, 119
Denver, John, 60
Denver Bears. See Bears, Denver
Denver Broncos. See Broncos, Denver, 27
Dilone, Miguel, 78
DiMaggio, Joe, 50, 51, 106, 114, 116, 122
Diplomats, Washington, 146, 149
Disney, Walt, 149, 156
Disneyland, 149
Dobson, Pat, 61
Dodgers, Brooklyn, 48, 51–52, 115, 164, 168
Dodgers, Los Angeles, 14, 20, 62, 169, 177, 186, 194–95
Dolich, Andy, 146, 149–53, 155–56, 196
Donohue, Tom, 98
Doubleday, Abner, 140
Doubleday Field, 161
Dougherty, Chuck, 173

Downey Jr., Jack, 43
Downey, Joan (formerly Jenny), 7, 43, 81, 94, 218; See also Pisani, Jenny, and Salvini, Jenny
Downey, Joan (daughter), 43
Downey, John Thomas "Jack," 43, 81
Downey, Pat, 43
Doyle, Brian, 163, 173, 194
Drake Hotel, 5, 76, 116
Drumright, Keith, 194
Dunning, Steve, 16
Durham, Bull, 97

Eagles, Philadelphia, 147
East Bay, 16, 29, 31, 38, 74, 90, 113, 123, 149, 155
Ebbets Field, 51, 115
Edgewater Hyatt House, 69, 70, 127
Egan, Tom, 59–60
Eisenhardt, Roy, 2, 101, 109, 113–20, 122, 124, 138, 143, 145–48, 150, 158, 161, 187, 193–94, 206–07, 211, 213–15
Embarcadero Center, 113
Emeryville, California, 50
Ermer, Cal, 55
Eskenazi, Gerald, 187

Essian, Jim, 17, 21, 76, 86, 88, 95, 99, 103, 132
Evans, Johnny, 203
Evans Diamond, 178
Events
Exhibition Stadium, 174
Expos, Montreal, 192, 215

Fallick, Alan, 27, 29, 32, 35
Feeney, Chub, 32
Fehr, Donald, 177
Fernando-mania, 169
Fingers, Rollie, 11, 192
Finley, Carl, 17, 26, 97, 146
Finley, Charlie, 5–8, 12–19, 21–23, 25–26, 35, 54, 56, 69, 71–76, 78–79, 84–85, 92–94, 97, 109–11, 114–20, 122–23, 130, 149–50, 152, 162, 178, 185, 196, 212, 214
Finley, Nancy, 26
Finley, Shirley, 74
Fisk, Carlton, 133
Ford, Gerald, 25
Ford, Whitey, 51, 52, 106, 114, 122
Ford C. Frick Award, 128
Ford Foundation, 112
Fort Collins, Colorado, 52
Fort Ord, California, 51
49ers, San Francisco, 97
Foster, Scott, 197

Fowler, Art, 54–55, 77, 84, 98, 131, 133, 158, 172, 199, 204
Fox, Howard, 54
Frey, Jim, 178
Frick, Ford, 27

Gale, Rich, 101
Galloway, Randy, 55, 58–60
Game of the Week, 101, 130
Gammons, Peter, 192
Garcia, Dave, 211
Garner, James P., 31
Garner, Phil, 138
General Foods, 152
Giants, San Francisco, 6–7, 15–18, 20, 29–33, 35, 51, 74, 82, 88, 110, 112, 117–19, 128, 131, 147–49, 158–59, 178, 199–200, 217
Glendale, California, 48
Golden Gate Bridge, 45
Golden Gate Ferry Company, 42
Golden State Warriors, 148, 167
Gold Rush, 112
Golenbock, Peter, 61, 63, 122, 207
Goodby, Jeff, 152–56
Good Morning America, 171, 208
Goodwin, Danny, 203
Gossage, Rich "Goose," 65, 130, 189–91
Grain Belt brewery, 53
Great Depression, 37–38, 43

Grebey, Ray, 176–77
Grich, Bobby, 93, 129
Griffith, Calvin, 18, 53, 55–56, 73
Grizzly Peak Boulevard, 45
Gross, Wayne, 21, 98–99, 101–03,
    130, 159, 173, 180, 184, 190,
    195, 208
Guerrero, Mario, 78, 95, 158
Guidry, Ron, 70, 104, 186, 188
Guinn, Jimmy, 136
Gura, Larry, 184

Haas, Betsy, 113
Haas, Peter, 112
Haas, Wally, 113–14, 116, 208
Haas Sr., Walter A., 112
Haas Jr., Walter A., 101, 111–16,
    119, 178, 191
Haas family, 112, 115–16, 118,
    125, 144, 148, 157–58,
    165–66, 180
Haas foundation, 112
Hagar, Ray, 66
Hagin, Wayne, 98–99, 121,
    127–28, 148, 156, 167–68,
    197, 206
Hancock, Gary, 217
Harvard University, 112, 146
Hawaiian island of Kauai, 38
Hayward High Farmers, 47

Heath, Mike, 21, 69–71, 86, 95,
    102, 118, 173, 176, 185, 190,
    199, 200, 202, 207
Heaverlo, Dave, 16, 20, 93, 126,
    130, 144, 172, 175, 179
Hecht, Henry, 64
Hegenberger Road, 29
Heinz pickle factory, 48
Henderson, Bobbie, 95, 135, 208
Henderson, "Krazy George," 166,
    167
Henderson, Rickey, 1–2, 21, 87,
    94–95, 99, 102, 107, 130,
    135–40, 159, 167–69, 184,
    188, 190–92, 194–95, 200–
    02, 204–05, 208–09, 217
Henderson Heights, 192
Hernandez, Pete, 47
Herzog, Whitey, 58, 143
Hickey, John, 15, 19, 34, 74, 78, 88,
    114, 157–58, 186, 191, 211
Hodges, Russ, 148
Holtzman, Ken, 15, 160
Hotel de France, 66
Howard, Elston, 63
Hubert H. Humphrey Metrodome,
    163
Hunter, Jim "Catfish," 13, 61, 70,
    110, 160

Ibanez, Mark, 40–41, 165–66
IBM, 152

Idaho Falls, Idaho, 48, 197

Idaho Falls Russets, 48, 210

Illinois, 66

Indians, Cleveland, 57, 131, 159, 161, 164, 168, 181, 202, 211, 213

Jack London Square, 143

Jackson, Reggie, 15, 62–64, 70, 79, 84, 186–87

James, Bill, 193, 196

James Kenney Park, 44

Javier, Stan, 217

Jenkins, Bruce, 8, 20, 75, 102, 133, 145, 156, 170, 178, 183, 185, 204–05

"Jeremiah," 110

Jersey City, 110

Jocketty, Walt, 84, 144

John, Tommy, 133, 187–89

Johnson, Cliff, 65, 158, 167, 173, 217

Johnson, John Henry, 21, 136

Jones, Jeff, 133, 168, 189, 202–03

Jordan, Michael, 154

Joseph County, Indiana, 74

Kaat, Jim, 144

Kaiser Aluminum, 100, 113–14, 116–17, 166

Kaiser Center, 114–15, 147

KALX-FM, 17

Kansas City, Missouri, 6, 8, 15, 20, 22, 42, 52, 64, 73–74, 103, 117, 180–81

Kansas City A's. See A's, Kansas City

Kansas City Blues. See Blues, Kansas City

Kansas City Royals. See Royals, Kansas City

Kauai, 38

KCBS radio, 213

KDIA radio, 96–97

Kennedy, Bob, 54

Kennedy, Jackie, 25

Keough, Matt, 21, 87, 90, 94, 97–98, 130–32, 135, 139–40, 159–60, 163–64, 169–72, 174, 188–90, 195, 200–02

King, Bill, 2, 94, 127, 147

King, Clyde, 212

King, Mike, 158

Kingman, Brian, 21, 46, 87, 90, 119, 130–32, 134, 160, 169–70, 189, 200

Kinney, Dennis, 203

Kissinger, Henry, 25

Klutts, Mickey, 76, 90, 95, 101–02, 104, 120, 127, 132, 134, 173, 179, 191, 194, 198, 202, 213, 217

KNBR radio, 147

Kool & the Gang, 147

Korach, Ken, 1–3
Korean War, 52
Koselke, Norm, 19, 84
KPIX-Channel 5, 97
KSFO radio, 147–48, 206
KTVU (television), 40, 165
Kubek, Tony, 130, 187
Kuhn, Bowie, 13, 15, 24, 31–32, 66, 117

Lacey, Bob, 11–12, 49, 83, 87, 95, 123, 131, 133, 161–62, 203
Lachemann, Rene, 19, 23–24, 26, 132
Lake Merritt, 115
Lakers, Minneapolis, 58
Lancaster, California, 137
Langford, Rick, 21, 90, 95, 103, 107, 130–32, 140, 159–60, 162–64, 170, 175, 184, 188–89, 200, 202–03
Lansford, Carney, 217
La Russa, Tony, 217
Laws, C. L. "Brick," 47–48
Lemon, Bob, 64–65, 186
Lemon, Jerry, 65
Leonard, Dennis, 181, 184
Levine, Matt, 34, 149–53, 170–71
Levi Strauss & Co., 111, 113, 118–19
Lodigiani, Dario, 49
Lopes, Davey, 194

Los Angeles, California, 7, 33, 35, 99, 169
Los Angeles Dodgers. See Dodgers, Los Angeles
Lucchesi, Frank, 60
Lurie, Bob, 7, 29–30, 32–34, 112, 119, 158–59
Lurie, Marty, 2
Lyle, Sparky, 61
Lysander, Rick, 133

MacPhail, Lee, 6–7, 17, 28, 32, 34–35, 72, 115, 120, 174, 177, 188, 208
Madison, Wisconsin, 197, 210
Maier, Cornell, 100–01, 111, 113–14, 116, 121–22, 166–67
Major League Baseball Players Association, 14, 91
Major League Scouting Bureau, 23
Maltester, Jack, 116, 120
Manhattan, New York, 123, 172, 175
Mantle, Mickey, 51, 52, 67, 77, 106, 114, 116, 122, 128, 207, 209
Marichal, Juan, 110
Mariners, Seattle, 2, 19–20, 24, 88, 96, 158, 167–68, 172, 179, 208
Maris, Roger, 106, 114, 122
Marshall, Jim, 8, 19, 76, 78, 83

marshmallow salesman, 7, 66, 97, 195, 212

Martin Sr., Alfred Manuel, 38

Martin Jr., Alfred Manuel, 37, 44

Martin, Billy
army, 51–52
awards, 140, 191–92, 195–96
baseball strike, 175–77
"Billy Ball," 9, 89, 121, 140, 145, 152–53, 156, 164–66
Billy Martin Appreciation Day, 114, 121–23
childhood, 37–38, 41, 44–45
death, 218
early management jobs, 53–60
faith, 126–27
fans, 151–53, 157, 166, 167
fights/temper, 7, 44–45, 47, 49–50, 56, 66, 96–97, 102, 126, 134, 174, 200
firings, 7, 56, 57, 60, 62, 66, 71, 73, 105, 159, 186, 207, 212–14
Kansas City A's, 52
marshmallow salesman, 7, 66, 97, 195, 212
Oakland (city), 121–25
Oakland A's, 3, 6, 8, 24, 69, 71–79, 81–90, 93–107, 111, 114–17, 125, 129–36, 143–45, 157–75, 177, 179, 183, 185, 192–210, 217

Oakland Oaks, 47–50
personality, 1, 2, 5, 37, 44, 48–50, 54–56, 75, 79, 89, 96, 102–03, 126–28, 152, 153, 156
Tigers, 73
Yankees, 8, 50–52, 61–66, 70, 72, 77–78, 87, 90, 104–06, 124–26, 140, 145, 159, 186–88, 206–07, 211–15, 217–18

Martin Jr., Billy, 38–39, 43, 45, 51–54, 59–60, 121, 124–25, 154

Martin, Dean, 18

Martin, Gretchen, 40, 53, 54

Martin, Kelly Ann, 53

Maryland, 150

Maryland Arrows. See Arrows, Maryland

Mathews, Eddie, 144, 199

May, Rudy, 61, 188–89

Mays, Willie, 18, 128, 135

McCatty, Steve, 8–9, 17, 21, 78, 87, 90, 93, 95–96, 112, 120, 124, 126, 129–32, 159–60, 163–64, 167, 170, 172, 184, 188–89, 192–93, 197, 199–201, 203, 207

McCoy, Larry, 96

McGwire, Mark, 144, 217

MC Hammer, 17

McKay, Dave, 106–07, 179, 191, 194–95, 208

McKeon, Jack, 18–19, 162

McLaughlin, Bo, 203

McNamara, John, 56–57, 72–73

Medford, 210

Medich, George "Doc," 14, 18, 22, 24, 208

Mele, Sam, 53

Merced, California, 137

Messer, Frank, 106

Metro, Charlie, 205

Metropolitan Stadium, 73, 97, 163

Michael, Gene, 212

Michaels, Al, 184

Mickey Mouse, 156

Midsummer Classic, 204

Mieuli, Franklin, 167

Mile High Stadium, 25, 27

Miller, Marvin, 14, 91–92, 175, 177

Miller, Norm, 99

Milwaukee, Wisconsin, 23, 52, 74, 106, 136, 141, 172, 186, 208

Milwaukee Brewers. See Brewers, Milwaukee

Minetto, Craig, 133, 162, 168

Minneapolis, Minnesota, 53, 56, 195

Minneapolis Lakers. See Lakers, Minneapolis

Minnesota Vikings. See Vikings, Minnesota

Mitterwald, George, 84, 97, 158, 175

Modesto, 210

Montgomery, John, 74

Montreal Expos. See Expos, Montreal

Moore, Jackie, 40, 43, 82, 127, 158, 165–66, 185, 187, 191, 195, 198, 204, 209, 213

Moore, Kelvin, 179

Moore, Monte, 94

Morabito, Mickey, 85, 125, 141, 146, 170, 211

Moretti, Ray, 161

Morgan, Joe, 62

Morgan, Mike, 158

Morris, Jack, 99, 100

Moscone, George, 29, 32

Moxley, Rick, 170

Munson, Diane, 67

Munson, Thurman, 61–63, 65, 69

Murphy, Dwayne, 21, 87, 95, 99–102, 107, 130, 137–38

Mustad, Eric, 161

Myers, Jim, 148

Nahas, Robert T., 29–33, 117

National Geographic, 64

National Labor Relations Board, 173

National Lacrosse League, 149

NBA, 149

NBC, 101, 120, 130, 171

Negron, Ray, 63–66, 79, 126, 186, 212

Nettles, Graig, 61, 144, 189, 190

Newhan, Ross, 130, 143

Newhouse, Dave, 17, 40, 49, 69, 77, 89, 100, 112, 131, 139, 144, 156

Newman, Jeff, 6, 18, 20–21, 82, 86, 95, 99–102, 107, 134, 159, 168, 176, 190, 195, 200, 217

New Mexico, 27

New Orleans, 147

Newton, Doug, 74, 79

New York, 63, 65, 71, 76, 81, 85, 90, 105–06, 113, 115, 121, 123–26, 133, 171–72, 186, 189, 195, 211–14, 218

NFL, 35, 73, 197

NHL, 149

Nike, 154

Norris, Mike "Jeremiah," 110

North, Billy, 16, 22

North American Soccer League, 146, 149

Number 1 (autobiography), 45, 122

Oakland, California, 5–8, 11, 18, 20, 23–27, 44, 48, 69, 73, 77, 94, 101, 111–18, 121–25,

143, 165, 181, 184, 187, 192–93, 214

Oakland-Alameda County Coliseum. See Oakland Coliseum

Oakland A's. See A's, Oakland

Oakland Baseball Park, 50

Oakland Chamber of Commerce, 29

Oakland Coliseum, 1–2, 11, 16–17, 20, 26–35, 41, 73, 81, 87, 93, 95–96, 98–104, 114, 116–20, 122, 127, 131, 143, 146–47, 153–54, 165–67, 170–71, 180, 184–85, 190, 192, 194, 196, 199, 202–09

Oakland Coliseum board, 26–28, 30–35, 101, 118, 120, 146

Oakland International Airport, 186, 189

Oakland Oaks, 8, 47–51, 75, 77, 90, 123, 203

Oakland Raiders. See Raiders, Oakland

Oakland Technical High School, 21, 135–36

O'Brien, Dan, 60

Odom, Blue Moon, 160

Ogden, Utah, 70

Ogilvy, David, 156

Ogilvy & Mather, 151–52, 156

O'Hare Airport, 64

Ohio University, 146, 149

Old-Timers' Day, 61, 64–65, 105–06, 159

Orioles, Baltimore, 15, 73, 99, 104

Owchinko, Bob, 162, 169, 189

Pacific Coast League, 8, 11, 50, 54, 123, 210

Pacific Heights neighborhood, 112

Pacific Select Corporation, 149

Packard Baseball Stadium, 155

Padres, San Diego, 12, 15

Page, Mitchell, 21, 99–101, 130, 159, 162

Palmer, Pamela, 208

Palm Springs, California, 31

Papiano, Neil, 31

Parker, Dave, 138, 178

Parrish, Lance, 99–100, 144

Pascual, Camilo, 144

Patterson, Mike, 173

Paul, Gabe, 61, 211

Paulus, Lorraine, 146, 150

People magazine, 101

Pepe, Phil, 145, 204, 212

Pepto-Bismol, 105

Perez, Tony, 62

Phelps, Ken, 96, 131, 137

Philadelphia, Pennsylvania, 136, 143

Philadelphia A's. See A's, Philadelphia

Philadelphia Eagles. See Eagles, Philadelphia

Philadelphia Phillies. See Phillies, Philadelphia

Philadelphia 76ers. See 76ers, Philadelphia

Phillies, Philadelphia, 177

Phillips, B. J., 171

Phillips, Tony, 161, 203

Phoenix, Arizona, 65, 154, 196, 198

Phoenix Municipal Stadium, 197, 199

Phoenix Senators, 49

Picciolo, Rob, 22, 95, 98, 158, 194, 200, 202–03

Pirates, Pittsburgh, 72, 130, 137–38, 162, 164, 168

Pisani, Donato, 42

Pisani, Francis "Tudo," 42, 43

Pisani, Jenny, 42, 43; See also Downey, Joan and Salvini, Jenny

Pittsburgh Pirates. See Pirates, Pittsburgh

Player Relations Committee, 175

Plunk, Eric, 217

Pony Express, 37

Province of Foggia, Italy, 40

Puerto Piritu, Venezuela, 138

Raiders, Oakland, 7, 16, 33, 35, 69, 90, 99, 101, 113, 122, 147–49, 187

Raines, Tim, 192

Ramey, Hal, 94

Randle, Lenny, 168

Randolph, Willie, 62, 190

Rangers, Texas, 8, 15, 21, 40, 58–60, 62, 77, 103, 106, 136, 140, 158, 175, 191

Ratto, Ray, 88

Reds, Cincinnati, 62, 96, 161, 183

Red Sox, Boston, 15, 60, 104, 133, 175, 217

Reiser, Pete, 87

Remy, Jerry, 144

Righetti, Dave, 70, 186, 188, 189

Rigney, Bill, 155

Rijo, Jose, 217

Riney, Hal, 151–53

Rivers, Mickey, 62, 103

Robinson, Frank, 159

Robinson, Jackie, 51

Robinson, Ted, 34, 97, 116, 120, 213

Rocky Mountains, 26

Rolls-Royce, 152

Romo, Joe, 198

Royals, Kansas City, 22, 62–63, 101, 104, 106, 129–31, 177, 180–81, 183–85, 200, 209

Royals Stadium, 184

Rubinstein, David, 150, 166

Rudi, Joe, 13

Rush, Red, 94, 97

Ruth, Babe, 202

Sacramento, California, 148

Safari Hotel, 161

St. Louis Cardinals. See Cardinals, St. Louis

Salina, Kansas, 22

Salter, Stephanie, 85–86, 91, 103, 123, 140, 155, 160, 171, 191

Salvini, Jenny, 37–40, 42; See also Downey, Joan and Pisani, Jenny

Salvini, Nicola, 39–40

Salvini, Raphaella, 38–40, 42

Salvini family, 42, 45

San Diego, California, 87

San Diego Padres. See Padres, San Diego

San Francisco, California, 6, 45

San Francisco Bay, 6, 11, 15, 41

San Francisco 49ers. See 49ers, San Francisco, 97

San Francisco Giants. See Giants, San Francisco

San Francisco Peninsula, 149

San Francisco Recreation and Park Commission, 30

San Francisco Seals. See Seals, San Francisco

San Jose, California, 92, 148, 189

San Jose Missions, 11
San Jose State University, 148
San Leandro, California, 221
Santa Clara, California, 152
Sapir, Eddie, 17, 64, 66, 72, 74–76,
    111, 115, 123–24, 188–89,
    213–14
Sardi's Restaurant, 123
Saul, Jim, 78
Sausalito, California, 43
Schwarz, Glenn, 119, 139, 158,
    166, 169, 179, 197, 199, 203,
    208
Scott, Rodney, 21
Scottsdale, Arizona, 8, 79, 81–82,
    87–88, 161, 196
Scottsdale Stadium, 81–82, 87, 92,
    160
Seals, San Francisco, 50
Seattle, Washington, 15, 205
Seattle Mariners. See Mariners,
    Seattle
Seitz, Peter, 13
Seventh Street (West Berkeley),
    37, 81
76ers, Philadelphia, 149
Short, Bob, 58–59, 77
Silverstein, Rich, 152–54
Simmons, Lon, 94, 128, 147–48
Simmons, Ted, 208
Smalley, Roy, 95
Sofield, Rick, 95
Sons of Champlin, 113

Souza, Mark, 133
Spencer, Jim, 173, 175, 203
Spider-Man, 179
Spokane, Washington, 19
Sport magazine, 171
Sporting News, 157, 171, 191, 195
Sports Illustrated, 101, 166, 169,
    170
Sports Spectacular (CBS), 171
Stange, Lee, 84
Stanley, Fred "Chicken," 158, 173,
    194, 195, 200
Star of France, 42
Statler-Hilton Hotel, 54
Steele, Roy, 94
Steinbrenner, George, 7, 61–66, 69,
    71–72, 76, 105–06, 122, 125,
    159, 186–88, 195, 207, 212,
    214, 218
Stengel, Charles Dillon "Casey," 8,
    37, 48–52, 55, 61–62, 191
Stier, Kit, 83, 102, 123, 133, 137,
    194, 209
Stone, Steve, 131, 139–40
Strauss, Levi, 109, 112
Stringer, Lou, 50
Super Bowl (Raiders), 187
Super Bowl XV, 147
Superteams, 195
Swingers, 116

Tanana, Frank, 135, 144
Tenace, Gene, 15
Texas League, 49
Texas Rangers. See Rangers, Texas
Thompson, Jason, 144
Ticketron, 196
Time magazine, 170–71
Today Show, 208
Toronto, Ontario, 30, 34, 43, 101, 103, 174, 209
Toronto Blue Jays. See Blue Jays, Toronto
Trader Vic's, 50
Trammell, Alan, 144
Triple-A ballclubs, 11, 19, 54, 70, 78, 110
Triple-A Tacoma, 179, 200, 202–03, 210
Triple-A Vancouver, 110

US District Court, 175
UC Berkeley, 45, 112–13, 178
Underhill, John, 44
University of California, 17, 39, 46
University of Michigan, 215
Urban Cowboy, 157

Valentino, Dom, 97, 146
Valenzuela, Fernando, 169
Veeck, Bill, 111
Venezuela, 83, 137, 138, 163, 193

Versalles, Zoilo, 53
Vertlieb, Dick, 150
Vikings, Minnesota, 73
Vince's Restaurant, 186
Virdon, Bill, 61, 71, 159

Waikiki, 195
Walker, Wayne, 97
Walls, Lee, 84, 136, 158
Warren, Mike, 203
Washington, Claudell, 21
Washington Capitals. See Capitals, Washington
Washington Diplomats. See Diplomats, Washington
Wathan, John, 101–02, 184–85
Wax, Mel, 32
Weinberg, Barry, 198
Weir, Tom, 20
Weiss, George, 52
Weiss, Walt, 217
Werker, Henry F., 175
West Berkeley, California, 37, 42, 44–45, 81
West Haven (CT) Yankees. See Yankees, West Haven (CT)
White, Frank, 184
White, Roy, 61
White Sox, Chicago, 64, 72, 103, 111, 164, 168, 174–75
Wiencek, Dick, 24, 53, 144, 197
Wilber, Del, 144

Wiley, Ralph, 81, 88–89

Williams, Dick, 18, 56–57, 71–72, 162

Williams, Ted, 157

Wills, Maury, 136

Wilson, Artie, 203

Wilson, Lionel, 25, 29, 31, 116

Winfield, Dave, 189

Winkles, Bobby, 16, 18–19, 22, 71

Wirth, Alan, 133

Wonka, Willy, 97

Works Progress Administration, 43

World Airways, 122

World Series
  "Billy and George" showdown, 187
  1970s, 17
  Oakland A's, 3, 6, 17, 57, 88, 186–87, 217
  Royals, 183, 185
  St. Louis vs. Milwaukee, 212–13
  Yankees, 8, 50–52, 62–63, 65, 79, 115, 186, 190, 194–95, 212, 218

World War I, 38

World War II, 45, 50

Wyoming, 27

Yankees, New York
  and Billy Martin, 8, 50–52, 61–66, 70, 72, 77–78, 87, 90, 104–06, 124–26, 140, 145, 159, 186–88, 206–07, 211–15, 217–18
  and Casey Stengel, 50, 51
  and George Steinbrenner, 7, 61, 64, 66, 195
  in 1927, 170
  players, 13, 15, 61–62, 69–71, 79, 85, 110, 130, 158, 187, 217
  playoff berths, 177
  press reports, 63
  scouts, 48, 180
  uniform, 82
  vs. the A's, 104, 171–73, 187–91, 194–95, 204
  vs. Brewers, 185, 186

Yankee Stadium, 61–62, 64–65, 70, 90, 105, 159, 172, 186, 188–89

Yankees, West Haven (CT), 69, 210

Zisk, Richie, 205

ABOUT THE AUTHOR

DALE TAFOYA IS AUTHOR OF *BASH BROTHERS: A LEGACY SUBPOENAED* (Potomac Books, 2008) and has followed Oakland A's baseball for thirty years. His work has appeared in the *Oakland Tribune, Contra Costa Times, Orlando Sentinel, Modesto Bee, The Source,* and *Beckett Baseball Card Monthly.* In addition to his writing credits, Tafoya has been a guest on ESPN Radio, FOX Sports, Cumulus Media and Comcast Sports. Tafoya resides in the San Francisco-Bay Area.